AFTER LACAN

This book draws on the distinct phases of Jacques Lacan's career to show his way of thinking in and beyond his lifetime. It is an examination of the past, present, and futures of psychoanalysis, as these are developed beyond the routes of analysis in the clinic and in the dimensions of language, literature, logic, philosophy, visual culture, identity and sexuality, and politics. The interdisciplinary approach of the volume allows it to work across clinical, sociological, philosophical, and literary fields to both add dimensions to the literary/critical reception of Lacan and enable the system of Lacanian psychoanalysis to have a wider conversation. Reexamining the fundamental concepts of Lacanian theory in its historical contexts through the topological structures he inaugurated, *After Lacan* makes innovative critical interventions in contemporary debates on racism, Islam, the Communist Party, poetry, new media, disability identity, and queer theory. It is a key resource for students, graduates and instructors of literary theory, psychoanalysis, and the works of Lacan.

ANKHI MUKHERJEE is Professor of English and World Literatures at the University of Oxford and a Fellow of Wadham College. She is the author of *Aesthetic Hysteria: The Great Neurosis in Victorian Melodrama and Contemporary Fiction* (2007) and *What Is a Classic? Postcolonial Rewriting and Invention of the Canon* (2014), which won the British Academy Rose Mary Crawshay Prize in English Literature in 2015. She has edited *A Concise Companion to Psychoanalysis, Literature, and Culture* (2014, with Laura Marcus).

T0370791

AFTER LACAN

*Literature, Theory, and Psychoanalysis
in the Twenty-First Century*

EDITED BY

ANKHI MUKHERJEE

University of Oxford

CAMBRIDGE
UNIVERSITY PRESS

CAMBRIDGE
UNIVERSITY PRESS

University Printing House, Cambridge CB2 8BS, United Kingdom

One Liberty Plaza, 20th Floor, New York, NY 10006, USA

477 Williamstown Road, Port Melbourne, VIC 3207, Australia

314-321, 3rd Floor, Plot 3, Splendor Forum, Jasola District Centre, New Delhi - 110025, India

79 Anson Road, #06-04/06, Singapore 079906

Cambridge University Press is part of the University of Cambridge.

It furthers the University's mission by disseminating knowledge in the pursuit of education, learning and research at the highest international levels of excellence.

www.cambridge.org
Information on this title: www.cambridge.org/9781108466486
DOI: 10.1017/9781108650311

First published 2018

A catalogue record for this publication is available from the British Library

ISBN 978-1-316-51218-0 Hardback
ISBN 978-1-108-46648-6 Paperback

Contents

Notes on Contributors

Clint Burnham is Professor of English at Simon Fraser University. His research interests include cultural studies (film and popular culture), contemporary poetry, and theory (psychoanalysis and Marxism in particular). He is the author of *Does the Internet Have an Unconscious? Slavoj Žižek and Digital Culture* (Bloomsbury, 2018), *Fredric Jameson and the Wolf of Wall Street* (Bloomsbury, 2016), and *The Jamesonian Unconscious: The Aesthetics of Marxist Theory* (Duke University Press, 1995), and he has published works of poetry such as *Pound @ Guantanamo* (Talonbooks, 2016). Burnham has co-edited *Digital Natives* (Other Sights, 2011) and *From Text to Txting* (Indiana University Press, 2012) and is one of the founding members of the "Lacan Salon," a psychoanalytic study group based in Vancouver, Canada.

Merrill Cole is Professor of English at Western Illinois University, specializing in poetry, modernism, queer studies, and creative writing. He has published *The Other Orpheus: A Poetics of Modern Homosexuality* (Routledge, 2003) and his critical articles have appeared in collaborative volumes such as *The Psychoanalysis of Race* (Columbia University Press, 1998) and the *Cambridge History of Gay and Lesbian Literature* (Cambridge University Press, 2015) and peer-reviewed journals including *Women's Studies, Twentieth-Century Literature*, and *American Imago*. Cole is also a published poet. His translation from the German of Anita Berber and Sebastian Droste's *Dances of Vice, Horror, and Ecstasy* was published in 2012 by Side Real Press.

Jodi Dean is Professor of Political Science at Hobart and William Smith Colleges. Her areas of specialization are contemporary political theory, communism, theories of digital media, psychoanalysis, feminist theory, and climate change. She is the author of multiple critical works, including *Crowds and Party* (Verso, 2016), *The Communist Horizon* (Verso, 2012), *Democracy and Other Neoliberal Fantasies* (Duke University Press, 2009), and *Žižek's Politics* (Routledge, 2006). Dean has edited *Reformatting Politics* (with Jon Anderson and Geert Lovink; Routledge, 2006), *Empire's New Clothes: Reading Hardt and Negri* (with Paul Passavant; Routledge, 2004), and *Cultural Studies and Political Theory* (Cornell University Press, 2000), and she is the former co-editor of *Theory and Event*.

Mladen Dolar is professor and a senior research fellow in the Department of Philosophy at the University of Ljubljana, Slovenia, and Professor of Philosophy at the European Graduate School (EGS). His areas of research are German idealism, psychoanalysis, structuralism, and the philosophy of music and film. Together with Slavoj Žižek and others, Dolar founded what has become known as the "Ljubljana School of Psychoanalysis" in the late 1970s. The author of twelve books and more than a hundred articles, his works in English are *Opera's Second Death* (co-authored with Slavoj Žižek; Routledge, 2001) and *A Voice and Nothing More* (MIT Press, 2006).

Nouri Gana is Professor of Comparative Literature and Near Eastern Languages and Cultures at the University of California, Los Angeles (UCLA), and a current recipient of a New Directions Fellowship awarded by the Andrew W. Mellon Foundation in the United States, dividing his time between Tunisia and Turkey. He has published numerous articles and chapters on the literatures and cultures of the Arab world and its diasporas in such scholarly venues as *Cultural Politics*, *PMLA*, *Public Culture* and *Social Text*, and he has also contributed op-eds to magazines and international newspapers, such as *The Guardian*, *El Pais*, *Internazionale*, *Electronic Intifada*, *Jadaliyya*, and *CounterPunch*. Gana is the author of *Signifying Loss: Toward a Poetics of Narrative Mourning* (Bucknell University Press, 2011), and the editor of *The Making of the Tunisian Revolution: Contexts, Architects, Prospects* (Edinburgh University Press, 2013) and *The Edinburgh Companion to the Arab Novel in English* (Edinburgh University Press, 2013). He is currently completing a book manuscript on the politics of melancholia in the Arab world and another on the history of cultural dissent in colonial and postcolonial Tunisia.

Azeen Khan is Assistant Professor in the Department of English and Creative Writing at Dartmouth College. She specializes in postcolonial literatures and theory, feminist and critical theory, continental philosophy, and psychoanalysis. Her book project, "The Subaltern Clinic," draws on the history of colonial medicine and psychiatry, feminist studies, and critical race theory to trace the movement of psychoanalysis from its birthplace in Europe to the "rest of the globe" – to Algeria, India, and South Africa, among other places. Her publications include "Extimate Enemies," a translation (with Fredric-Charles Baitinger) of Jacques-Alain Miller's writings in the *Lacanian Review* (Summer, 2017) and "An Alibi of Reason," in *Novel: A Forum on Fiction* (48/2, 2015).

Anna Kornbluh is Associate Professor in the English Department at the University of Illinois at Chicago. Her research and teaching interests center on Victorian literature and critical theory. She is the author of *Realizing Capital: Financial and Psychic Economies in Victorian Form* (Fordham University Press, 2014) and her articles have appeared or are forthcoming in *ELH, Novel: A Forum on Fiction, Henry James Review, Mediations*, among others. Kornbluh is a founding member of the V21 Collective, a group of Victorianist scholars with shared interests in critical theory and what they term "strategic presentism." She has co-edited a special issue of Boundary 2 Online on "Presentism, Form, and the Future of History," and edited "Lukács 2016: *The Theory of the Novel* at 100," a special issue of *Mediations*.

Todd McGowan is Professor of Film and Television Studies at the University of Vermont. He teaches courses in theory and film and his areas of interest include Hegel, psychoanalysis, and existentialism. McGowan is the author of several books, including *Only a Joke Can Save Us: A Theory of Comedy* (Northwestern University Press, 2017), *Capitalism and Desire: The Psychic Cost of Free Markets* (Columbia University Press, 2016), and *Enjoying What We Don't Have: The Political Project of Psychoanalysis* (University Press of Nebraska, 2013), And he has written on a wide range of topics, including Christopher Nolan, David Lynch, and Spike Lee.

Tracy McNulty is Professor of French and Comparative Literature at Cornell University. Her research interests include twentieth-century French literature and comparative modernism, psychoanalytic theory (especially Freud and Lacan), contemporary French philosophy, and political theory. In addition to these fields, she regularly teaches interdisciplinary courses on the origins of language, myth and symbolic thought, eroticism and perversion, and philosophical, scientific, and psychoanalytic theories of subjectivity and human agency. McNulty is the author of two books, *The Hostess: Hospitality, Femininity, and the Expropriation of Identity* (University of Minnesota Press, 2007) and *Wrestling with the Angel: Experiments in Symbolic Life* (Columbia University Press, 2014).

She has co-edited a special issue of *Diacritics* ("Taking Exception to the Exception", 2008) and edited a special issue of *Differences* ("Constructing the Death Drive", 2017).

Anna Mollow is an independent scholar whose research interests include disability studies, fat studies, feminism, queer studies, and critical race studies. She is the co-editor of *Sex and Disability* (with Robert McRuer; Duke University Press, 2012) and *DSM-CRIP* (with Merri Lisa Johnson; *Social Text Online*, 2013). Mollow's articles on disability, queerness, feminism, race, and fatness have appeared or are forthcoming in *African American Review*, *Hypatia: Journal of Feminist Philosophy*, *Journal of Literary and Cultural Disability Studies*, *The Disability Studies Reader*, *Michigan Quarterly Review*, the Wiley-Blackwell *Companion to Critical and Cultural Theory*, *Disability Studies Quarterly*, *Huffington Post*, and others.

Ankhi Mukherjee is the author of *Aesthetic Hysteria: The Great Neurosis in Victorian Melodrama and Contemporary Fiction* (Routledge, 2007) and *What Is a Classic? Postcolonial Rewriting and Invention of the Canon* (Stanford University Press, 2014), which won the British Academy Rose Mary Crawshay Prize in English Literature in 2015. She has published articles on a wide range of topics – Victorian literature and culture, intellectual history, modern fiction, postcolonial studies – in journals such as *PMLA*, *MLQ*, *Paragraph*, *Parallax*, *Contemporary Literature*, and the *Cambridge Journal of Postcolonial Literary Inquiry*, and co-edited *A Concise Companion to Psychoanalysis, Literature and Culture* (with Laura Marcus; Wiley-Blackwell, 2015). Mukherjee is currently working on an AHRC- and Wellcome Trust-funded research project, "The Psychic Life of the Poor in Mumbai, London, and New York," which is the basis of her third monograph, *Unseen City*.

Dany Nobus is Professor of Psychoanalytic Psychology at Brunel University London. He is also a clinical psychologist, psychoanalytic psychotherapist, and Chair of the Freud Museum London. His main research interests are the history, theory, and practice of psychoanalysis, the history of psychiatry, and the intersections between psychoanalysis, philosophy, and the arts. In 2017, Nobus was awarded the Sarton Medal of the University of Ghent for his outstanding contributions to the history of psychoanalysis. He is the author of more than 150 journal articles and book chapters, and his monographs in English include *Jacques Lacan and the Freudian Practice of Psychoanalysis* (Routledge, 2000), *Knowing Nothing, Staying Stupid: Elements for a Psychoanalytic Epistemology* (Routledge, 2005), and *The Law of Desire: On Lacan's "Kant with Sade"* (Palgrave, 2017).

Introduction

Ankhi Mukherjee

One of the opening caveats of *After Lacan: Clinical Practice and the Subject of the Unconscious* (2002), co-authored by Willy Apollon, Danielle Bergeron, and Lucie Cantin, is that "the academic appropriation of Lacan can function as an obstacle to understanding key Lacanian concepts."[1] The editors of the work, Robert Hughes and Karen Ror Malone, seem to be attributing Lacan's ill-deserved reputation as "all theory" in clinical circles to the stranglehold on Lacan studies literary critics and cultural theorists enjoyed in the late twentieth century. The distinction between "theory" and "praxis" is key to understanding the grounds of this indictment:

> Certainly differences in the theoretical understanding of clinical work in Lacanian circles as well as the differences in technique (variable sessions being iconic in this regard) have made some North American practitioners wary. The warm reception by academics reinforces other suspicions.[2]

To counteract the kiss of death that is the "warm reception by academics," *After Lacan* (2002) presents a collection of essays by clinicians who lead the École Freudienne du Québec and the GIFRIC group, a non-profit organization founded in 1977 to develop psychoanalysis at the intersection of sociocultural research and social work. The "suffering addressed by psychoanalytic practice"[3] is the touchstone that differentiates critical Lacanism from the clinical in this reckoning. The "After", in this predecessor *After Lacan*, reflects not only the aftermaths of Jacques Lacan's life and legacy, but also the introductory elaborations of Lacanian theory that have come before, by theorists such as Bruce Fink, Slavoj Žižek, Joan Copjec, Juliet MacCannell, Ellie Ragland, and Charles Shepherdson as well as academic/practitioner figures like Dany Nobus and Philip Hill. The editors concede that the work is not a systematic exposition of Lacanian concepts because extant scholarship has freed it up to focus on Lacan's clinical teaching instead. Ironically, therefore, the 2002 *After Lacan*'s showcasing of Lacan's enduring relevance and salience for contemporary clinical practice is posed as a beneficiary of the very philosophical, philological, and literary critical interventions in Lacan's thought and theory that it simultaneously disavows. Published fifteen years later, this present collection of essays, also titled *After Lacan*, undertakes a syncretic critical articulation from the vantage point of academic humanities of the theory, analytic practice, and pedagogy of Jacques Lacan. For a figure who spectacularly emerged in 1953 and 1964[4] as a renegade in the Freudian institution of psychoanalysis, the *savoir* or propositional knowledge of Lacan's non-normative oeuvre is indissociable with its *savoir-faire*, its know-how, or knowing how to make.

Jacques Derrida's "For the Love of Lacan" is one of three essays in *Resistances of Psychoanalysis* (1996) where he seems to be writing private autobiography against great transferential figures: Sigmund Freud, Michel Foucault, and Jacques Lacan.[5] We could say that Derrida is playing with the psychoanalytic notion of transference neurosis, or the unconscious transfer, in long-term therapy, of the analysand's original neurosis to the figure of the analyst. The dynamics of transference, which acknowledges the presence of the other even where it is unnamed, has a parallel in the mode of deconstruction, which relinquishes the self-identical subject in favor of the expropriating self. In "For the Love of Lacan," Derrida is reminiscing about his first encounter with Jacques Lacan in 1966 in the United States, "to which both of us had been for the first time exported."[6] He makes a sly reference to the alter-egos Lauzun and Saida, thinly veiled caricatures of Lacan and Derrida, respectively, in Kristeva's 1992 novel, *The Samurai*. Lacan and I, Lacan with me, "were both of us 'adulterated products fit for exportation'," Derrida observes.[7] While Kristeva, the bad novelist, had relegated Lacan and Derrida to the promiscuity of the same export container, the essay suggests that the relationship between the psychoanalyst and the philosopher is better represented by a chiasmus. Philosophy finds in psychoanalysis all the motifs that were offering themselves, although not without resistance, to a "genealogico-deconstructive interpretation":[8] psychoanalysis, in turn, finds itself at home with philosophy despite all sorts of disavowals (within philosophy) on this subject. Speaking of *his* role in this criss-crossing of opposed trajectories, the philosopher sounds psychoanalytical himself, bypassing egological consciousness for unconscious and accidental patterns:

> My theoretical coming-to-terms with Lacan consisted in pursuing my own work according to its specific pathways and requirements, whether or not this work should encounter Lacan's, and Lacan's – I do not at all reject the idea – more than any other today.[9]

"Was this not a way of saying that I loved and admired him a lot? And of paying homage to him, in a way that pleased me?" Derrida asks. Derrida's tribute to Lacan, besides emphasizing the significance of Lacan's contribution to poststructuralist thought, raises two key questions about the way in which scholarship creates intellectual genealogies and affiliations and self-situates in their intersections. How does one say "we" when speaking all alone, as Derrida observes, after the death of the other? The second question is that of archivization. How does one archive he who does not remain? What remains of the historical Jacques-Marie-Émile Lacan (1901–1981), who does not remain? Psychoanalysis, Derrida observes in *Archive Fever* (1998), is inherently a thinking of the archive: the term "archive" here refers to not simply the systematized textual corpus of psychoanalysis but a memory system or mnemotechnology. As Simon Morgan Wortham observes:

> Derrida . . . moves us away from the idea that the archive simple accommodates, violates, monumentalises, and amortizes the event. Certainly in *Archive Fever*, the question of the psychoanalytic archive is bound to a thinking of the psychoanalytic event to come, an event which not only marks "in advance" the entire landscape of our intellectual, disciplinary, historical and cultural "archive," but which is still destined to transform it.[10]

The psychic procedures of archivization associated with psychoanalysis are not merely conservational, monumentalizing the past, but also intent on the erasure of memory or for history that is written in the future anterior. The aggression–destruction–death drive of psychoanalysis, which is its peculiar logic of supplementarity, binds it to its own finitude, its other, and to the arrival of the event. Keeping in mind the specificity of Lacan's contribution to the letteration of psychoanalysis, this collection of chapters, titled *After Lacan*, addresses the archive as well as the "archive fever" of Lacan's output in the academy and psychoanalytic clinic, both the archivable corpus and its anticipation of the "psychoanalytic event to come."

"Without written documents, you know you are in a dream," Lacan stated in a lecture at Yale University.[11] Élisabeth Roudinesco addresses Lacan's relationship with the archive in *Lacan: In Spite of Everything*. She interprets "archive," as I have done, as the moment of movement between filed, monitored, carefully considered history – pedagogic history – and the performative history of creativity.

> Between these two impossibilities, which are like two boundaries of the same prohibition – prohibition of absolute knowledge, prohibition of the interpretive sovereignty of the ego – it must be accepted that archives – destroyed, existing, excessive or erased – are the precondition of history.[12]

The way in which this collection approaches the oral and written oeuvre of Lacan reflects what Roudinesco rightly identifies as Lacan's own ambivalence about written traces: neither subscribing to the positivity of the inventoried whole, nor denying the need to bequeath to posterity a body of work associated with his teaching and his person. The belatedness implied by the *After* in this book's title is mobilized as a privileged entry point to examine the unthought elements and the unlived-out amplitude of Lacan's theory of the 1950s, 60s, and 70s in new fields of inquiry, such as disability, race, or new media studies. These thriving elaborations of or critical departures from the classical theory informing Lacanian work are examined in their varied, often non-synchronous, cultural, geopolitical, and disciplinary contexts. This critical retrospective also adds a multidimensional understanding to the epistemologies the historical Lacan came after and returned to, the Freudian field of psychoanalysis in particular. In its wider aims, *After Lacan* is a focalized examination of the futures of psychoanalysis, as they are developed beyond the routes of analysis in the clinic, and in the dimensions of language, literature, logic, philosophy, visual culture, gender and sexuality, and politics. Along the way, we reexamine some of the fundamental concepts of Lacanian psychoanalysis, both the topological structures he inaugurated, and the regimes of the imaginary, symbolic, real, and the symptom that these structures give temporal and spatial delineation to. We examine the objective of analysis and the nature of truth associated with the Lacanian School of psychoanalysis, with its difficult negotiation of idealism and materialism, and its logic of the real, whose impossibility leads to a structural impasse. The chapters consider also Lacanian concepts of aporetic subjectivity which have gained traction in postmodern literary studies and its cognates: the gaps in the body, jouissance, sinthome, object a, drive, the divided/barred subject, and the four discourses, among others.

If the twentieth century was Freudian, "the twenty-first century is already Lacanian," according to Roudinesco.[13] In recent years, Jacques Lacan has been readily and creatively used to talk about the political: Holocaust to the Arab Spring, capitalism, neoliberalism, consumerism, publics, post-democracy, advertising, new media, entertainment, sex change, and Donald Trump. Lacanian theory in the twenty-first century is indeed a theory in action, but its politics cannot be limited or reduced to "the level of strategic-pragmatic interventions," as Slavoj Žižek terms it.[14] In fact, Lacanian theory as political act is impossible, Alenka Zupančič has written; not impossible in the sense of "impossible to happen," but in the sense of "an impossible *that* happened," an "impossible gesture of pure expenditure" that, to quote Žižek again, changed "the very coordinates of what [was] strategically possible within a historical constellation."[15] This is hardly unexpected of a theorist who imagined history (*histoire*) itself as hystory (*hystoire*), a story with hysterical potential.[16] As in the last decade and a half of Lacan's teaching, the emphasis in Lacanian psychoanalytic theory has steadily moved beyond the transcendental logic of the signifier to the predominance of the drive, the non-linguistic or extra-discursive dimension of language and subjectivity: jouissance, excess, enjoyment, or the Lacanian real, which Ellie Ragland describes as "the algebraic x, inherently foreclosed from direct apprehension or analysis."[17] *After Lacan* analyses and interrogates the trajectory from the signifier to the symptom through the wide-ranging reading protocols which reveal the transformative ethico-political possibilities of Lacan's enduring concepts. Like the Lacanian analyst, Lacanian discourse does not impose prescriptive interpretations but allows the (analysand's) unconscious to analyze itself. As Roudinesco observes, "in the end, the true form of the patient's desire becomes interpretable to the patient, in his or her own terms, for his or her own ends."[18]

Lacanian theory is testing for psychoanalysis in particular and the history of consciousness in general for the way in which it introduces to the cognitive register and reading practices "the impossible thing" that will turn them upside down. Whether it is in his theories of the gaze, voice, desire, jouissance, or the category of the real, which does not refer to reality, objects in the world, or some phenomenological thing-in-itself, Lacan documents the overlap of traumatic knowledge or lack with symbolic or imaginative orders. "Every truth has the *structure* of fiction," Lacan argued in Seminar VII, *The Ethics of Psychoanalysis*.[19] This traumatism at the heart of signification is not, for Lacan, a primordial scene but, to cite Ellie Ragland, "an interior knowledge that breaks up the imaginary consistencies to which a given subject clings in a willed *méconnnaissance* (misrecognition)."[20] Jacques Lacan is the confidence trickster who privileges *lettre* over being, who plunders literary language for the sense that lies outside its historical reality, a *sens jouis*, and who seems to say that psychoanalysis is an impossible and unrealized art. He "emphasizes *accommodation* of the id rather than its *assimilation* by the ego," as Mark Bracher puts it.[21] Lacan is also notorious for locating the truth of the symptom in the future, not the past, claiming for psychoanalysis, as he does in his Rome discourse, "the future perfect of what I shall have been for what I am in the process of becoming."[22] Instead of being programmed by events completed in the past, Lacanian analysands "are given the key to their own destiny," states the psychoanalyst Dany Nobus. Instead of the "classical analytic question, 'What has happened to me . . . that could possibly explain my present misery?'," Lacanian analysis, Nobus adds, "ushers the patient to ask 'What is going to happen to me that will explain both my current situation and my life-history?'"[23]

Jacques-Alain Miller has divided Lacan's theory into three phases: the 1950s and early 1960s, 1964–1974, 1974–1981. *After Lacan* draws selectively on these distinct archives to show the exfoliation of Lacanian thought and the ways in which Lacan, in his lifetime, outlived, outgrew, or outdid his discourse. In that sense, the book should be titled *After Lacans*, tracing, as it does, the afterlives of different, self-othering Lacans, including the Lacans posited retroactively in the course of our ongoing critical evaluations. *After Lacan* alludes also to Lacan's term for the Freudian word "Nachträglichkeit," which means deferred action, *a posteriori*: "après-coup," or afterwardness, through which an event becomes significant (or traumatic) retroactively, in the act of looking back. It could be argued that *After Lacan* embodies the logic of après-coup, coming after psychoanalysis and acting out its capacity to endow events with significance retrospectively. The logic of "après-coup" is related also to a reordering or "remémoration" of history. While Freud cast doubt on the hysteric's reminiscences, despite busily articulating the same into the coherent purposiveness of the talking cure, Lacan maintained that the ambivalence of the hysterical revelation was not due to a vacillation between the imaginary and the real: the ambivalence was due to the fact that the utterance belonged to both registers. As he states in *Écrits*, "in psychoanalytic anamnesis, it is not the question of reality, but of truth," whereby past contingencies are re-collected and re-ordered in full speech "by conferring on them the sense of necessities to come."[24] Lacan defines the act of re-collection and re-ordering as the "assumption of his history by the subject, in so far as it is constituted by the speech addressed to the other":[25] this is a foundational moment for Lacanian psychoanalysis, dealing, as it does, a death blow to the intersubjective constitution of its Freudian predecessor.

Fundamental Concepts

The book has three parts. The first, "Fundamental Concepts," alludes to Lacan's Seminar XI, also known as the *Four Fundamental Concepts of Psychoanalysis*. Arguably his most influential work, *Four Fundamental Concepts* draws on four basic Freudian concepts – unconscious, repetition, transference, and drive – to arrive at unique formulations and foundational ideas. This section examines the medical and intellectual history that (fore)shadows the Lacanian operational field and is often radically rewritten by it. Examining the genesis of Lacanian revolutionary psychoanalytic thinking in the works of Sigmund Freud, poets, and philosophers, in literature, clinical theory, and analytic practice, "Fundamental Concepts" provides the context (the "before" for the "after," if you will) of the profound impact Lacan has had in the interpretive humanities, and in the shaping of psychoanalytic discourse and a wider psychoanalytic culture. This part of the book contains four chapters, by Mladen Dolar, Anna Kornbluh, Tracy McNulty, and Dany Nobus, respectively. Mladen Dolar's "Voice after Lacan" examines the fundamental Lacanian concept of "voice." As Jacques-Alain Miller points out, psychoanalysis had been oriented by a diachronic scheme of object relations – the developmental stages defined by oral and the anal objects – until the "structural" turn ushered in by Lacan, which highlighted the unfolding of the unconscious in the structure of language.[26] The voice qua object, the object little *a* in the Lacanian algebra, is not to be found in the audible register. It is to be glimpsed – or heard – in the interstice of sense and presence, Dolar argues, and marks not their intersection but divergence. Voice, in Lacan's thought, is associated not with full presence, but with the negative entity of the subject. It is a leftover of the symbolic, its meaningless byproduct. The subject "emerges only in an impossible relation to that bit that cannot be present," Dolar argues in an earlier essay, titled "The Object Voice." "Only insofar as there is a Real (Lacan's name for that bit) as an impossibility of presence is there a subject."[27] Dolar's chapter in this collection is a further elaboration and provocation of the "almost nothing" of the hallucinatory and paradoxical object voice, as glimpsed through literary works by William Shakespeare, Italo Calvino, and Samuel Beckett.

Anna Kornbluh's "Freud's Return to Lacan" examines Freud's works as a corpus of language and a literary form to be worked through and rethought repeatedly. Scholars such as Juliet Mitchell and Jane Gallop have long asserted that only after reading Lacan can one read Freud and truly understand what Freud was saying. Lacanian theory is often interpreted as a "return to Freud," a return *to* the meaning of Freud, or a retrieval and reclaiming of Freudian doctrine that can itself be analyzed as a return *of* the repressed. Lacan's return addresses unresolved questions in Freud's writings relating to the ego and the subject of knowledge, the Oedipus complex, feminine sexuality, society, and law. That said, he does not exactly gloss or translate Freud: instead, Lacan symptomatically repeats the untranslatability of Freud. Lacan's reinterpretation of Freud, or the repetition of Freud's own persistent reworking of psychoanalysis, makes for what Jean-Michel Rabaté calls "an endless task of rereading."[28] The chapter critically questions received ideas about Lacan as a Freudian as well as Lacan's reinvention of Freud. Freud after Lacan is "Freud plus language," Kornbluh formulates, defamiliarized, refined, and disfigured at the same time. The chapter pays attention to the symptoms and fictions in Freud's designation of the laws of psychoanalysis (as revealed in Lacan's rewriting), to its political unconscious and aberrant relationship to the social, all of which go beyond the schematic reductions or what Freud, in *Beyond the Pleasure Principle*, called the "artificial structure of hypotheses" constituting psychoanalytic thought.[29]

Tracy McNulty, like Kornbluh, discusses the Dora case and the dynamics of transference, but in a substantially different way. For instance, if in Kornbluh's chapter "transference" ushers in the inter-subjective dimension of psychoanalysis, and its return to the social, in McNulty's reading transference is the expedient modality linking the imaginary to the symbolic, or "the complaint to the transference properly speaking (the address to the locus of the Other as the locus of knowledge)." McNulty's "Beyond the Oedipus Complex" addresses another crucial facet of the revisionism that defines Lacan's Freudian genealogy while also demarcating his departure from his disciplinary origin. In the seminars of the 1960s, in particular, Lacan had proposed that the function of the symbolic is to be sought not in the Oedipal prohibition. In Seminar XVII, for instance, Lacan called the Oedipus complex "Freud's dream," one whose universalism needs to be interrupted by the theory of the four discourses (the master's, the university's, the analyst's, and the hysteric's). Focusing on Lacan's reading of Freud's case study of Dora and his interpretation of Antigone, McNulty outlines the anti-Oedipal or feminine-Oedipal logic of Lacan's "Discourse of the Hysteric" as his manifesto of symbolic law. The chapter revives and refines the Lacanian definition of the "symbolic" as an enabling constraint that can usher in genuine "creativity, invention, and novelty," as McNulty puts it in an earlier work.[30] It also demonstrates the process of the "worlding" of psychoanalysis through literature, reminding us of a neologism coined by Lacan – "lituraterre" – meaning writing and/as erasure on earth, and the ways in which the subject creatively renegotiates the lack in the Other to articulate its desire and freedom.

Elizabeth Wright delineates two perimeters of Lacanian literary criticism, the pro and the anti: "criticism in the mode of Lacan and criticism of and beyond the mode of Lacan."[31] Both bear testimony to Lacan's virtuoso reading of psychoanalysis with literature – the ancient classics, Shakespeare, Joyce, Kafka, Blanchot, and Duras, among others – and his extensive knowledge of literary genres, not just tragedy, comedy, and rhetoric, but also the essay and symposium forms. As the scholarship of Jean-Michel Rabaté, among others, has demonstrated, this essay implicitly claims that Lacanian psychoanalytic theory is not only a hermeneutic but a literary event in itself. Dany Nobus's chapter, on psychoanalysis and/as poetry in Lacan's late clinical paradigm, examines the similarities between the interpretive and analytic acts as they apply to poetry and psychoanalysis, respectively. If meaning-making in poetry necessarily involves a loss, a translation that is not-all, psychoanalysis provides an analogue of this lack in the impossible logic of the real, helping the analysand come to grips with the most valuable element of the treatment. Nobus draws on Lacan's reflections on poetry in public seminars, his response to the French essayist and poet Léon-Paul Fargue in particular, and his own youthful poetic dabbling to examine the "'field of language' in psychoanalysis" and "'the field of meaning' in the direction of treatment."

After Lacan

The chapters in Part II, titled "After Lacan," examine the chronological and qualitative effects of Lacanian theory. They show how the relevance and influence of this theory have been instrumental in linking psychoanalytic reason and treatment to literature, the arts, identity politics, and cultural production. The chapters by Merrill Cole and Todd McGowan explore Lacan's reinvention of the unconscious and its implications for the psychoanalysis of language and image, pertaining to their discursive organization as well as their relationship to phenomena irreducible to symbolization. They examine the deployment of Lacan, especially his writings on sexuality in the field of vision, power, and fantasy, in the psychoanalysis of cinema, and the development of queer theory. McGowan's chapter, and that contributed by Jodi Dean – a psychoanalytic reading of the party form – also shed light on the enormous impact Slavoj Žižek's version of Lacan had in the 1990s and beyond, and on Lacan studies after the high noon of the Slovenian School. The final chapter, written by Azeen Khan, reclaims Lacan's scattered speculations on race and poses the same as a vital contribution to critical race studies. Deploying the concept of jouissance, and the hatred of the Other's jouissance, Khan deftly demonstrates how racism is the libidinal economy of being linked to a foreign body.

For Lacan, sexuality is indissociable from language and linguistic processes, and is a matter of speech and discourse, not biology. Sexuality, whose Lacanian definition, according to Elizabeth Grosz is "a pleasure marked by a lack," is the privileged field where desire is played out as a search for meaning, or particular meanings.[32] In fact, it could be argued that Lacanian theory foreshadows discourses of sexuality where the gender of object-choice is inconsequential. Lacan's seminar on "sinthome," which yokes the psycholinguistic dimensions of the imaginary, symbolic, and real, lays the groundwork for future elaborations of what Lee Edelman calls the economy of "*sinthom*osexuality," as it applies to the reinstallation of gender and transgender norms.[33] Whether it is in his critique of ego psychology and normative sexuality, his reconceptualization of the unconscious, or his imbrication of the death drive with jouissance, Lacan, Tim Dean has argued, makes psychoanalysis look rather queer.[34] The chapter by Merrill Cole offers a genealogy of the field of queer studies to examine its avoidance of Lacanian psychoanalysis despite several influential interventions, notably Tim Dean's *Beyond Sexuality* (2000). Focusing on repression – and queer theory's curious rejection of the discourse of repression – Cole offers a Lacanian reading of unconscious desire. This chapter offers a valuable overview of the disagreements between psychoanalysis and queer theory, and suggests alternative deployments of psychoanalysis that promise to disrupt the "commodified homonormative, heteronormative, and cis-gender continuums of the present." Cole reinforces his argument with a reading of the foreclosure of psychoanalysis in Paul B. Preciado's "postqueer" manifesto, *Testo Junkie*.

As Stephen Heath stated, cinema, especially after the psychoanalyzing of cinema by the Slovenian Lacanian School, is not merely "the vehicle of an exposition" but "a matter of experience."[35] The Lacanian meditation on optics in particular, and the centrality of the image and apparatus in Lacan's psychoanalysis in general, have both drawn on cinema and proved enormously influential for film theory. Metz turned to Lacan for an account of the "*other mirror*, the cinema screen,"[36] and cinema, in turn, has been widely used in discussions of imago, image, and identity, or image and identification in psychoanalysis. The chapter by Todd McGowan, which looks at film theory after Lacan, shows how the point of connection between psychoanalysis and cinema is often in the modality of shock as each commutes the unrepresentable into language, image, signs. In "Cinema after Lacan," McGowan analyzes the importance of

Lacan's theory of the gaze, which presents the subject as an object of the visual field, not its master. He argues that while popular cinema avoids the gaze to preempt a disturbing experience on the part of the cinegoer, the greatest films force a confrontation with it. Drawing on classic and contemporary works – *Vertigo, Citizen Kane, Tokyo Story,* and *La La Land* – McGowan lingers on disfigurations of the visual field caused by the gaze, seeing in this tense negotiation of aesthetics and politics a possibility for political emancipation.

How does Lacanian psychoanalysis stand up to the *antiphusis* or antinature, that constitutive excess of the human, in the dimension of the political? In *Four Fundamental Concepts of Psychoanalysis,* Lacan posits psychoanalysis as "a beyond to [this] identification."[37] The end of psychoanalysis is not in the identification with the analyst as an exemplar of social or political good: in fact, analysis is terminated when such an accident occurs. Jodi Dean's "Lacan and Politics" analyzes some of the ways in which both psychoanalytic theory and practice have tapped into the material of the political, including the political unconscious. Dean uses Lacan to theorize what she calls the "psycho-dynamics of collectivity" galvanizing the party form. Focusing on the work of sociologist Robert Michels (a student of Max Weber's) on political formations, and with the help of Lacanian theory, she examines how no party is identical with itself. It is in this dehiscence – this gap, which Lacan theorizes as a social space – that the enabling prerequisites and conditions of political collectivity may be rediscovered. Dean's is also an elaboration of the theory of transference examined by McNulty and Kornbluh in Part I, and here she uses it to describe collectivities around political leaders that do not necessarily lead to authoritarianism. Dean points out that Lacan associates the Freudian unconscious with a gap, "a gap where something happens but remains unrealized." It is a space where the unrealized makes itself felt, and Dean argues that the communist party bestows political form "for the press of the unrealized struggles of the people."

Is psychoanalytic theory relevant to race? Critics, such as Charles Shepherdson, have argued that race is comparable to sexual difference in psychoanalytic theory in that, like the latter, race is neither a biological entity nor a symbolic construction. As an entity which is both discursively posited and extradiscursive, the perplexity of race lends itself to psychoanalytic readings, as evidenced in the rich scholarship on this topic by Anne Anlin Cheng (*Melancholy of Race*), Christopher Lane (*The Psychoanalysis of Race*), David Marriott (*Haunted Life*), Hortense Spillers (*Black, White, and in Color*), Darieck Scott (*Extravagant Abjection*),

Kalpana Sheshadri-Crooks (*Desiring Whiteness*), Michelle Stephens (*Skin Acts*), Claudia Tate (*Psychoanalysis and Black Novels*), Antonio Viego (*Dead Subjects*), and Shannon Winnubst (*Way Too Cool*). Acknowledging, though not revisiting, this valuable scholarship on the usefulness or irrelevance of psychoanalysis to questions of race, Azeen Khan examines instead the singularity of the Lacanian intervention into race and racism. Developing the concept of segregation, she examines Lacanian theory alongside Jacques-Alain Miller's interpretation of the same, especially Miller's elaboration of the Lacanian concept of "extimité" to interpret racism as an exemplary form of social group formation. Bringing to the fore lesser known works by Lacan – the essay "L'étourdit" or "Address on Child Psychoses" – or recasting well-known ones such as Seminar XVII, *The Other Side of Psychoanalysis*, and *Television* in new light, Khan's chapter is bold and original in the way it addresses head-on Lacan's thoughts on race and racism (instead of applying Lacanian theory to the knotty question of race). The inassimilable jouissance of the Other, Khan argues, is an obscure cause of racism.

Beyond Lacan

The final part, "Beyond Lacan," showcases new consequences of Lacanian psychoanalysis in contemporary critical and cultural theory. These topics, which show how some of the discoveries of Lacan's clinical teaching have been refined and expanded beyond the contexts in which they were originally used, include Lacanian readings of new media (Clint Burnham), positive disability identity (Anna Mollow), and Islam (Nouri Gana). Not only do these revaluations unsettle the lexicon and axiomatics of the interpreted Lacanian text, and the hegemonies of schools of Lacanian thought that perpetuate the same, they powerfully communicate the need to acknowledge new and recombinant categories of human as well as non-sentient subjects of psychoanalysis.

To echo Jacqueline Rose on the topic of psychoanalysis and history, psychoanalytic ideas about causality, time, identity, and repetition undermine the historical concept of the event, showing how fantasy "plays a central, constitutive role in the modern world of states and nations."[38] Lacan's dialectic opposition to the materialist logic of historicism is widely accepted: the Lacanian subject is not the Foucauldian self (*le soi*) articulated by panoptic power or by an *eros* coming after desire. In a famous response to the Lacanian psychoanalyst Jacques-Alain Miller in 1977, Michel Foucault said psychoanalysis is "not the theory of development, not the sexual secret behind the neuroses and psychoses, but a logic of the unconscious."[39] Anna Mollow's chapter reads, through the lens of disability studies and psychoanalysis, bodily issues such as subject formation, specularity, identity, and sexuality. Reading Lacan's oft-cited "The Mirror Stage" (1932) alongside disability activist Connie Panzarino's memoir, *The Me in the Mirror*, Mollow discovers parallels and complicities between disability studies and psychoanalysis that speak to a mutual investment in the destabilization of ideal ego and identity. The promise of this alliance, if that is indeed the right term for the fraught relationship between psychoanalysis and disability studies, however, is a tentative one. Mollow's astute reading of the hysterical symptom, which is posited as psychoneurotic in Freudian and Lacanian epistemologies, reveals the ableist paradigms and Cartesian models of causality in psychoanalytic thought. For a person with an undocumented disability, as was the case with Panzarino, this attitude lent credence to her parents' and caregivers' charge that her symptoms were withholding psychic information, and that they were her own fault. As Mollow demonstrates, at odds with the non-identitarian and non-totalitarian thinking of the "Mirror Stage" essay, Lacan's theories of hysteria perpetuate an asymmetry of power between the analyst, "a-subject-presumed-to-know," and the analysand posed as a passive sufferer who hasn't, in the words of Lacan, understood anything.

How do Lacan's theories hold up in the hypermediated world we live in? How does his concept of psychic realities as networks resonate with ideas like hypertext or with the realities of our virtual lives? Can the key elements psychoanalysis – gaze, objet *a*, the webs of desire, intersubjectivity, the Other, paranoia – be revised through a cyberanalysis of Lacanian theory? Scholarship on Lacan and the new media shows that not only is Lacan a prophet of the "paranoid knowledge" of cyberspace, but that millennial psychoanalysis can help us imagine a posthumanism that is neither apocalyptic nor anti-social. Clint Burnham's chapter on the selfie, the cloud, and the dialectics of lack looks at ways in which the dematerialized materialism and the affective world of the internet, digital culture, and social media can reframe and reorder our understanding of Lacanian psychoanalysis, in particular its mainstays such as the mirror stage and the big Other. Burnham's chapter, like that of Mollow before it, develops the mirror stage, although he does so with the help of digital portraiture and postmodern aesthetics. Using resources as disparate as Kim Kardashian's selfies, the artist Tim Lee's "Duck Soup," John Gerrard's digital simulations, and architecture criticism, Burnham outlines a desiring or lacking dialectic – "the dialectic qua connectivity that also disconnects" – between the selfie, a photographic self-portrait, and the cloud, a data storage service provider. In this Lacanian reading, the unconscious is structured like a data set (or the other way around).

Just as Lacan had "silent partners," as Žižek observes, borrowing from philosophy to perfect his own conceptual apparatus, Lacanian thought connects with philosophy and theology in their mutual concern over the unconscious, the non-human and inhuman, the uncanny, life and death, love, and self-knowledge. Jacques Derrida claimed in *Resistances of Psychoanalysis* that the resistance to psychoanalysis (pervasive in philosophy) should be thought alongside the resistance to analysis at the heart of psychoanalysis, an auto-immune process, as he identified it. The relationship between Lacanian theory and the philosophers, whether it is Levinas, Foucault, Agamben, or Derrida, has often been read along these lines of analysis and resistance. In the final chapter of this volume, "Islam after Lacan," Nouri Gana examines Fethi Benslama's 2002 book, *La psychanalyse à l'épreuve de l'Islam* (later translated into English and published in 2009 as *Psychoanalysis and the Challenge of Islam*), which provides a sensational account of translating Islam into Freudian and Lacanian psychoanalysis. For Benslama, the Rushdie affair, where the celebrated novelist Salman Rushdie, by virtue of authoring *The Satanic Verses*, became the hapless victim of the speech-act that was the Iranian Ayatollah's death sentence or *fatwa* on February 14, 1989, was a "rude awakening." It spurred him on to develop an intellectual project that led to an investigation of the question of origins of Islam, and his deployment of psychoanalysis, both clinical and theoretical, was challenged as the discipline was transported to a cultural context dramatically different from that instrumental in its emergence. Benslama's dalliance with psychoanalysis raises questions about the applicability of the theory to Islam, a religion that received little more attention than Freud's passing remarks in *Moses and Monotheism*. The institution of psychoanalysis, in that sense, could be held responsible for the present-day "resistance to the intelligibility of Islam." Benslama points out that historically, psychoanalysis did little to decipher the complexities of Islam, which would have promoted its intelligibility, for better or worse, and made it more culturally mainstream. Gana demonstrates how, because of the missed encounter between psychoanalysis and Islam, Benslama's method is necessarily translational, attempting, as it does, to read Islam and psychoanalysis in tandem. With critical reservations, the chapter uses Benslama's use of Lacanian psychoanalysis to reexamine the notion of origins in Islam.

This collection of essays provides a historical and critical account of how the institution of psychoanalysis has negotiated critical and clinical Freudian frameworks and how it has fared *after* Lacan: the ways in which psychoanalysis has transmitted Lacan's theory, amplifying its promise, and also its disagreements with Lacan's ideas, technique, and lexicon, his bon mots included. Its contribution is distinctive in three key ways. Firstly, it allows students and scholars of psychoanalysis to make a searching reassessment of Jacques Lacan's writings in detail and depth, with close attention to chronology and immediate context, and in the expanding framework of its intellectual genealogies and legacies. This commitment to the complex resonances of the Lacanian text offers a corrective for the way in which Lacan, often read by deputy and through the mediation of populist cultural translations of his vatic utterances, is the object of fleeting youthful enthusiasm at university, only to be eventually tossed aside for more serious, discipline-bound work.

Secondly, while there are many influential critical interventions – by Peter Brooks, Shoshana Felman, Maud Ellmann, Barbara Johnson, Claudia Tate, Jeffrey Mehlman, Jean-Michel Rabaté, Joan Copjec, Laura Marcus, and Ankhi Mukherjee – on the question of the cultural impact of psychoanalysis, *After Lacan* disaggregates and disambiguates Lacan's contribution from that of his predecessors (primarily Freud), contemporaries, and successors. Taking care not to automatically posit causality in these generational chains or lateral networks, as the case may be, it studies the ways in which psychoanalysis, as multi-authored theory, method, and praxis, has been singularly developed by Lacan (and after Lacan). Finally, scholarly appraisals of the legacies of Lacan (and Freudian–Lacanian psychoanalysis) tend to be exclusively critical or clinical. *The Subject of Lacan: A Lacanian Reader for Psychologists*, edited by Karen Malone and Stephen Friedlander, or the above-mentioned *After Lacan: Clinical Practice and the Subject of the Unconscious*, co-authored by Willy Apollon et al., which self-consciously eschew critical and cultural expositions of Lacanian theory in favor of Lacan's clinical teaching, are cases in point, as is Jean-Michel Rabaté's *Jacques Lacan: Psychoanalysis and the Subject of Literature*, which offers valuable insights into Lacan as a literary and cultural counter-power instead. Despite its literary orientation, *After Lacan* explicitly addresses both varieties of knowledge, the one ensuing from a generalizable theory and the other performed case-by-case in clinical practice. It achieves this through the involvement of theoretical clinicians such as Nobus and Khan in this project and through references to records of clinical treatments. Drawing on Lacan's own differentiation between the university and analytic discourses, the chapters of *After Lacan* examine the productive tension between psychoanalytic theory and the analytic clinic with the advent of the figure of the "Lacanian." It asks how Lacanian thought is negotiated in the academy and the consulting room, and whether there can be any dialogue between, say, the theoretical abstractions on the Lacanian "real" in academic psychoanalysis and clinical encounters with the real.

Psychoanalytic practice and writing of every persuasion "sounds a bit like religion, a bit like metaphysics, a bit like anthropology, a bit like science," says the noted British psychoanalyst and writer Adam Phillips.[40] And, of course, a bit like literature. The approach of this book is interdisciplinary, working, as it does, across clinical, sociological, philosophical, and literary fields to allow the system of Lacanian psychoanalysis to participate in wider cultural conversations. In "For the Love of Lacan," with which I framed my introduction, Derrida states:

> I consider it an act of cultural resistance to pay homage publicly to a difficult form of thought, discourse, or writing, one which does not submit easily to normalization by the media, by academics, or by publishers, one which rebels against the restoration currently underway, against the philosophical or theoretical neo-conformism in general (let us not even mention literature) that flattens and levels everything around us, in the attempt to make one forget what the Lacan era was, along with the future and the promise of his thought, thereby erasing the name of Lacan.[41]

Derrida acknowledges Lacanian theory as "a difficult form of thought," a rare complexity of style and subject matter that has prevented its easy transmission. In 1973, Lacan notoriously claimed that he named his work *Écrits* because, in his opinion, a writing ("un écrit") is "made not to be read."[42] What he meant was that the essays in the collection should be treated as utterances instead, "sayings" that are not to be *read* but to be reinstated in conjunction with their lost performative contexts. The difficulty of Lacan, thus, does not encourage blind transference, or seek to make devotees out of his readers. Jane Gallop cites Roland Barthes's distinction between the readerly and writerly texts, aligning Lacan's work with the latter, scriptible category, wherein the reader is "not a consumer but a producer of the text."[43] This, I'd argue, is possible because of the ethics of Lacanian theory, a veritable ethics of the real. If, by ethics, we understand the prohibitionist structure that rations and disciplines desire, Lacan shows how excess is a component of ethics. As Alenka Zupančič observes, "ethics is by nature excessive," an adversary to the "smooth course of events" or the "reality principle."[44] Tracing Lacan's changing position on ethics across the different seminars, notably Seminar VII (*The Ethics of Psychoanalysis*) and Seminar XI (*The Four Fundamental Concepts of Psycho-Analysis*), Zupančič shows the logic of desire in Lacanian analysis eventually ending in the dimension of the drive. The ethical in Lacanian theory goes beyond the pleasure principle and field of intersubjective relations, and its subject, the subject of drive, is articulated in relation to the order of the real, which disarticulates the imaginary and the symbolic through impasses and knots. It evokes a mode of *inhuman* subjectivity ordered not by the dialectic of desire, but by the desire of the Other, the Other as *das Ding* or the Thing. Rereading ethics by acknowledging the encipherments of the real in Lacan's work (during his lifetime and in his wake), *After Lacan* offers a series of provocations to the founding fantasies of psychoanalysis, literature, and politics. As Derrida says, to pay homage publicly to Jacques Lacan is in itself an act of cultural resistance.

Notes

1 Willy Apollon, Danielle Bergeron, and Lucie Cantin, *After Lacan: Clinical Practice and the Subject of the Unconscious*, ed. Robert Hughes and Kareen Ror Malone (New York: SUNY Press, 2002), 1.
2 Ibid., 2.
3 Ibid., 3.
4 In 1953, Lacan's unorthodox theory and practices, especially the variable-length session, led to a vote of no-confidence by psychoanalysts belonging to the IPA (International Psychoanalytical Association). In 1964, he founded the École Freudienne de Paris after the SFP (Société Française de Psychanalyse), a splinter group of the IPA formed in 1953, was coerced by the IPA into expelling Lacan from its list of analysts.
5 Jacques Derrida, *Resistances of Psychoanalysis* (Stanford University Press, 1998).
6 Ibid., 49.
7 Ibid.
8 Ibid., 55. Derrida uses "genealogical" in "genealogico-deconstructive" in the sense of interpretation or investigation. The Derridean genealogist is an investigator, not a hermeneutician, and the meaning they seek is historically situated, not absolute.
9 Ibid., 56.
10 Simon Morgan Wortham, "The Archive, the Event, and the Impression," in *Libraries, Literatures, and Archives*, ed. Sas Mays (New York: Routledge, 2013).
11 Élisabeth Roudinesco, *Lacan: In Spite of Everything* (New York: Verso, 2014), 51.
12 Ibid., 52.
13 Alan Badiou and Élisabeth Roudinesco, *Jacques Lacan, Past and Present: A Dialogue* (New York: Columbia University Press, 2014), 28.

14 *Iraq: The Borrowed Kettle* (New York: Verso, 2005), 80.

15 Alenka Zupančič, *Ethics of the Real: Kant, Lacan* (New York: Verso, 2000),
    235. Slavoj Žižek, "What Some Would Call . . . A Response to Yannis
    Stavrakakis," *Umbr(a): Ignorance of the Law*, 8 (2003), 133.

16 Cited in Richard Feldstein, Bruce Fink, and Maire Jaanus (eds.), *Reading
    Seminars I and II: Lacan's Return to Freud* (Albany: State University of New
    York Press, 1998), 262.

17 Ellie Ragland, *Jacques Lacan and the Philosophy of Psychoanalysis* (Michigan:
    University of Illinois Press, 1986), 188.

18 *Lacan: In Spite of Everything*, 87.

19 Jacques Lacan, *The Ethics of Psychoanalysis: 1959–1960* (New York:
    Routledge, 2013), 12.

20 Ellie Ragland, *Jacques Lacan and the Logic of Structure: Topology and
    Language in Psychoanalysis* (New York: Routledge, 2015).

21 Mark Bracher, "How Analysis Cures According to Lacan," in *The Subject
    of Lacan: A Lacanian Reader for Psychologists*, ed. Kareen Ror Malone and
    Stephen R. Friedlander (Stonybrook: SUNY Press, 2012), 192.

22 Cited in Dany Nobus, *Jacques Lacan and the Freudian Practice of
    Psychoanalysis* (Philadelphia: Psychology Press, 2000), 86.

23 Ibid.

24 Jacques Lacan, *Écrits: A Selection*, trans. Alan Sheridan (New York: W. W.
    Norton, 1977), 48.

25 Ibid.

26 See Jacques-Alain Miller, "Jacques Lacan and the Voice," in *The Later Lacan:
    An Introduction*, ed. Veronique Voruz and Bogdan Wolf (Albany: SUNY
    Press, 2012).

27 Mladen Dolar, "Lacan and the Voice," in *Gaze and Voice as Love Objects*,
    ed. Renata Salecl and Slavoj Žižek (Durham, NC: Duke University Press,
    1996), 42.

28 Jean-Michel Rabaté, *The Cambridge Companion to Lacan* (Cambridge
    University Press, 2003), 22.

29 In this context, Freud is comparing the hypotheses of psychoanalysis to
    biology, suggesting that these speculations may be unseated by empirical
    evidence from physiology or chemistry. Sigmund Freud, *Beyond the Pleasure
    Principle* SE 18 (1920), 60.

30 Tracy McNulty, *Wrestling with the Angel: Experiments in Symbolic Life* (New
    York: Columbia University Press, 2014), 11.

31 Elizabeth Wright, "Another Look at Lacan and Literary Criticism," *New
    Literary History* 19, 3 (1988), 617–627, 617.

32 Elizabeth Grosz, *Jacques Lacan: A Feminist Introduction* (New York:
    Routledge, 2002), 81.

33 Lee Edelman, *No Future: Queer Theory and the Death Drive* (Durham, NC:
    Duke University Press, 2004), 59.

34 Tim Dean, "Lacan and Queer Theory," in *The Cambridge Companion to
    Lacan*, ed. Jean-Michel Rabaté (Cambridge University Press, 2003), 238.

35 Stephen Heath, "Cinema and Psychoanalysis: Parallel Histories," in *Endless Night: Cinema and Psychoanalysis, Parallel Histories*, ed. Janet Bergstrom (Berkeley: University of California Press, 1999), 36. 25–56.

36 Christian Metz, *The Imaginary Signifier: Psychoanalysis and Cinema* (Bloomington: Indiana University Press, 1982), 4.

37 Jacques Lacan, *The Four Fundamental Concepts of Psycho-analysis*, ed. Jacques-Alain Miller and trans. Alan Sheridan (London: Penguin Books, 1994), 271.

38 Jacqueline Rose, *States of Fantasy* (Oxford University Press, 1998), 5.

39 Cited in Jan Goldstein, *Hysteria Complicated by Ecstacy: The Case of Nanette Leroux* (Princeton University Press, 2011), 203.

40 Adam Phillips, *Promises, Promises* (London: Faber and Faber, 2016).

41 Derrida, *Resistances of Psychoanalysis*, 45–46.

42 Cited in Jane Gallop, *Reading Lacan* (Ithaca: Cornell University Press, 1985), 44.

43 Ibid.

44 Zupančič, *Ethics of the* Real, 5.

PART I

Fundamental Concepts

CHAPTER I

Voice after Lacan

Mladen Dolar

The voice has never really been an object of theoretical scrutiny in itself. To be sure, there have been scattered reflections on its mysterious power, on its aesthetic value, its overwhelming power in music, on the inner voice of conscience, etc. In the literary studies one used it as a metaphor for an author's specific and unique quality, an instantly recognizable tone or style, and one used it particularly in regard to poetry where the sound value is of at least equal importance as signification. "A poem: a prolonged hesitation between sound and sense," such was Paul Valéry's famous definition of poetry, extolled by Roman Jakobson.[1] These reflections were often interesting, engaging, and inspiring, yet one could hardly extricate from them a sustained theory of the voice nor did one quite envisage a pressing need for one.

This all changed *after Lacan*. Indeed Lacan is a major watershed in the treatment of the voice given that he took the voice to be one of the privileged "embodiments" of the *object a*, the object that stands at the core of psychoanalysis, and he considered the theory of *object a* to be his major contribution to psychoanalytic theory. To the list of Freudian objects he famously added the object gaze and the object voice, and this extension of the list may well seem to be a modest addition, yet he thereby provided a concept where so many strands and loose ends of Freud's theory come together, converging in this "bit of the real" that doesn't quite coincide with any given entity, with any existing thing, yet tenuously and tenaciously perseveres within them – and it took the psychoanalytic experience to single it out. This insight, this conceptual invention proved to be immensely fruitful for a number of other areas. It instigated a quickly expanding area of voice studies[2] and gave a completely new inflection to literary studies. Taking the voice as the object, the object in the precise Lacanian sense, points beyond the major preoccupations of literary studies with interpretation and signification, and on the other hand with unraveling the enigma of the aesthetic value. For this object is irreducible to meaning, to the signifier, and irreducible to the aesthetic value – its aesthetic value rather serves as an obfuscation of what is at stake. Furthermore it entails far reaching philosophical questions about the nature of presence, beyond interpretation and aesthetics.

In what follows I will take up three literary examples that can hopefully provide a simple demonstration of how to conceive this object voice and what use one can make of it. The three examples are treated briefly, with modest aims, as demonstrational devices, with no attempt to give a sustained analysis and do justice to them. They are considered only in a limited and focused perspective to disentangle the specificity of the object voice.

Juliet, standing on the balcony and talking into the night, says: "What's in a name? ... It is nor hand, nor foot, / Nor arm, nor face, nor any other part / Belonging to a man."[3] Juliet doesn't see Romeo, hidden in the darkness of the garden, not yet; she speaks into the dark, and Romeo listens to "his Mistress's voice" addressing the night. This is first of all a scene of voices, voices heard in the dark, and at the same time, emblematically, a scene of names: precisely the drama of the disparity between voices and names. She will recognize Romeo, a moment later, by his voice, and they will commune with their voices in the dark, not quite seeing each other. They will swear their love in this scene of voices, the canonical scene which has defined so much of what we understand under the name of love. The scene can be taken as a cue for the understanding of the voice, for the rather dramatic understanding of the discrepancy, the opposition between the voice and the name, that is, between the voice and the signifier.

In this scene, at the simplest, the name is the enemy and the voice is the ally. "'Tis but thy name that is my enemy," says Juliet. Both the name and the voice point to individuality, they pinpoint our uniqueness, our singularity, but in opposing ways: the name points to the inscription of our individuality into the social, into the network of social divisions, hierarchies, and obligations; it ascribes us a social place, a symbolic identification. The voice, on the other hand, seems to escape the social network and its vicissitudes, it appears to be beyond the symbolic, it speaks from heart to heart, it is of such stuff that love is made of. Each voice is unique, it has the fingerprint quality. It is far more singular than the name, since the name is shared, it obeys social and family codes, and it is always generic – one is always a Montague or a Capulet. By the name one is inscribed in a symbolic network, but the voice presents something that the symbolic network cannot account for, the specter of an "inner treasure." By the name one always impersonates someone else, one is always a representative of a class of people bearing certain names, a family, a nation, a tradition, but with the voice one always impersonates only oneself, as it were. "Impersonating oneself" may seem a paradox, but it is perhaps not a bad description of the use of one's own voice, as we will see.[4] But for the Veronese lovers it is a matter of life and death to sever this unity. The uniqueness that the voice evokes and testifies to is the uniqueness which is at stake in love, love aiming precisely at the exclusive trait that cannot be quite spelled out or pinned down by the symbolic. Voice is its harbinger, voice is the pledge, and the two lovers in the night have no problems communing in their voices: everything would be all right, or so it seems, if only they could be confined to the voice; it is the name that is the source of all trouble. "In what vile part of this anatomy / Doth my name lodge?" asks Romeo later in the play (III/3). "Tell me that I may sack / The hateful mansion." And he draws his sword, as the stage directions indicate, prepared to cut off that vile bodily part, to cut off his name with the sword, castrate himself of his name, the name of the father,[5] but to no avail. To cut off the name and to retain the voice – the name is expendable, the voice is not: "Deny thy father and refuse thy name" – in order to fully assume the voice? This is the fantasy of the Verona lovers – love beyond names and signifiers, the communion of "voices and nothing more."

So what's in a voice, to extend Juliet's question? What does the voice bear witness to? And which part of the anatomy does it inhabit? It is also "nor hand nor foot nor arm nor face nor any other part belonging to a man." And how does "what's in a voice" differ from "what's in a name"? There is a dichotomy, an antinomy of the voice and the signifier, something that this scene dramatizes most spectacularly, by pitting the voice against the master signifier, indeed that of the name of the father. But what is brought here to a dramatic pinnacle happens on a more modest and elementary level all the time: there is a drama, a miniature drama, carried out in virtually every sentence we may utter. For the signifier, this could serve as its definition, is that in language which can be replicated – its replication, repetition, iterativity enables speech. It is that in language which can be linguistically classified, pinned down, and dissected into a web of differences; it upholds a logic which functions well enough, despite its pitfalls and flaws with which we must make do. But the voice which sustains the speech, the voice which is the vehicle and the means whereby we can speak, cannot be linguistically described as such, although it stands at the very core of speaking. What can be linguistically dissected is the phoneme, a particular discrete sound, i.e. the voice as it is molded by the signifier, cut down to size so that it can produce meaning, in view of production of meaning. For it is only with signifiers that one can make sense; signifiers are there, as their name indicates, in order to signify. The voice is another matter: it is that in language which doesn't contribute to signification; it is what doesn't help making sense.[6] And this could serve as its provisional definition – it is what cannot be said, although it enables saying. It is the means in the ascent toward meaning, to be eventually discarded, like Wittgenstein's ladder, once we have climbed to the peak of meaning. The voice is unique, unrepeatable, singular, and therefore not subject to linguistic description; it is what cannot be universalized – and linguistics seizes only that part of the voice that can be universalized. Hence it can serve as the pledge of one's ineffable being in the midst of repetition and replication, the pledge of love – this is where the linguistic drama intersects the drama of lovers, linguistics meets love. But in its unrepeatable singularity, and for that very reason, it is also immediately vanishing, evanescent, disappearing the moment it appears, and hence bringing up the question of presence at its most acute.

The voice is the junction of presence and sense. Perhaps nowhere is the sense of presence more incisive, more invasive and acute, than with the experience of the voice. There is an overwhelming sense of presence in the voice, be it in the voice heard which cuts directly into the interior, to the point that the very notion of interior can be put into question (and the most frequent experience of psychosis, that of "hearing voices," only takes on and amplifies something which is there in the most common functioning of the voice, blurring the line between the exterior and the interior); be it in emitting one's own voice – and for Derrida hearing one's own voice, "hearing oneself speak," is concomitant and coextensive with the very notion of consciousness – there is no consciousness unless one can hear one's own voice, in a loop of self-affection. Both are spectacularly there from the first moment on, since emitting one's voice is the first sign of life, the first opening to the other, and hearing voices is the first experience of the presence of the other. There is something striking and immediate in the experience of the voice, with the impossibility to maintain distance to it (as opposed to the visual world); one cannot close one's ears the way one can close the eyelids, one is constantly exposed and available to the voice. It hits the interior and it stems from the interior, so that sorting out the divide between the interior and the exterior is always endowed with a puzzle, a riddle. It constitutes the predicament of the first massive epistemic and affective "decision" one has to deal with in life, the line to draw. At the same time the voice is the epitome of passing, it's gone the moment it is emitted, as well as the epitome of changing, of constant becoming and elapsing, being on the move. It is intimately involved with the very notion of time and hence with our hold on presence. The voice is both immediate and treacherous, treacherous in its immediacy.

But if the voice epitomizes presence *par excellence*, it is also most immediately and inextricably linked with making sense, the other part of our provisional alternative. It is the most immediate and general means we have for conveying a meaning, for "expressing oneself," in the broadest sense. The voice is singled out among the innumerable sounds and noises by being a means of "expression," by bringing forth the inside, externalizing the interior, and hence conveying, wanting to say something. From the first moment on, the moment of a baby's cry, the voice is the first and the most prominent bearer of signification, its vehicle, but one which at the same time, while conveying and signifying, in the very same process, also conveys itself in its singularity and materiality. This can be described as the dichotomy or the antinomy of the voice and signifier, where the signifier is that part of the voice which contributes to signification, and the voice proper, the object voice, is that part which doesn't take part in the signifying process, but maintains a paradoxical and intense relationship with presence as the other part of our alternative. There is an intimate drama of presence and sense which is being played out with every use of the voice.

I will take up two literary examples as two models of conceiving this drama. The first one is a short story by Italo Calvino, "A King Listens," one of the last things he wrote, in 1984, just before his death (in 1985). It is a story which should have been part of a collection of stories on the five senses, but he finished only three before his death.[7] The story was also part of a collaboration with Luciano Berio, one of the most prominent modern composers, who actually wrote an opera, *Un re in ascolto*, based on this story (and some other sources). What is interesting for our purpose is the way that the story is entirely built on the alternative "sense or presence," the way it pits the two functions of the voice against one another, and in this dilemma it clearly takes sides, it endorses the "return to presence" as opposed to making sense.

There is a king lonely on his throne, the sovereign in the place of power, in the middle of the palace, with all the insignia, the scepter, the crown, the hosts of servants. He has come to occupy the throne by a coup, dethroning the previous ruler; he has achieved the highest post that a man can achieve in this empire, in this world; he is duly adulated, all his needs are amply seen to. So what is left to be done once there? Well, all he can do is to wait and to listen.[8] The king is not the emitter of the voice, the conveyor of the commanding voice of power, the Master's voice; the king is not the voice but the ear. All days long he listens to the sounds of the palace, the footsteps of servants, the morning trumpet blares, the people going about their business, the ceremonies, the visitors to the palace, the clocks, the clicks, the music, mostly played in his honor, the flattering words; and beyond the palace, the sounds of the city, the parades, the distant echoes, but also the riots and their stifling. "All the acoustical routes converge on the throne room" (38). All the voices and noises flow into king's ears.

Why does the king listen? His position at the top is most precarious: he deposed the previous ruler and can be himself deposed at any moment. This is the world of power and it is in its nature to be the world of usurpation and conspiracy, so all the voices are submitted to a gigantic hermeneutics of power. The point of the king's listening is to scrutinize all the voices and sounds in order to sort out the recalcitrant, the mutinous, the non-compliant, rebellious voices, to draw an elusive line. The king is the permanent listener and the permanent interpreter – to rule is to listen and to interpret. He is constantly on the watch for the hidden meaning. What do voices say? The trouble is not so much their explicit meaning, their positive and immediate messages – this is the easy part. The trouble is the undecidable hidden part which pertains precisely to the voice, to its inflections, its shadings, its tone, its cadences, the panoply of its infinite possibilities. They may appear docile and compliant, but this may be just a mask concealing subversion, mutiny, and conspiracy. He doesn't listen to the semantic part, but precisely to the voice as a bearer of semantics beyond semantics, the semantics beyond signifier. They are saying this, but what do they really want? *Che vuoi?*[9] This duplicity runs through all the sounds he hears, the duplicity of appearance and its hidden underside. The king is the ear intercepting the sounds of the Other, and no matter how sharply he listens there is something in the Other which is elusive. There is a dark spot in the Other, something unfathomable, and all the voices and sounds of all kinds are tainted by this. No sound is what it seems. This is a permanent stakeout which tries to discern the most obscure, the meaning of what structurally and necessarily escapes, that in the voice which is, by definition, beyond meaning, conveying something else than the signifiers it is attached to. It's not just voices; also the pauses between them are suspicious. "You cannot help looking for meaning, concealed perhaps not in single, iso-lated noises but between them, in the pauses that separate them" (43). Silences are even worse: the absence of sounds is threatening, a fateful sign of conspiracy. And also if the sounds are all ordinary and follow the routine pattern round the clock, this is highly suspicious; the conspira-tors may be lying low and creating the pretense of normality.

> Perhaps everything continues as before, but the palace is already in the hands of the usurpers; they have not arrested you yet because, after all, you no longer count for anything. They have forgotten you on a throne that is no longer a throne. The regular unfolding of palace life is a sign that the coup has taken place, a new king sits on a new throne ... (45)

The king doesn't listen alone: he has his secret service, his CIA, his Stasi, the web of spies who listen throughout the kingdom, with all the technology. The king is an ear with many extensions which reach into the most remote recesses of the country. But this doesn't help, it only makes things worse. Not just because of the massive extent of material that has to be carefully inspected, but because it is in the nature of spies to be double agents. There is a mole in every spy, they may be themselves the perpetrators of conspiracy.

> It is pointless for you to read [the secret reports]: your spies can only confirm the existence of the conspiracies, justifying the necessity of your espionage; and at the same time they must deny any immediate danger, to prove that their spying is effective. (39)

So all the reports are saying the same thing: they are useless as a way of pinning down meaning. One would have to eavesdrop on the eavesdrop-pers, and so forth into infinity.

The primal scene of power is an acoustic scene, a scene of constant lis-tening. Practically all the voices here are acousmatic voices, so the trouble is not only to assign them a meaning, but also to assign them a source at all. They can come from all quarters, from anywhere, and even more disturbingly, it can never be quite clear whether they are coming from the outside at all or just from one's head.

> You are wise to listen, not to let your attention lapse even for an instant; but you must be convinced of this: it is yourself you hear, it is within you that the ghosts acquire voices ... You are not convinced? You want abso-lute proof that what you hear comes from within you, not from outside? Absolute proof you will never have. (48–49)

So it is not even clear that these are not the voices in the head, the vocal ghosts. Or rather, it is clear that the ghost part cannot be detached from them. There is a hallucinatory moment involved which is structurally part of power, there is a moment where power cannot quite escape hearing voices. It listens to the voice of the people, *vox populi*, and tries to draw an impossible demarcation line in it, but which is always prey to fantasy and hearing voices.

Foucault proposed Bentham's Panopticon as a model for a certain functioning of power, and here we have its counterpart, the Panacousticon. In both, the decisive thing is the dividing line between seeing and being seen, and hearing and being heard. Maintaining the position of power depends on clearly maintaining this line.[10] But if Panopticon seems to be doomed to success – it appears to function well by imposing detachment and transparency through the mere mechanism it puts into place – then Panacousticon seems to be doomed to failure: it can never achieve detachment and transparency, for the more it listens, the more blurred things become, the less it is clear what all those voices really mean, the more it appears that total control is powerless. The king is quite literally the subject; he is subjected to the mechanism he imposes to control the subjects. The more power he has, the more powerless he is.

One could say: the king is the analyst of the empire. He tries to discern his subjects' voices in order to pin down their unconscious which pertains to the secret recesses of what they say. He spies on the gaps of their speech, on the secrets of their noises. Everything means, this is the analysis as the paranoia of meaning. And this is where he is the furthest removed from the position of the analyst and presents its caricature, its reverse side, since the point of analysis is precisely to undo the ties of meaning, to decompose them, to work to counter the paranoia of meaning.

So this is the first model of dealing with the voice, which one could call the *hermeneutical paranoia*. Every meaning is a potential threat, every interpretation leads to a delirium of interpretation. Maybe there is a part of paranoia in every hermeneutics insofar as it endeavors to capture the elusive meaning, but there always appears the phantom of more meaning beyond meaning: semantics breeds semantics beyond semantics, the elusive dark spot in the Other that one can't quite reduce by interpretation. The meaning one gets hold of breeds more meaning which escapes. The scene of power can be conceived as a double hermeneutical paranoia: on the one hand, the subjects who try to decipher the messages of power, to figure out the signs that the power emits, but they can never quite succeed ("they are telling us this, but what do they really want?"). On the other hand, the power which tries to decipher the voice of the people, but can never come to the bottom of it; it keeps hearing voices in its own head, and acts out with preemptive strikes. So everybody unhappily gets their own message from the other in the inverted form, in a double missed communication.

But there is a way out of this paranoiac universe. Among all the voices that the king listens to, there appears actually the voice of the Other, the Other voice, a voice different from all others. It is the voice of a woman singing in the night, and this voice doesn't raise the question of what does it really mean. It doesn't raise any hermeneutical question at all, but appears just as "voice as voice."

> You are attracted by that voice as a voice, as it offers itself in song. That voice comes certainly from a person, unique, inimitable like every person; a voice, however, is not a person, it is something suspended in the air, detached from the solidity of things. The voice, too, is unique and inimitable, but perhaps in a different way from a person: they might not resemble each other, voice and person. Or else, they could resemble each other in a secret way, not perceptible at first: the voice could be the equivalent of the hidden and most genuine part of the person. (53)

Here is the fantasy surrounding the voice in a pure form: there is a discrepancy of the voice and the person, but the uniqueness of the voice brings out what is in person more than her, the inner treasure, the most genuine part, the quintessential uniqueness, the pure exteriorization of the most intimate. The voice, detaching itself from the person, spreading invisibly in the air, is more real than this person herself. It is this split which produces a new and intensive kind of presence, endowed with the enigmatic power which pertains to the acousmatic voice. There is a real at stake in the split.

> ... what attracts you ... is the throbbing of a throat of flesh [*la vibrazione d'una gola di carne*]. A voice means this: there is a living person, throat, chest, feelings, who sends into the air this voice, different from all other voices. A voice involves the throat, saliva, infancy, the patina of experienced life, the mind's intentions, the pleasure of giving a personal form to sound waves. What attracts you is the pleasure this voice puts into existing: into existing as voice. (54)

So the incorporeal is the quintessence of corporeality – the throat, the saliva, the flesh. The voice is the surplus of the body, and at the same time the quintessence of spirit – the childhood, memories, life experiences, intentions, in one word, the soul. It's like the overlapping of the surplus-body and the spirit, the embodied soul. This is linked with two essential traits. Firstly, voice is self-referential. It only means itself, the pure externalization of interiority; it means its proper act of production. It is a self-revelation, it doesn't reveal anything but itself as becoming.

Secondly, voice is unique. It means: precisely this voice, this person, different from all others, in the singularity of this moment.

So the king, who is constantly in the terrible position of anguish, of spying on the voices of others, finally hears a voice he doesn't have to interpret, a voice whose meaning is not a threat. He is overwhelmed by this new magic, the magic of this self-referentiality and uniqueness which spells sheer joy: it is immediately understandable because there is nothing to understand, nothing to decipher. And with its overpowering appeal, there is suddenly no position of power to defend, defending power loses all sense, one can only let go.

This voice, not meaning anything, is at the same time pure interpellation, a provocation, an address, which instigates a desire for participation; it solicits a response. Insofar as it doesn't demand anything, it is a pure demand, an appeal for an answer, and one can only answer it by giving one's own voice; the only thing that can measure up to the appeal of the voice is one's own voice. So the king cannot but try to answer, in his own voice, that is, he can only sing in return, he can join the singing voice in the dark with his own voice. This is a purely phatic communication, not expressing anything but voice as expression, not communicating anything but communication, or rather a communion in the co-sounding of two voices in the dark. Like in *Romeo and Juliet*.

The king who sings is not a king who listens and deciphers. The singing king ceases to be a king. Solicited by this other voice he abandons his post, his throne, his hermeneutical paranoia and domination; he goes out in search of the bearer of this other voice, he leaves the palace, he loses himself in the labyrinth of paths and sounds, his own voice now one among many, he turns into a mere bearer of a unique voice, deprived of all insignia. In the rising dawn he is one with the multiplicity of voices in which he loses himself, that is, he finds himself. This is how this story ends.

So the story hinges on two paradigms of the voice, directly pitted against one another: the paradigm of deciphering, the paranoiac and vain attempt to reduce voice to signification, to pin it to the signifier, and because this is structurally impossible it can only breed more paranoia. And the paradigm not of listening, but of hearing the voice, which immediately translates into responding to the voice, for one can decipher this voice only by replying to it with one's own voice, taking part instead of interpreting. The voice conveys the joy of its own expression, which inspires the joy of responding with one's own expression. But isn't there something missing between these two paradigms, in this all too smooth transition from the one to the other?

Indeed, there is some cause for skepticism already in the fact that this Other voice, the call of the Other, happens to be the voice of a woman. Is the Other the Woman? Isn't there a tacit, or not so tacit, fantasy of the Other at work in this? There is a whole tradition and imagery which weighs heavily on the woman's voice, something that a feminist commentary on this story puts into a brief slogan: "The woman sings, the man thinks."[11] Calvino makes two assumptions that for the present purpose one could sum up as follows: (1) The Woman exists. (2) There is a sexual relationship. Whereas Lacan, with his knack for striking slogans, notoriously maintained exactly the opposite: (1) The Woman doesn't exist. (2) There is no sexual relationship.

The fascination with the woman's singing voice is of terribly long standing; it is inscribed in one of the most inveterate fantasies which runs through our culture. The bearer of pure and genuine voice happens to be a woman, the voice beyond logos, with the sexually determined opposition between the masculine logos and the feminine voice. The power is the affair of deciphering, hermeneutics, and control, hence "culture," while the woman is on the side of the genuine joy and uniqueness of the voice, its overwhelming magic, hence "nature," beyond culture, law, and its vicissitudes. There was a massive tradition of fighting, exorcizing the insidious dangers of the effeminate voice and its boundless jouissance, and of attempts to pin it down to logos – a classical "patriarchal," "metaphysical," "logocentric" fantasy, but which in this story serves as a call of redemption, exactly with the reversed value. What was seen as damnation should now serve as salvation. The woman's voice should serve as the antidote to male preoccupations with power and interpretation.

The historic pattern of this was provided by the Sirens, the voice which reputedly makes us lose our mind and judgment, the irresistible voice which makes one run into shipwreck (cf. also Lorelei, etc.). It is most curious, by the way, if we read the source of this in Homer (*Odyssey* xii, 186–191), that the Sirens are not at all presented merely as the source of fatal infatuation with sensual jouissance, but that they actually present the figures of knowledge. In their song, they boast about their omniscience: they know everything about past events and can offer knowledge about the future, they know about what is going on at distant places, etc. There is another figure in play, the disturbing figure of feminine knowledge, not of the overwhelming sensuality of feminine voice, or more precisely the figure of omniscience within the sensual and the feminine. There is a most curious amnesia that has beset the host of interpreters, Adorno and Horkheimer included, who all reduced Sirens to the voice and the sensuous.[12] What Calvino ultimately wants is a good Siren, the Siren as the savior. The loss of control in face of this unstoppable seductive voice which made people lose control is the very thing that is dearly needed. The meaning, the preoccupation with its endless deciphering, and hence the signifier which is supposed to spell it out, are the source of domination and of all the power games.

The two paradigms clearly embody our alternative: either sense or presence. It is the voice as presence which enables a relationship – ultimately a successful sexual relationship – a relationship of appeal and response, a congruence of voices, a harmony in their very difference and uniqueness, their happy match. Their match is only possible insofar they can circumvent the signifier and meaning, in an encounter beyond signification, beyond the signifying cut. The voices can meet in the material real beyond the symbolic; this enables their communion. But doesn't one thus enter into pure fantasy, doesn't one thus elude the real which is at stake in the voice and immediately translate it into the imaginary? Isn't the dive into pure materiality and uniqueness a dive into pure fantasy? Doesn't the alternative "either sense or presence" present a choice between the symbolic and the imaginary, the third term missing in this being precisely the real? But where does this real emerge?

Let me take another literary example which also very much hinges on the voice, but in a strikingly different way. I can think of no more appropriate statement about the problem of the voice than a passage from Samuel Beckett's *The Unnamable*. I can just briefly remind that this is the third part of a trilogy, which comprises *Molloy*, *Malone Dies*, and *The Unnamable*. With each consecutive part there is a reduction, more things are taken away. In *Molloy* we still have some characters and some plot, while in *Malone Dies* we have just a dying man endlessly rambling on, confined to a room; and finally in the third part there is not even that – there is just a voice whose source remains enigmatic, it is literally unnamable, a nameless voice that cannot even be ascribed to a person (it abandons the opposition between the voice and the name that was the backbone of the balcony scene; this is an unnamable voice). Plots and characters are all gone, this is a novel which has just "a voice and nothing more" as its protagonist, a voice persevering, continuing till the last page, to the famous "you must go on, I can't go on, I'll go on." The whole point is that the status of this voice remains uncertain, one cannot quite make out whether this is a voice like talking to someone or a voice going on in someone's head (or whether this is pertinent at all). The particular passage I have in mind is the following:

I'll have said it, without a mouth I'll have said it, I'll have said it inside me, then in the same breath outside me, perhaps that's what I feel, an outside and an inside and me in the middle, perhaps that's what I am, the thing that divides the world in two, on the one side the outside, on the other the inside, that can be as thin as foil, I'm neither one side nor the other, I'm in the middle, I'm the partition, I've two surfaces and no thickness, perhaps that's what I feel, myself vibrating, I'm the tympanum, on the one hand the mind, on the other the world, I don't belong to either ...[13]

This is the most succinct statement about the voice that I can think of. One couldn't be more precise: the voice is the very principle of division, itself not on either side and yet on both sides at once, at the intersection of the inner and the outer, yet unplaceable in that division, the thinnest of foils which connects and separates the two. It persists merely as the transition. There is a standard way to describe certain procedures of modern literature under the heading "the stream of consciousness," when a writer supposedly follows the inner rambling and faithfully records it as a scribe, putting down its meanderings in a raw form as they appear to consciousness before being made presentable and coherent. As far as Beckett is concerned, the term is misleading and inappropriate, for the stream of consciousness presupposes consciousness as a realm neatly separate from the outside world; the whole point with Beckett is that this inner voice maintains itself as unplaceable, at the very edge of the mind and the world, the speech and the body, cutting into both and being cut by both. Its inner split immediately translates into an outer split and vice versa. It is not that the consciousness is incoherent; rather the very line that separates consciousness and constitutes it as such is constantly blurred and indistinct. The voice is the cutting edge of both consciousness and the world.

The voice which literally embodies the dividing line is something that one can never quite claim as one's own, one can ultimately never speak in one's own voice: it may seem to be the most intimately mine, my own innermost possession, the inner treasure, but it is also something which disrupts our self-presence, the very notion of the self, and refers it to virtuality. Stemming from the interior, it brings out more, and other things, than one catered for. Beckett is here an excellent point in the case: there are now many schools of creative writing which endeavor to teach people how to find their own author's voice; this is their guiding metaphor: to find your own voice in writing, what is specifically and originally yours, proper to you only. Beckett's problem was exactly the opposite: how to lose one's own voice, how to write neutrally, anonymously, how to get rid of style, how not to be an author. (Hence, Foucault used Beckett's line "*Qu'importe qui parle*" as the cue for his famous lecture "What is an author?") For him the voice is precisely not something intimate or proper, but something that disrupts the illusion of one's self-presence in the voice, something that disturbs the interiority of consciousness. At the same time, if one of the most salient properties of the voice is to make sense, as the most common bearer of meaning, then Beckett brought the paradox of the voice to the extreme by gradually and radically reducing sense. It is just a voice which rambles on, all sense gradually becomes completely irrelevant, and what is left is the sheer persistence of the voice, at the limit of making sense. That is, at the limit where it doesn't go beyond language into the inarticulate, the scream, the laughter, the hiss, etc., but persists as the extreme point within language.

In this universe it is more appropriate to say that the voice, far from being a self-expression, a harbinger of interiority and individuality, is more like an intruder, a foreign body, a prosthesis, a bodily extension, an artificial limb – it is never "authentic", it is never just an expression. The voice has something like a spectral autonomy: it never quite belongs to the body we see, the voice never sounds like the person emitting it, there is always a gap, a *Verfremdung*, a mismatch, a ventriloquism. In its spectrality it is something both intimate and external: Lacan invented an excellent word for this, *the extimate*.[14]

I have used recurrently in my work on the voice[15] the scheme of the intersection of two circles, a very simple didactical device that Lacan proposed at a certain stage, in Seminar XI,[16] as a way of understanding the basic alienation that the subject undergoes when submitted to the symbolic. This scheme can serve various purposes, where the point is that there are two areas which are linked by something that doesn't simply make part of them, although it is something they have in common and presents the area of their overlapping. The two areas, in the broadest sense, can be taken as language and body, which intersect in the voice, or more generally nature and culture, the somatic and the symbolic, *phone* and logos, the subject and the Other, interiority and exteriority. In all these dualities voice is always placed at their intersection. But this is perhaps a misleading way of looking at it, misleading insofar as it seems to presuppose that we are confronting two areas which are already constituted in themselves and stand opposed to one another, facing each other, so that we are then looking for their link, the link that would bridge their utter divergence, their incommensurability. But here lies the major paradox of psychoanalysis and the major difficulty of understanding its object: the voice is precisely the operator of the split, it inhabits the split, and by its operation actually produces the two areas which it is supposed to bring together in the overlapping. The overlapping produces the very areas which overlap. There is no clear division into interiority or exteriority, no symbolic or biology, no nature or culture which would simply preexist this intersection as independent areas. At the same time, what they have in common is not some positive element which would simply belong to either of them – hence Lacan's insistence that the object, *objet a*, is not at the disposal of the Other any more than it is at the disposal of the subject; it is there as if a quirk, an addition, an intrusion. It presents a dimension which is neither interior nor exterior, neither nature nor culture, neither somatic nor symbolic, but where the one intrudes upon the other, it emerges at their interface. Beckett says, "I have two surfaces but no thickness" – there is no ontological thickness or substance to this interface. It embodies their borderline, but a borderline which is constantly renegotiated and doesn't exist as a clear line of demarcation. In the voice the language infringes upon the body and the body infringes upon language, as it were, and the area of their overlap is the area of production of pure divergence. It produces two sides which don't have a common measure, irreducible to one another. Their intersection is something that articulates them and binds them together while holding them apart in their utter heterogeneity. It connects and disconnects at the same time. In a more general perspective, this is the area that Freud and Lacan have seen as the proper location of the drives, those mythical beings, as Freud says, which we can never get to directly, which cannot be isolated by themselves, but can only be detected and pursued through the paradoxes of both areas they produce, at the interstice of "nature" and "culture." This is why this object voice, which belongs to the most common experience, at the same time points to an "ontological paradox" – it requires a new kind of ontology, or rather a new kind of topology.

This is where the experience of the voice can never be quite adequately grasped and described either in terms of sense or in terms of presence. It is rather something that we can only glimpse, or hear, in the oscillation between the two, and the simplest way of presenting it may well be the device of the two intersecting circles, the circle of sense and the circle of presence. This is where sense doesn't simply make sense, but appears as something cumbersome, like a quirk in making sense, an obstacle to the flow of sense, and this is the part where presence is never simply there in its magic and intensity, but is referred to the signifying cut, the cut which enables making sense. So the intersection is something which is precisely eluded in both sense and presence, the part which cannot be positively present as such nor does it makes sense, but is constantly evoked by the glitches of both presence and sense. The voice as an opening is not an opening to either sense or presence, but an opening to their pure divergence.

Espousing presence to escape the traps of meaning and its hermeneutical paranoia, like the king in Calvino's parable, is always prey to a disavowal, the disavowal of the cut that it is based on. Its overwhelming fascination, its power to overpower, its auratic presence, stems from a void which opens at the intersection, and it is by being placed in this void that the presence of the voice gains this power. It is the power not simply of what it displays, of what it brings forth, what it presents, but it gains part of its power from what it occludes, what it comes to cover, and what cannot be presented as such. When it starts functioning as the token of individuality, of uniqueness, of the inner treasure, the full assumption of one's being, the communion with the other, then its seeming escape from the signifier and from making sense rather endorses sense as such, full meaning as such, the advent of meaning, the epiphany of meaning, the filling of the void which holds open the divergence of sense and presence as the very place of subjectivity. This is where Beckett's relentless pursuit of "almost nothing," the "unnallable least," which escapes both presence and sense while being at their core, is exemplary for the new topology that Lacan's invention of the voice as *object a* has made possible.

Notes

1 Roman Jakobson, "Linguistics and Poetics," in *Style in Language*, ed. Thomas Sebeok (New York: Wiley, 1960), 364.

2 Here is a brief list of some important work, wholly or partly inspired by Lacan, with no ambition for completeness and no doubt with important omissions: Michel Poizat, *L'Opéra ou le cri de l'ange* (Paris: Métalié, 1986; English translation, Ithaca: Cornell University Press, 1992); Poizat, *La voix du diable* (Paris: Métalié, 1991); Poizat, *La voix sourde* (Paris: Métalié, 1996); Poizat, *Variations sur la voix* (Paris: Economica, 1998); Poizat, *Vox populi, vox Dei* (Paris: Métalié, 2001); Bernard Baas, *De la chose à l'objet* (Leuven: Peeters, 1998); Baas, *La voix déliée* (Paris: Hermann, 2010); Jacques Nassif, *L'écrit, la voix* (Paris: Aubier, 2004); Michel Chion, *La voix au cinéma* (Paris: Cahiers du cinema, 1984; English translation, New York: Columbia University Press, 1999); Chion, *Le son* (Paris: Armand Colin, 1998, 2010; English translation, Durham, NC: Duke University Press, 2016); Gérard Wajcman, *Voix* (Caen: Nous, 2012); Francois Sauvagnat (ed.), *La voix*, Actes du Colloque d'Ivry (Paris: La lysimaque, 1989); Steven Connor, *Dumbstruck: A Cultural History of Ventriloquism* (Oxford University Press, 2001); Connor, *Beyond Words: Sobs, Hums, Stutters and Other Vocalizations*

(London: Reaktion, 2014); Jorge Salcido-Romero and Sylvia Mieschkowski (eds.), *Sound Effects: The Object Voice in Fiction* (Leiden: Brill, 2015); Jonathan Sterne (ed.), *The Sound Studies Reader* (New York: Routledge, 2012); Mika Ojakangas, *The Voice of Conscience* (New York: Bloomsbury, 2013); Doris Kollesch and Sybille Krämer (eds.), *Stimme* (Frankfurt: Suhrkamp, 2006); Friedrich Kittler, Thomas Macho, and Sigrid Weigel (eds.), *Zwischen Rauschen und Ofenbarung* (Berlin: de Gruyter, 2002); Mladen Dolar, *A Voice and Nothing More* (Cambridge, MA: MIT Press, 2006); and many more.

3 "'Tis but thy name that is my enemy; / – Thou art thyself though, not a Montague. / What's Montague? ... O, be some other name! / What's in a name? That which we call a rose, / By any other name would smell as sweet; / So Romeo would, were he not Romeo call'd, / Retain that dear perfection in which he owes / Without that title: – Romeo, doff thy name; / And for that name, which is no part of thee, / Take all myself." "O Romeo, Romeo! Wherefore art thou Romeo? / Deny thy father and refuse thy name; / Or, if thou wilt not, be but sworn my love; / And I'll no longer be a Capulet" (*Romeo and Juliet*, II/2).

4 The word person, *persona*, according to a popular (although very doubtful) etymology, comes from *per-sonare*, to sound through, namely to sound through a mask, to emit the voice through a mouthpiece – the uniqueness of a voice has to sound through a mask to invoke the person. One could say that the name is like wearing a mask; the mask is generic, it highlights the characteristic features, the type, while the voice is unique, yet its uniqueness is voiced through a mask, so that the person is the troubled unity of the two.

5 What part of the body might he purport to cut off when he draws his sword? Does he tacitly assume that "the phallic signifier" resides in his phallus? Is this not the spontaneous assumption that the audience inevitably makes? This is like an almost caricature Lacanian *Urszene*, bringing together the name of the father, the phallic signifier, castration, and the nature of love. The fate of the Veronese lovers may actually be sealed by this assumption that true love resides in the immediacy, by getting rid of the phallic signifier of the name as the intruder into the purity of heart.

6 In Lacan's notorious graph of desire, one can find a line that runs from the signifier on the left to the voice on the right (Écrits, New York: W. W. Norton 2006, 684, 692). One way to read this would be that the voice is put in the position of the product, the leftover of the signifying operation, as opposed to the voice that seems to be the starting point, the "natural given" that has to be molded by the signifier. The object voice is the remainder of the incidence of the signifier.

7 They were published posthumously as *Sotto il sole jaguaro* (1986), *Under the Jaguar Sun* (London: Vintage, 2001), from where I quote (with page numbers given in the text).

8 "In sum, the throne, once you have been crowned, is where you had best remain seated, without moving, day and night. All your previous life has been only a waiting to become king; now you are king; you have only to

reign. And what is reigning if not this long wait? Waiting for the moment when you will be deposed, when you will have to take leave of the throne, the scepter, the crown, and your head" (36).

9 This is precisely where Lacan places fantasy: you are saying this, but what do you really want? *Che vuoi?* Fantasy is what supplies an answer to this question, it provides the framework in which one strives to come to terms with the dark spot of the non-transparency of the other, the enigma of its desire. Cf. *Écrits*, 300.

10 Foucault proposed Panopticon as the model of power after the deposition of kings (Michel Foucault, *Discipline and Punish: The Birth of the Prison*, tr. Alan Sheridan (New York: Vintage, 1977). Calvino inversely proposes a model of the modern mechanisms of power – telephones, bugging, and technology are mentioned – but the point for him is that this modern set-up retains the pre-modern Master at its hidden core. This goes against the grain of Foucault's theory of power.

11 Adriana Cavarero, *A più voci. Filosofia dell'espressione vocale* (Milan: Feltrinelli, 2003), 12. I am indebted to her reading of this story, although my take on it sharply differs from hers.

12 Cavarero, *A più* voci, 115–129.

13 *The Beckett Trilogy* (London: Picador, 1979), 352.

14 Beckett was not Lacan's author, one is tempted to add curiously and unfortunately. It took a very long time for the scholarship to take up this topic which seems to strikingly impose itself. Now we have the magisterial monograph by Llewellyn Brown, *Beckett, Lacan and the Voice* (Stuttgart: Ibidem Press, 2016). The present chapter was written before that volume was available; it is a very inspirational source for the work that has to be done.

15 Dolar, *A Voice and Nothing More* (Cambridge, MA: MIT Press, 2006).

16 Lacan, *The Four Fundamental Concepts of Psychoanalysis* (London: Penguin, 1979), 211.

CHAPTER 2

Freud's Return to Lacan

Anna Kornbluh

After Lacan, we read Freud. Lacan named his life's work "the return to Freud": a reimmersion in Freud's ideas, Freud's language, and perhaps even Freud's unconscious, in order to counter the post-Freudian tendencies in psychoanalytic and psychological circles. Lacan had been working as a psychoanalyst for almost twenty years and was arriving at the realization that the Freudian discoveries had been abandoned, that "things have come to such a pass that to call for a return to Freud is seen as a reversal."[1] Only, it's a bit misleading to describe the return in this way, since the force of Lacan's corrective to his contemporaries was not "go back, do your homework, get Freud right" – but rather an exhortation to feel out "a return" in language, to become sensitized to language's routes, turns, detours, circuits, and dead-ends. Go back, return, retrace, repeat the movement in language. Marking this arc of repetition, Lacan defined the return circuitously: "The meaning of a return to Freud is a return to Freud's meaning."[2] Vertiginous tautologies, chiasmic reversals, and compulsive repetitions of this sort do not deliver a longed-for meaning, instead casting us on to the *defiles* of the signifier – plunging us into a tail-chasing turning (*un tour*) in which sense eludes us but sensation compels us. "What can Lacan mean by this? What does he want?" we ask ourselves, and this position of questioning the other's desire, this suspension of certainty about experts, this dwelling in language as a medium of opacity in excess of communication – this is some of what he means. After Lacan, we know many new things about Freud, but the ultimate point of returning to Freud is not knowing *more* so much as knowing *differently*, palpating this agency of language to be simultaneously too much and too little. Freud's work is not to be summarized or mastered; it is to be turned around in, reveled in, detoured; "One never goes beyond Freud … One uses him. One moves around within him. One takes one's bearings from the direction he points in."[3]

41

After Lacan's return, today's readers should keep returning to Freud, rereading the letter of his language, touching what in his texts says too much and what says too little, attending to the ways his own texts bespeak or perform, rather than master, the very phenomena he was trying to discover. This chapter returns to Freud to illustrate some of what can be done with Freud after Lacan. After Lacan, we read Freud's written word not as philosophy or gospel, but much as though Freud himself were speaking two enigmatic discourses at once: that of the analyst, who punctuates what the analysand speaks, *and* that of the analysand, whose desire derails speech. We read Freud's words as though they are addressing us, inviting us into lacunae. We activate reading as a process of attunement to the form, contour, gap, and surface of discourse. What is being spoken? How does the shape and rhythm of what is being said point us to what hasn't found its way to being said? How, at even its most ostensibly summative moments, does Freud's discourse proliferate questions, enigmas, and overdeterminations? After Lacan, Freud is a work to be worked through, a corpus of language to be rethought again and again.

In characterizing our state after Lacan as a position of ongoing return, I intend that we not take Lacan as a master any more than Freud. This is a big temptation. There are dozens of introductions to Lacan aimed at helping readers become experts in his work, explaining his transformations of Freudian psychoanalysis, and many of these are very smart guides. An essay could devote its entirety to summarizing those guides: Lacan makes available Freud as philosopher, Freud as structuralist, Freud as revolutionary; above all, Lacan adds the dimension of language to Freud's discovery of the unconscious. This is the simplest formulation of Freud after Lacan: Freud plus language. Where Freud's medical background and fascination with biological life lead him to speculations about the body and existence which many have read as pronouncements about human nature, Lacan's return to Freud educes the linguistic quality of Freudian phenomena such as the symptom, the dream, desire, fantasy, and emphasizes the linguistic quality of the Freudian revolution: the talking cure. Freud discovered the unconscious and Lacan discovered that the unconscious is structured like a language. As Lacan himself describes this parallel: "Freud's discovery was that of the field of the effects, in man's nature, of his relations to the symbolic order and the fact that their meaning goes all the way back to the most radical instances of symbolization in being. To ignore the symbolic order is to condemn Freud's discovery to forgetting and analytic experience to ruin."[4] Lacan's notion of the symbolic order names language but also the relationships for which language is at the base: laws, institutions, norms, traditions. In approaching the psyche as crucially activated by the symbolic order, Lacan deromanticizes the dynamics Freud studies; rather than charting individual eruptive, erratic flows of instincts and desires, Lacan charts the syntaxes of social connection in every individual's case. Underscoring language in this way, Lacan provides a framework for receiving Freud as a theorist of social context, including not only how languages are used in particular cultures, but also how societies are themselves constituted by relations to and in language (this is what Lacan calls "the symbolic order"). Where received readings of Freud cast him as a scientist, a universalizer, and a prophet of biology as destiny, the Lacanian reading enables new appreciation of the linguistic, social, and situated tenor of Freud's insights: he produced less an account of a transcendental vital force toward sexual satisfaction, and more a theory of sexuality as dissatisfaction, as a disturbance in the human animal, its inability to be uncomplicated in its necessary social relations.

In drawing out the language aspects of Freud's concerns, Lacan opens Freudian psychoanalysis to broad connections with linguistics, semiotics (the study of signs), aesthetics (especially literary theory), anthropology, philosophy, and social theory. Already, Freud was not necessarily modest in describing his innovations, characterizing psychoanalysis as sister to "the history of civilization, mythology, the psychology of religions, literary history, and literary criticism."[5] Lacan's highlighting of the role of language in Freud's thought expands this scope even more: "I would be inclined to add: rhetoric, dialectic, grammar, and poetics – the supreme pinnacle of the aesthetics of language."[6] After Lacan, Freudian psychoanalysis can be appreciated as this incredibly expansive engagement with human experience, from law and society to literature and language. Scholars such as Adrian Johnston, Julia Kristeva, Lorenzo Chiesa, and Markos Zafiropoulos have traced out these branches with great lucidity and brilliance. The psychoanalyst properly practicing is sometimes a historian, sometimes a mythologist, sometimes a doctor, and always a highly sensitized linguist:

> We must thus take up Freud's work again starting with the Traumdeutung to remind ourselves that a dream has the structure of a sentence, or, rather, to keep to the letter of the work, of a rebus – that is, of a form of writing ... which reproduces ... the simultaneously phonetic and symbolic use of signifying elements found in the hieroglyphs of ancient Egypt and in the characters still used in China ... what is important is the version of the text, and that, Freud tells us, is given in the telling of the dream – that is,

in its rhetoric. Ellipsis and pleonasm, hyperbaton or syllepsis, regression, repetition, apposition – these are the syntactical displacements; metaphor, catechresis, antonomasia, allegory, metonymy, and synechdoche – these are the semantic condensations; Freud teaches us to read in them the intentions – whether ostentatious or demonstrative, dissimulating or persuasive, retaliatory or seductive – with which the subject modulates his oneiric discourse.[7]

For Lacan, turning around in Freud's discourse necessarily evokes the turning of *tropes* (etymologically, trope derives from the Greek trepein, "to turn"), those figures in language that mobilize words for senses beyond the proper. The subject's ordinary language makes use of rhetorical tropes in abundance, and this very quality of proliferating repetition and metaphor, allegory and ellipsis, reveals that the unconscious is not a place or presence, but rather, as Samuel Weber puts it, "a representation that in turn refers to other representations."[8] This propulsive movement of language's turning, its always offering more words in lieu of meanings, animates Lacan's own notoriously evasive language, and underlies his refusal to define the return to Freud as a quest for accuracy, getting back to the source. Consequently, rather than spending this chapter summarizing the various ways that Lacan's return to Freud was a repetition with a difference, I want to stage something of my own return. I hope that, in enacting a return rather than cataloguing Lacan's return, the argument will achieve greater effect than it might otherwise, since it is this prospect of essays acting out their own ideas, instead of authoritatively delineating them, that Lacan pursues in advocating that Freud's writings had not yet been adequately encountered.

In trying to consider Freud after Lacan in terms of Lacan's return, Lacan's exhortation to repeat, we must return to Freud's language, and we might take as a starting point one of Lacan's rare overarching statements about Freud's oeuvre:

> From the beginning to end, from the discovery of the Oedipus complex to *Moses and Monotheism*, via the extraordinary paradox from the scientific point of view of *Totem and Taboo*, Freud only ever asked himself, personally, one question – how can this system of signifiers without which no incarnation of either truth or justice is possible, how can this literal logos take hold of an animal who doesn't need it and doesn't care about it – since it doesn't at all concern his needs? This is nevertheless the very thing that causes neurotic suffering.[9]

Lacan helps us to see that Freud's entire project, from his first to his last works, is driven by the question of why human beings are bound to language and broad social frameworks. If the unconscious is structured like a language, Freud seems almost equally interested in the "is structured" part as in the "unconscious" or "like a language" part: he continuously poses the question of structure, of "the system of signifiers," of the mutual constitution of the psyche and the social. Whence this interest? How is it that Freud's discovery of the unconscious somehow also entailed new questions about the essence of sociality?

Lacan's discourse gives us Freud's language in its fuller dimensionality and broader (as it were, interdisciplinary) scope, but Freud's language itself already gives us a perpetual emphasis on this intrinsically social character of psychoanalysis, what might be called the "objective" register that complements its "subjective" focus. For Freud, unlike Lacan, composed numerous works specifically addressed to the psychoanalytic contributions to social theory, specifically addressed to the psychoanalysis of culture, specifically addressed to the uniquely psychoanalytic purview on to human collective history. He acknowledged the special status of these texts in referring to them as his "metapsychology": forays into the meta level of context for the unconscious. The works of political metapsychology include *Totem and Taboo, Thoughts for the Times on War and Death, Group Psychology and the Analysis of the Ego, Civilization and its Discontents*, and *Moses and Monotheism*, and they span from 1912 to 1939, relatively early in his career to the very end. As a group, these texts are speculative, searching, and even outlandish, going so far as to conjure the myth of the primal horde of brothers who murder their father for sexual access to his women, the omnipresent possibility for humans to fall sway to demagogues, and the existential impossibility of happiness. Inflected by the very real threat of world war, these texts recur again and again to the question of peace – to how it can be possible to formulate societies that acknowledge their own origins (in acts of arbitrary if not violent founding) and their own incompletion (in chronic discontent). Freud's wildly imaginative and repeatedly undertaken political metapsychology strives to represent the social as the proper object of psychoanalysis. This is Freud's return to Lacan.

Freud returns to Lacan the emphatically social quality of the language Lacan returns to Freud. In authoring works of overt political theory of a type from which Lacan himself demurred, but whose centrality to psychoanalysis can never be sidestepped, Freud returns to Lacan the positivized sociopolitical dimension of Lacan's own work. This implicit dimension in Lacan has been skillfully explicated by Slavoj Žižek, Joan Copjec, Todd McGowan, and others. As a mode of inquiry, Freud's metapsychological works consistently probe the logics and sutures of the collective psyche, turning again and again to the role of constituted frameworks for social life. As readers of Freud after Lacan, we also read Lacan after Freud, read the political insights in Lacan's own discourse that continue to clamor for punctuation. In an effort to illustrate Freud after Lacan, the remainder of this chapter pursues, in a Lacanian fashion, the perennial Freudian question of "how . . . this system of signifiers . . . is possible."

Origins of Origins

In claiming Lacan's return to Freud as an opportunity to return to Freud's social thought, I take some inspiration from the way that the social concerns of psychoanalysis already prompted Lacan's very first call for the return. He made the call in a 1951 paper on transference, in which he conducted a close-reading of the Dora case study narrative to demonstrate that "by rethinking Freud's work, (it is possible to) find anew the authentic meaning of his initiative and the means by which to maintain its salutary value."[10] Transference, the distribution or displacement of psychic energy toward the analyst, provided the perfect topic for hailing the return, and for substantiating the return as a turn, a twist, a complex trajectory: Lacan traced Dora's positioning of Freud and Freud's positioning of Dora in order to advocate "the return" as an activation of the transference *toward* Freud, a deliberate and ecstatic *positioning* of Freud. Closely following the case history narrative, Lacan's paper underscores the fact of the failure in the case; though Freud acknowledges the failure, Lacan reads in Freud's acknowledgment a different cause than Freud himself does. Where Freud looks to Dora's desires, Lacan looks to Freud's own desires, broaching the question of the countertransference, "the sum total of the analyst's biases, passions, and difficulties, or even of his inadequate information, at any given moment in the dialectical process."[11] For Lacan, Dora, like all the case studies, ultimately relays less the desire of the analysand, and more the desire of the analyst, the desire of and for psychoanalysis.

Lacan is able to read the desire of the analyst in a number of important features of the Dora case study that we might call "formal," pertaining to the way the case study is composed. Specifically, he emphasizes that Freud chose a failed treatment to be elevated as one of his very few case studies; that Freud later amended the text with significant and weighty footnotes; that the text proceeds through a series of repeated "dialectical reversals." To Lacan, these aspects lend an uncertain and unfinished quality to the Dora study: Freud had not quite said what he meant – he had not been able to identify countertransference, "the sum total of the analyst's biases, passions, and difficulties, or even of his inadequate information, at any given moment in the dialectical process."[12]

The case concerns the issue of Dora's involvement as a subject in the scenarios which she reports herself as an object, but Lacan adds that it concerns as well the issue of Freud's involvement in the scenarios in the clinic, his own investment in the analytic relationship. The work of Freud's case study is to attend to the subject's own part in her narrative of objectification; Dora complains of the plots and triangulations to which she is exposed, but does not avow her own desire within them, hence those desires speak through her hysterical symptoms, and the task of the analyst is to receive this speaking as discourse. Similarly, Freud makes dramatic reversals and amendments to the case narrative, and acknowledges the treatment's failure, but does not avow his own desire within them. The case poses the question of hysteria – "who am I for this other who desires?" – and poses it for both Dora and Freud. A narrative is not without a subject – this is the lesson of Dora for Freud, and the lesson of Freud's *Dora* for Lacan.

Just as Freud reads for Dora's secrets and investments, Lacan reads for Freud's, prioritizing the analysand–analyst relationship at the heart of the clinic. "What must be understood about psychoanalytic experience is that it proceeds entirely in this subject-to-subject relationship, which means it preserves a dimension that is irreducible to any psychology considered to be the objectification of certain of an individual's properties."[13] Dora's story is not Dora's individual story, but the story of her relating her story to Freud, and Freud relating back to her as well as relating the story to his imagined reader, and of these relationships as themselves the space of sexuality; sexuality is not an individual's idiosyncracy but the opaque energies in a social field. "Transference" serves as a "fundamental concept" of psychoanalysis (it becomes one of the four in Lacan's Seminar XI *The Four Fundamental Concepts of Psychoanlaysis*) because it captures the social quality of the analysand's desire becoming available for interpretation in relation to the analyst and to the analyst's own desire – it captures the clinic as a social space, it captures psychoanalysis as a practice of language that builds new social links. These social studies on transference and countertransference are the perfect origin for the desire for a return to Freud, reinvigorating the social, subject-to-subject distinction of psychoanalysis, as against the personal of ego-psychology. Reading for the transference and the countertransference becomes a way of reading for the intersubjective distortions that we cannot escape, for the ineluctably *mediated* character of all relations. From the beginning, then, we can note that the return to Freud is tacitly a return to the social.

To further punctuate these social commitments of the return, we should also note that Lacan's very same essay first articulating the return to Freud also argues for Freud's proximity to the great social thinker Claude Levi-Strauss. "Isn't it striking that Levi Strauss – in suggesting the involvement in myths of language structures and of those social laws that regulate marriage and kinship – is already conquering the very terrain in which Freud situates the unconscious?"[14] The linguistic revolution, the return to Freud's language and return to the Freud of language, is co-extensive with political consciousness, with returning and reawakening to Freud's political vision. Freud studied the hysteric, the neurotic, the psychotic *in culture* ("the uneasiness in culture" is a more literal translation of the German *Das Unbehagen in der Kultur*, the text the Anglophone world knows as *Civilization and its Discontents*); he probed that which in intersubjectivity causes the subject's enjoyment and the subject's suffering. The "cultural context" that matters to Freud is not local norms and particular customs, but the general realm of regulated subject–other relationships. Slavoj Žižek's return to Lacan crystallizes Freud's foundational political insight:

> One of the big reproaches to psychoanalysis is that it is only a theory of individual pathological disturbances ... When Freud says "the uneasiness" in culture, he means not that most of us are normal, we socialize ourselves normally, some idiots didn't make it, they fall out, oh, they have to be normalized. No. Culture as such, in order to establish itself as normal, what appears as normal, involves a whole series of pathological cuts, distortions, and so on and so on. There is, again, a kind of *unbehagen*, uneasiness, we are out of joint, not at home, in culture as such, which means, again, that there is no normal culture. Culture as such has to be interpreted.[15]

What Freud's consistently social interests endeavor to grasp are the violent occlusions and displacements of any given social formation. Psychoanalysis addresses itself to the impossibility of a fit between cultural constellations and the lacking nature that precipitates them, to the reasons why all cultures are uneasy. Freud's repeated and outlandish representations of the origins of culture bespeak the very absence of origins – the constitutive incompletion – of culture as such. Lacan's return encircles this radical kernel of psychoanalysis at its origin, so in returning to Lacan's return, we would do well to recur again and again to the social dimension of Freud's work.

Totem in Extremis

Freud first turned to the political as an overt topic when he was already in the middle of the concerted reflections on psychoanalysis that he called "metapsychology." Right before *Totem*, he wrote *Five Lectures on Psychoanalysis* and numerous "Papers on Technique"; right after it he wrote "On the History of the Psychoanalytic Movement," "Papers on Metapsychology," and *Introductory Lectures on Psychoanalysis*. This timing seems important: he made his "first" explicit political reflections in the midst of grappling with what could be generalized about psychoanalysis; one could say that the question of the general and of the level at which psychoanalysis intervenes in the whole field of human relations is at stake for him in this period, as it would be at stake at the outbreak of World War I mere months after *Totem*. He marks his turn to the topic as a turn: in *Totem*'s very first paragraph, he confesses to making a "first attempt" to "bridge the gap" between psychoanalysis and social studies (xxviii),[16] and he marks as well the speculative and outlandish character of this first attempt, disclaiming "if in the end [my] hypothesis bears a highly improbable appearance, that need be no argument against the possibility of its approximating more or less closely the reality which it is so hard to reconstruct." As if he did not have big enough fish to fry in discovering the unconscious and experimentally developing the metapsychological constructs that could possibly inscribe the enormity of that discovery, Freud is compelled to take on the arguably bigger task of developing political origin stories, and original theories of political dynamics. It is this compulsion itself – repeated in his multiple works of political meta-psychology, each of which returns to *Totem* – which shows the breadth of Freud's commitment to the intricacy of the subjective and objective, the psychic and the political.

After Lacan, we read *Totem and Taboo*, Freud's first political theory, as the place of his unworked, what has not yet been "worked-through." As Lacan read the form of the Dora case study for indications of Freud's desire to discern countertransference, we might read the form of the repetition of political theories for indications of Freud's desire to reckon with the unaccountable factors in political relations. Noting that Freud deemed *Totem* "his favorite ... his greatest triumph," Lacan highlights this triumph as both "a neurotic product" and "nothing other than a modern myth, a myth constructed to explain what remained gaping in his doctrine, namely 'Where is the father?'"[17] The myth provides an answer to the question of place and origin of the law (and the signifier as its avatar), an unanswerable question, pertaining to the order of the real. "Not the slightest trace has ever been seen of the father of the human horde. Freud holds that it was real. He clings to it. He wrote the entire *Totem and Taboo* in order to say it."[18] Lacan minces no words in his appraisal of the text: "to study how it is composed, it is one of the most twisted things I can imagine ... one has to return to Freud – it's in order to perceive that if it's twisted in this way, given that he was a chap who knew how to write and think, there must be a good reason for it."[19] These twists are the essential formal matter that must be read, for a myth is "manifest content ... not latent" and *Totem*, as neurotic product, is owing to what is "impossible to formulate in discourse."[20] The myth suffers symptoms, it speaks the unspeakable: the position of discursive installation, the origination of the social relation. It is "impossible" to say from within a given social order where that order originates, because this requires reference to some element outside the order; as a consequence, attempts to tell origin stories twist discourse. It might be appealing to dismiss *Totem* as extreme and irrelevant, to set it aside in favor of the less twisted, more straight psychological works like *The Interpretation of Dreams*, but Lacan helps us see that this extremity is organic to the very question of where social relations start. *Totem* must be read for, not despite, its extremity.

Indeed, the extremity offers itself for the kind of interpretation modeled by Freud in *The Interpretation of Dreams*, the kind of formal rearrangement modeled by Levi Strauss in "The Structural Study of Myth": "it is possible to put a myth on index cards that one then stacks up to see what combinations unfold."[21] That is, Lacan repeats Levi-Strauss's method for myth analysis in his own analysis of Freud's myth, a method of formal analysis that identifies central units of meaning across levels of a text (or even versions of a text) and then clusters them together to make new meanings. Just as Levi-Strauss clusters the multiple stories of Oedipus (Rex and Colonnus and Antigone), Lacan aligns *Totem* with Freud's other mythmaking project, his identification of "the Oedipus complex." Stacking up the index cards, Lacan fixates on the gap between the two myths: whereas in Oedipus the law precedes enjoyment, in *Totem* enjoyment precedes the law.[22] Reading the myths together allows this gap to speak: there is a chicken–egg problem, an undecidability in the connection between law and enjoyment, the objective and the subjective. Lacan's formal reading of the redoubled reliance upon myth, and the reversed causality across *Totem* and Oedipus, leads him to the insight that for Freud the discovery of the unconscious is paralleled by the quest for the origin of the socio-symbolic order.

Lacan's interlocution with Levi-Strauss proved so pivotal to his return to Freud precisely because Lacan perceived the Freudian origins of Levi-Strauss's concept of culture. As Lacan saw it, Freud's frequent quest for the origins of the social anticipates Levi-Strauss's own centralization of sexuality in social life:[23]

> Freud's discovery went right to the heart of this determination by the symbolic law, for in the unconscious – which, he insisted, was quite different from everything that had previously been designated by that name – he recognized the instance of the laws on which marriage and kinship are based, establishing the Oedipus complex as its central motivation already in the Traumdeutung ... Indeed, it is essentially on sexual relations – by regulating them according to the law of preferential marriage alliances and forbidden relations – that the first combinatory for exchanges of women between family lines relies, developing the fundamental commerce and concrete discourses on which human societies are based in an exchange of gratuitous goods and magic words.[24]

Freud's centralization of the Oedipus complex demonstrates that the unconscious is galvanized by the social rules that govern kinship, the traffic in women, sexual freedom, and sexual constraint. The revolutionary quality of Freudian psychoanalysis stems from its intrinsic regard for the social relations that determine the unconscious. What might appear as the personal core of Freudian psychoanalysis is actually at the same time a social core, since the subject of the unconscious is situated at the unpronounceable intersection of the body and language, structurally comparable to the undefinable emergence of culture from nature. The mysterious, inexplicable origin of the social cannot be narrated into sense or mythologized away; the individual subject's enjoyment is not only structurally comparable to this mystery, but also linked to it, insofar as it is the encounter between the body of the subject and the field of the other which engenders enjoyment.

Mind the Gap

Lacan provides excellent resources for more thoroughly appreciating the social and political consequences of Freudian psychoanalysis, and he does so at a time when ego-psychology was the most intent on domesticating Freud. Yet, as I have suggested, Lacan's own work seems to take up these aspects less explicitly than Freud did. This political explicitness, which I will substantiate more below, is what I am arguing that we receive, after Lacan, as Freud's return to Lacan.

Freud wrote several works of political metapsychology, and the sheer fact of this repetition warrants interpretation. In conducting such an interpretation, we might take some inspiration from both the conclusions derived, and the method employed, by Joan Copjec, in her analysis of repetitions between *Totem* and another metapsychological text (though not in the political grouping), *Beyond the Pleasure Principle*. Just as Lacan arrives at structuralist insights by emphasizing the repetition of the role of myth across Freud's two primal texts, Copjec intensifies Lacan's political insights by emphasizing the repetition of what she identifies as a wild factor across Freud's two most important metapsychological texts. In her reading, the two texts' shared repetition of a "preposterous" element, one which is "objectively so" (the primal father in *Totem and Taboo*, the death drive in *Beyond the Pleasure Principle*), points to the working through of the problem of "the necessity of accounting aetiologically for an empirical field, where the pleasure principle reigns in one case, and where a fraternal order obtains, in the other."[25] The key dynamic is that Freud's "preposterous" element is performing the force of a factor that cannot be located in the field of reality: a real, a "surplus existence that cannot be caught up in the positivity of the social."[26] Whereas other political ontologies, namely Foucauldian historicism, apprehend the political as an immanent field, psychoanalysis uniquely refuses "the reduction of society to its indwelling network of relations of power and knowledge."[27] Instead, psychoanalysis insists on a transcendent element, an irreducibility of the social, which is nothing other than the gap in the social itself, the failure of social relations to emanate smoothly from nature. Freud's preposterous extremities are the rhetorical form of appearance of this incompletion of the social, the irreducible surplus of the real.

Copjec's illumination of the importance of this social insight in Freud's work can frame a reconsideration of the political metapsychology. What can emerge if we return to the last work of it, *Civilization and its Discontents*? In *Civilization and its Discontents*, Freud devotes his argument to the ways in which culture is "largely responsible for our misery" even as culture remedies what Freud presents as the inevitability of "aggressiveness."[28] Returning to the questions that motivated *Totem and Taboo*, after intervening years in which World War I obviously heightened impressions of social strife and human aggression, Freud is compelled to grapple yet again with the question of the origin of the social order. This time, it is the antisocial instincts that motivate a repressive or sublimating social formation ("civilization has to use its utmost efforts in order to set limits to man's aggressiveness"[29]), pressures need counterpressures in accordance with his dynamic hypothesis. He articulates profoundly that it is the nature of culture to be unnatural, disturbing, uneasy, yet he also makes claims about nature that read as psychologizing and universalizing: claims that human beings are inherently uneasy *because* inherently aggressive.

These psychologizing foundations should be seen as a compromise formation, not a true metapsychological insight. They name the idea of something insurmountable, but they blatantly contradict the "natural foundations" on which Freud has generally, since the *Project for a Scientific Psychology*, based his theories: the foundations of human cooperation and interdependence. Infantile helplessness is a material fact of the human animal, as elemental to its animal particularity as is sexuality. In *The Future of an Illusion* Freud ultimately credits this feeling as the cause of religion; we can recognize in his according it such causal force the parallel prospect that it is the cause of sociality. Such causality is material; the human animal is materially characterized by prolonged dependency (unlike birds or cows, etc.), but this dependency brings with it no correlative infrastructure (family or collective formation). It is this asymmetrical relation between the fact of dependence and the artifice of interdependence – the unordained quality of any framework for that relatedness – which instigates political antagonism, the contest over arbitrary origins of the socius.

Across his body of political metapsychology, this question of the ground of the social order repeats. Freud cannot arrive at a fully satisfactory answer, and the unanswerability itself effectuates a great insight of the political metapsychology: that there is no explicable groundedness of the social order in the psyche, there is no cause of sociality in drives, because the psyche is constituted in and through the social order that precedes it of necessity. Alenka Zupančič has succinctly observed that "the gap of the unconscious is the other name for the reality of the inconsistent Other,"[30] and we can add that this inconsistency is a direct object of Freud's inquiry in and as the discovery of the unconscious. Freud's discovery of the unconscious, I would argue, is a discovery of the inconsistency of the social, the enormity of which task compels his frequent returns to the reckoning with the origins of the social, to narrating, mythologizing, domesticating the uneasiness in all culture. This repetition in Freud's thought is not an ephiphenomenon; his speculative political theories were not ancillary to his project, but rather central, demanding close readings of their own, demanding workings-through and distinct new constructions of their own. Moreover, the emphatic social aspect of psychoanalysis entails that any movement toward a psychoanalytic cure must also be a movement for social change. Again, Zupančič is so succinct: "If something is to be changed in our unconscious, it has to be changed in the structure that supports it."[31] After Lacan, through the linguistic prism, psychoanalysis appears profoundly socialized; yet before Lacan, Freud himself had already, and more systematically, more compulsively, articulated this properly social purview of psychoanalysis.

If we return to Lacan in the manner of the return to Freud, we can notice something conspicuous about his own reading of *Civilization and its Discontents*, something which might provide an explanation for why Lacan did not fully return to the political aspect of Freud's oeuvre. Lacan's main reading of *Civilization and its Discontents* takes place in *Seminar VII: The Ethics of Psychoanalysis*, the most influential and widely cited of all his seminars in English (perhaps of the published seminars in French), and the "reading" there curiously departs from the reading method Lacan exemplifies for the return in his earlier seminars. Instead of the close reading of Freud's texts in pursuit of the unworked in them, Lacan reads *Civilization* much more distantly and narrowly. As result, it is not read as an account of the enigmatic confrontation between the enjoying subject and the objective social field. Rather, Lacan focuses on the internal ecology of the subject-in-the-social: the ethical dimension of superegoic functioning and of fidelity to the subject's desire.

> If we are following so closely the development of Freud's metapsychology this year, it is in order to uncover the traces of the theory that reflects an ethical thought. The latter is in fact at the center of our work as analysts, however difficult it may be to realize it fully ... a fundamental intuition that is taken up by each one of us. If we always return to Freud, it is because he started out with an initial, central intuition, which is ethical in kind.[32]

Later in the seminar Lacan ultimately defines this intuition as pertaining to the "paradox of the moral conscience":

> the moral conscience, as he (Freud) says, shows itself to be more demanding the more refined it becomes, crueler and crueler even as we offend it less and less, more and more fastidious as we force it, by abstaining from acts, to go and seek us out at the most intimate levels of our impulses or desires. In short, the insatiable character of this moral conscience, its paradoxical cruelty, transforms it within the individual into a parasite that is fed by the satisfaction accorded it.[33]

Arguably, this seminar is distinguished by Lacan's departure from his formal and structural readings of Freud's discourse, and thematically, of course, ethics are a different domain of relationality than politics. The most important seminar is also the least careful about its return to Freud, with the consequence that the unquiet antagonism of social life is overly psychologized and attributed heavy-handedly to the voraciousness of the superego. We might even say that, just as Freud violated his own theories of human cooperation in conspicuously turning to the motif of human aggressiveness, Lacan ignores his own insights into Freud's social theories by conspicuously narrowing his interests to the superego's aggression.

Freud's political metapsychology more directly, and more correctly, apprehends the social antagonism as a structural feature of social relations. What Freud offers after Lacan is less this psychological will toward morality and more the unbearable formalism of the law, the emptiness of sociality that provokes the plenitude of the superego. His myths inscribe this function. It is this formalism of sociality, this necessarily formed but unmotivated collectivity, which his political metapsychology radically chronicles.

After Lacan, we read Freud's political metapsychology for the essentiality of the signifier and its awesome power in installing social relations that exceed justification. In the very project for a political metapsychology in Freudian theory, in the repeated returns to origin myths, and repeated extremes of political suture, we can read behind the contingency of social installation the abyssal void in which the signifier emerges, the very "unground," if you will, of the social. It is the legacy of Freud, after Lacan, for psychoanalysis to advance its unique inscription of the formalism of the symbolic, of the formative power of the symbolic for sociality as such – a legacy quite at odds with contemporary theory's prevailing rejection of the symbolic, an ecstatic desire for formlessness uniting left anti-statism and right fascism. While current prominent theories in work by Gilles Deleuze, Bruno Latour, Michael Hardt, and Jane Bennett[34] prioritize flows of affects and anarchic assemblages, psychoanalysis continues, to its distinction, to highlight the social structures without which desiring bodies could not exist.

In a recent book, Tracy McNulty has brilliantly distilled this legacy, marking the political facets of the Freudian–Lacanian commitment to the symbolic that we have been tracing:

> the symbolic is an absolutely crucial dimension of social coexistence, but one that is neither reducible to social norms and ideals (specific contents or values) nor something that can be assumed to be functioning in a necessary and inexorable way. As a dimension of human existence that is introduced by language – and thus inescapably "other" with respect to the laws of nature – the symbolic is an undeniable fact of human existence.

The same cannot be said of the forms and practices that represent and sustain it, however. In designating these laws, structures, and practices as "fictions," Lacan makes clear that the symbolic is a dimension of social life that must be created and maintained, and that may also be displaced, eradicated, or rendered dysfunctional. The symbolic fictions that structure and support the social tie are therefore historicizable, emerging at specific times and in particular contexts and losing their efficacy when circumstances change.[35]

Those who wish to stage Freud's return to Lacan, to practice a relation to language that grips the horizon of politics, might lend their energies to the historicizing of specific symbolic fictions or the unsettling of particular norms and ideals. This has certainly been the predominant way in which humanists in the Anglo-American academic context in the past thirty years have understood the ultimate consequences of their work with language: to expose social constructedness, to puncture the pretenses of the universal, to trouble normativity. Yet, as McNulty makes clear, beyond such relativizing, there remains "an undeniable fact" of the symbolic that must be embraced as its own enabling universal. After Lacan, Freud returns, calling us to think this universal sociality, in all its obscene formalism.

Notes

1 Jacques Lacan, *Ecrits: The First Complete Edition in English* (New York: W. W. Norton, 2007), 335.

2 Ibid., 337.

3 Jacques Lacan, *The Seminar of Jacques Lacan, Book VII: The Ethics of Psychoanalysis* (New York: W. W. Norton, 1997), 206.

4 Lacan, *Ecrits*, 227.

5 Sigmund Freud, "The Question of Lay Analysis," in *The Standard Edition. Volume XX* (London: Hogarth Press, 1926), 246.

6 Lacan, Ecrits, 238.

7 Ibid., 221–222.

8 Samuel Weber, *Return to Freud* (Cambridge University Press, 1991), 3.

9 Lacan, *The Ethics of Psychoanalysis*, 242.

10 Lacan, *Ecrits*, 178.

11 Ibid., 225.

12 Ibid.

13 Ibid., 215.

14 Ibid., 236.

15 Slavoj Žižek, Žižek! Astra Taylor documentary. *Minute* 38, 41 (2005), 38.

16 Sigmund Freud, "Totem and Taboo" (1913), in *The Standard Edition, volume XIII* (London: Hogarth Press, 1950), xxviii.

17 Jacques Lacan, *Le Séminaire livre XVIII: D'un discours qui ne serait pas du semblant* (Paris: Seuil, 2007), 161; Lacan, *Le Séminaire livre IV: La relation d'objet* (Paris: Seuil, 1994), 210.

18 Jacques Lacan, *The Seminar of Jacques Lacan: The Other Side of Psychoanalysis*. Volume XVII (New York: W. W. Norton, 2007), 113.

19 Ibid., 111.

20 Lacan, *D'un discours qui ne serait pas du semblant*, 161.

21 Lacan, *The Other Side of Psychoanalysis*, 113.

22 Lacan, *D'un discours qui ne serait pas du semblant*, 160.

23 Claude Levi-Strauss, "The Structural Study of Myth," *Journal of American Folklore* 68, 270 (1955), 435.

24 Lacan, Ecrits, 359.

25 Joan Copjec, *Read My Desire: Lacan against the Historicists* (Cambridge, MA: MIT Press, 1996), 13.

26 Ibid., 4.

27 Ibid., 6.

28 Sigmund Freud, "Civilization and Its Discontents" (1930), *The Standard Edition. volume XXI* (London: Hogarth Press, 1968), 38, 71.

29 Ibid., 69–70.

30 Alenka Zupančič, *Why Psychoanalysis?* (Natchitoches, LA: NSU Press, 2008), 16.

31 Ibid., 29.

32 Lacan, *The Ethics of Psychoanalysis*, 38.

33 Ibid., 89.

34 Gilles Deleuze, *Pure Immanence* (New York: Zone Books, 2005); Bruno Latour, *Reassembling the Social* (Oxford University Press, 2007); Michael Hardt and Antonio Negri. *Multitude* (New York: Penguin Books, 2005); Jane Bennett, *Vibrant Matter: A Political Ecology of Things* (Durham, NC: Duke University Press, 2010).

35 Tracy McNulty, *Wrestling with the Angel* (New York: Columbia University Press, 2014), 12–13.

CHAPTER 3

Beyond the Oedipus Complex

Tracy McNulty

In his seminars of the 1960s, Lacan proposes that the function of the symbolic must be sought not in the Oedipal prohibition and the social order to which it gives rise, but in a reexamination of the "discourse of the hysteric" that founds psychoanalysis by revealing the transformative potential of the signifier (or the symbolic function of speech) as distinct from the "imaginary" of the social bond: the norms, values, and ideals with which the ego identifies in order to repress the fragmented body of the drives. Lacan marvels that, after years of listening to hysterics, Freud can come up with nothing better than the Oedipus complex to make sense of their experience: "Why did Freud mislead himself to this extent? ... Why does he substitute for the knowledge he gathers from all these mouths of gold – Anna, Emma, Dora – this myth, the Oedipus complex?"[1] (Lacan 2007:99).

As women who were not addressed by the prohibitions that metaphorize a man's relation to the lack in drive (for example, the incest prohibition that identifies certain sexual objects as impossible or forbidden), Freud's first hysterical patients were confronted with a jouissance not limited by the law. The fact that they were able to benefit from analysis, however, demonstrates that they encountered through the transference another modality of the symbolic, the elaboration of the signifying chain that functions to limit and constrain the jouissance of the symptom. The logic of the transference reveals that the assumption of castration is not solely a matter of internalizing the phallic laws of lack, but more fundamentally of encountering and assuming the lack in the Other, its structural decompletion. That there is no signifier for the singular and unsettling jouissance the subject experiences means there is a lack in the Other (in language as such), a defect in the signifier inasmuch as it cannot name – and so repress – that jouissance.

Freud's *Dora: An Analysis of a Case of Hysteria* (1905) is a case Lacan returns to several times as he works out his own understanding of the symbolic nature of transference, and of the symbolic more generally.[2] When Dora leaves the analysis after only six weeks, Freud concludes that he failed to appreciate early enough that Dora had made him the object of her transference-love, thereby confusing him with Herr K – who he supposes to be the object of her unconscious fantasy.[3] In his 1951 "Presentation on Transference," Lacan suggests that the case actually runs aground on Freud's own "countertransference," which leads him to oppose his own biases to Dora's unconscious desire. Freud's repeated efforts to prove to Dora her desire for Herr K, like his delayed realization of her homosexual love for Frau K, must for Lacan "be ascribed to a bias, the very same bias that falsifies the conception of the Oedipus complex right from the outset, making him consider the predominance of the paternal figure to be natural, rather than normative – the same bias that is expressed simply in the well-known refrain, 'Thread is to needle as girl is to boy.'"[4]

For Lacan the solution is not to identify the "true" object of Dora's desire, however (a quest that could only falsify the stakes of desire by assigning it to an object in the world, whether a man or a woman), but rather to examine the "real value of the object that Frau K is for Dora" by viewing her not merely as a possible object of sexual attraction, but as the representative of Dora's own unconscious question: "Frau K is not an individual, but a mystery, the mystery of Dora's own femininity, by which I mean her bodily femininity – as it appears undisguised in the second of the two dreams whose study makes up the second part of the case history."[5] The corollary is that transference is not merely the restaging of the analysand's relationships with other people, but the elaboration of knowledge concerning an unconscious question.

In his *Seminar XVII: The Other Side of Psychoanalysis*, Lacan returns to the case to suggest that the problem is not that Freud fails to notice in time the transference confusing him with Herr K, but rather that he fails to appreciate the symbolic dimension of Dora's "love for truth" and how it might become "a love for what the truth hides, which is called castration."[6] At issue is thus the difference between the imaginary and the symbolic dimensions of the transference, or the movement from the complaint that posits an imaginary Other as the source of the subject's troubles to the transference that addresses the symbolic (or lacking) Other as the locus of knowledge. Central to this argument is a reexamination of the paternal function, and the specificity of what Lacan calls the "symbolic father" as distinct from the real and imaginary fathers: a distinction that is central to his critical reappraisal of the Oedipus complex. The pseudonym Freud gives his most famous patient is the Greek word meaning "gift." Yet Lacan's argument is that Freud fails to appreciate the gift Dora really is, and what precisely she gives him: namely, an understanding of the symbolic father, and through it the nature of the symbolic itself. Unlike the imaginary dimension of the father revealed by the obsessional focus on "frustration" (the effect of the Oedipal prohibition), the "symbolic father" revealed by the hysteric is aligned with the stakes of desire as an effect of the castration implied in the signifying articulation.

What then is at stake in the "mystery of Dora's own femininity," and how does it illuminate the stakes of the symbolic? Willy Apollon develops Lacan's core insight about the difference between the masculine and feminine ways of relating to castration by suggesting that a man is confronted with a jouissance that language makes *impossible*, while a woman is confronted with a jouissance for which language renders all objects *inadequate*.[7] The corollary is that a woman is not wholly inscribed within the phallic logic of the signifier and the object it both proffers and maintains at a safe distance. For the man who stands under the phallic function, says Lacan, castration is experienced when he approaches a woman, since "what he approaches is the cause of his desire that I have designated as object a."[8] Conversely, he notes that "on the side of ~~The~~ woman, something other than the object a is at stake in what comes to make up for the sexual relation that does not exist."[9] Her attempt to "make up for" castration turns around the quest for a signifier that would limit jouissance, a signifier she seeks on the side of man.

Lacan's two readings of the case (in "Presentation on Transference" and Seminar XVII) might allow us to articulate Dora's fundamental question as follows: *What use is a man in a woman's relation to the jouissance for which language renders all objects inadequate?* The Ks, like Dora's own parents, are an unhappily married couple. At the time Dora enters into analysis, she is aware that her father and Frau K have been involved in an affair for some time, despite the fact that her father is sexually impotent as a result of a syphilitic infection. Herr K, on the other hand, has made repeated advances to Dora all through her adolescence. When Dora is eighteen he declares his desire to marry her, confiding: "you know that I get nothing out of my wife." While Freud is puzzled by Dora's refusal to take Herr K's words in earnest, Lacan's reading allows us to understand her reaction as a questioning of the phallus and its irrelevance for a woman's relation to jouissance. To Dora's ears, "I get nothing out of my wife" necessarily also means "my wife gets nothing out of me"; what Herr K's words reveal to her is thus the inadequacy of the phallus where a woman is concerned. This central problematic is doubled in the case by another, concerning the status of the signifier – and the paternal signifier in particular. Dora repeatedly characterizes her father as a "man of means" (*ein vermögender Mann*), a rich man. Yet as Freud notes, the irony of this label is that he is also "a man without means" (*ein unvermögender Mann*), sexually impotent.[10] If Frau K manages to be satisfied by this "man without means," then what does she get from him? And what relation could it have to the "mystery of her own femininity"?

From Complaint to Transference

Freud's analysis of the Dora case hinges upon two dreams: one that is recalled early in the analysis and another that comes just before its end. The first dream (in which the father tries to save his children from a burning house, and tells Dora's mother that he "refuses to let his two children go to ruin for the sake of her jewel-case") gives the structure of the seduction fantasy and links it to two of Dora's major symptoms: a childhood bout of bedwetting, and a vaginal catarrh.

The dream occurs following a scene at a lake house where Dora and her father are staying with the Ks. When Herr K takes advantage of the absence of Dora's father and Frau K to confess his attraction to Dora, she slaps him on the face and runs away. The dream is renewed on each of the three nights following the proposal, while Dora sleeps in a room whose unlocked door makes her vulnerable to Herr K's advances. In Freud's analysis, the repetition of the dream corresponds to the resolution Dora has made not to give in to Herr K's advances: a resolution confirmed by the signifier of the "jewel-case" (*Schmuckkästen*), which in colloquial German is the name for female genitals that are immaculate and intact.[11] Further associations to the same signifier, however (the pearl drop earrings her mother received as a present from her father, the gifts of jewelry that Dora received from Herr K), point in another direction: toward Dora's repressed desire to be "wetted" by Herr K, such that his "drops" would fall into her "jewel-case." Freud's conclusion: Dora wants to keep her "jewel-case" dry and intact, but at the same time desires that it be wetted through sexual intercourse. This ambivalence is further complicated by additional associations pertaining to "drops" and "wetness," which relate to the symptoms of the vaginal catarrh (a lesion produced by gonorrhoea) and of bedwetting, and thus evoke the dirtying of the genitals that Dora fears will result from sexual activity.[12] The dream thus expresses an unconscious desire for intercourse that Dora represses out of her disgust at its possible consequences.

On another level, which will be more important to Lacan's interpretation of the case, Freud notes that Dora's dream expresses the wish that her father protect her: against the advances of the man pursuing her, but also against her own desire for Herr K.[13] In reality, however, Freud observes that it was her father who had brought her into danger, by leaving her alone with Herr K and exposing her to his advances.[14] The dream exploits the day-residue of her father's fear of fire to draw the opposite conclusion. In Freud's words, its meaning could be translated as follows: "He foresaw the danger from the very moment of our arrival! He was in the right!"[15] The latent thoughts given expression in the dream therefore posit the father both as the source of her afflictions (he is the one who made her ill, who delivered her to Herr K to hide his own extra-marital affair), and as a potential savior (the one who will save her from the "fire," and so prevent her from "going to ruin").

Prior to the first dream, Dora had been asking herself why she had fallen ill, and had put the blame on her father.[16] Freud then learns that she is afflicted with a vaginal catarrh: the legacy of a gonorrhoeal infection her father gave to her mother, who then transmitted it to Dora through childbirth. Her symptom is thus a trace of the father's "crime," the venereal diseases he contracted from consorting with prostitutes.[17] Freud reconstructs its meaning as follows: "I am my father's daughter. I have a catarrh, just as he has. He has made me ill, just as he has made Mother ill. It is from him that I have got my evil passions, which are punished by illness."[18] The symptom expresses at once an *identification* with the father and an *accusation* of the father as the one who is responsible both for her illness and for her "evil passions."

Considered from a Lacanian perspective, however, we could say that the seduction fantasy is concerned not with sexual gratification (the "wetting" that Freud sees as the object of Dora's unconscious wish), but more fundamentally with the complaint that makes her father responsible for her ills, and so allows her not to confront the work of the drive in her own body. If her mother is sick (not only infected with venereal disease, but acutely neurotic), it is because her father was unable to give her what she needed; if Dora herself is sick, it is because her father was unable to save her. The seduction fantasy therefore positions the father as the imaginary Other who is at once held responsible for the drive and called upon to answer for its effects or provide a solution.

The second dream (in which Dora's mother writes to tell her that her father has died, and the others have already left for the cemetery) involves the traversal of a "thick wood" in pursuit of the station that will take

Dora to the family's home. Freud quickly realizes that the words for the different locations in the dream – *Bahnhof* (station), *Friedhof* (cemetery), and *Vorhof* (vestibulum), as well as the "nymphs" (*Nymphae*) visible in the background of the "thick wood" – are anatomical terms for different regions of the female genitals. The dream therefore expresses a "fantasy of defloration" involving Herr K. In Freud's words,

> Here was a symbolic geography of sex! ... But anyone who employed such technical names as "vestibulum" and "nymphae" must have derived his knowledge from books, and not from popular ones either, but from anatomical text-books or from an encyclopedia – the common refuge of youth when it is devoured by sexual curiosity. If this interpretation were correct, therefore, there lay concealed behind the first situation in the dream a phantasy of defloration, the phantasy of a man seeking to force an entrance into the female genitals.
>
> I informed Dora of the conclusions I had reached. The impression made upon her must have been forcible, for there immediately appeared a piece of the dream which had been forgotten: "*she went calmly to her room, and began reading a big book that lay on her writing-table.*" The emphasis here was upon the two details "calmly" and "big" in connection with "book." I asked whether the book was in encyclopedia *format*, and she said it was. Now children never read about forbidden subjects in an encyclopedia calmly. They do it in fear and trembling, with an uneasy look over their shoulder to see if someone may not be coming. Parents are very much in the way while reading of this kind is going on. But this uncomfortable situation had been radically improved, thanks to the dream's power of fulfilling wishes. Dora's father was dead, and the others had already gone to the cemetery. She might calmly read whatever she chose. Did this not mean that one of her motives for revenge was a revolt against her parents' constraint? If her father was dead she could read or love as she pleased.[19]

Freud construes the father in an Oedipal light as one who forbids, putting an obstacle between Dora and her illicit desire (for Herr K, but also for sexual knowledge). But while his analysis identifies a shift in the father's role from the first dream to the second, we are dealing in each case with what Lacan calls the "imaginary" father of the seduction fantasy: alternately construed as the cause of her woes, as a potential savior, and as the one who forbids – and so protects her from – her unconscious desire.

Lacan's rereading of the case offers a very different interpretation of the second dream, which emphasizes the father's symbolic role as a *support* for knowledge, and thus the difference between the imaginary character of her complaint and the symbolic dimension of the transference. In 1951, Lacan had already claimed that the latent content of Dora's second dream, with its "symbolic geography of sex," was the "enigma of her own bodily femininity" that also underlies Dora's fascination with Frau K. Here he develops that reading by emphasizing the symbolic dimension of the transference as an interrogation of the lack in the Other. Instead of expressing a fantasy of defloration, as Freud suggests (a fantasy that would make her "bodily femininity" nothing more than the anatomical object of a man's lust), Lacan argues that the dream articulates a *desire for knowledge*, signified by the encyclopedia whose calm perusal is the final detail Dora reports. In the process, he offers a fundamental reinterpretation of the father's psychical importance.[20]

While Freud construes the father as an obstacle to Dora's quest for *forbidden* knowledge (and thus as an agent of prohibition), Lacan reads him as the object of her appeal for "knowledge about the truth" (implicitly, the truth of her own femininity). The proof is that when Dora reaches the empty apartment of the dead father, vacated by those who have left for the cemetery, she "easily finds a substitute for this father in a big book, the dictionary, the one that deals with sexual concerns. This dream makes clear that what matters to her, even beyond the death of her father, is the knowledge he produces. And not just any knowledge – knowledge about the truth." It reveals that "the dead father is indeed the symbolic father," and that "one only accedes to him from an empty locus that is without any communication."[21]

If the first dream concerns the imaginary father (who is at once the source of her afflictions and a potential savior), the second dream evacuates this image by substituting the "big book" for the person of the father. In the movement from the first dream to the second, the intersubjective dimension of the transference as an address to the locus of the Other begins to displace the imaginary staging of the complaint and the seduction fantasy. It reveals a symbolic understanding of the paternal signifier and its function that aligns the father with the Other as the "empty locus" of speech.

The dream gives form to an equivocation. (Lacan underscores it by turning the "encyclopedia" of Dora's associations into a "dictionary," as if to make a point about the limitations of the signifying articulation with respect to truth.) Dora appeals to the father for knowledge about the truth, but her search leads her to a "dictionary": a book in which every word merely leads to other words. Like the apartment of the dead father, it is an "empty locus without any communication," a repository of signifiers that does not communicate with the things of this world. The image suggests that the knowledge produced by the signifying articulation has *nothing to do with the truth*, and in particular the truth at stake in jouissance. When Freud characterizes the dream as a "symbolic geography of sex," the upshot of Lacan's reading is that "symbolic" must be taken in its most structural sense. Mapped on to the "big book," the "symbolic geography of sex" opens on to the larger question of the relationship between language and sexuality, or the failure of knowledge (the order of the signifier) to address the truth of feminine jouissance. It points to the incommensurability between what can be located in the real of sexuality (the different parts of the female anatomy) and what cannot (the errant jouissance of femininity, which is not localized in an organ or system). While the dictionary is full of words for sexual organs, bodily functions, and so forth, it has no word for the jouissance of the fantasy. The image suggests that although the hysteric appeals to the father for "knowledge about the truth," he in fact "knows *nothing* of the truth"[22]: not as a result of some personal deficiency, but because structurally he cannot know anything about it. The dream therefore reveals the lack in the Other, the fact of a truth (jouissance) that cannot pass through the signifier.

Dora never attempts to construct the lack in the Other to which the second dream leads, however. Shortly after its appearance in the analysis, she decides to terminate the treatment. This is where Freud claims that he mishandled the transference, by failing to realize early enough that Dora was confusing him with Herr K. While Lacan agrees that Freud bungled the transference, he interprets the problem differently. The implication of his reading is that Freud misses the movement in the second dream from the imaginary to the symbolic, or from the complaint to the transference properly speaking (the address to the locus of the Other as the locus of knowledge). In misrecognizing this symbolic father as the imaginary father (the father of the prohibition), Freud also misses the figure of the symbolic to which Dora's dream gives access.

Oedipus Revisited

In Lacan's reading, hysteria implies a recognition (albeit unconscious) that castration is the essence of the father, and that the castrated father is the only one who can fulfill the paternal function in its symbolic guise: that of supporting the subject's relation to castration, rather than modeling her relation to the object or sustaining the ideal ego through identification. The hysteric addresses the father in the truth of his castration, and not as all-powerful. But she also reveals that his function is tied to a "potency of creation" linked to the signifier, rather than to the imaginary omnipotence that gives its force to the Oedipal prohibition.

For Lacan, "the idea of positing an all-powerful father as the principle of desire is very adequately refuted by the fact that Freud extracted his master signifiers from the desire of the hysteric. We must not forget that this is where Freud begins."[23] Freud's myth of the father dissimulates the fact that "once he enters the field of the master's discourse ... the father, from the outset, is castrated ... Freud gives us the idealized form, which is completely masked. However, the experience of the hysteric – if not her words, then at least the configurations she offered him – ought to have guided him here rather than the Oedipus complex."[24] What then does her experience reveal? When Dora refuses the jouissance Herr K. offers her, she makes clear that what she wants from a man is not the phallus, but knowledge: "what she wants is knowledge as a means of jouissance – but in order to make it serve truth, the truth of the master that she, Dora, incarnates. And this truth ... is that the master is castrated."[25]

This truth is not merely the object of a triumphant unmasking, however. The hysterical symptom has two faces: the revelation of the father's castration, and the assumption, by the hysteric, of the "jouissance of being deprived,"[26] in which she identifies with the father *in* his castration. Lacan describes Dora's childhood bedwetting as the "stigmata" of the imaginary substitution of the child for the impotent father,[27] an identification with the castrated father.

Later in Seminar XVII, Lacan develops the link between hysterical desire and castration through a lapidary rereading of the Oedipus myth. Its focus is not the murder of Laius and wedding of Jocasta, but the second part of the Theban trilogy: the story of *Oedipus at Colonus*. In other words, it considers Oedipus not as the son of a father, but as the father of a daughter, Antigone. Oedipus is now a blind old man facing death. For Lacan, the fate of his eyes shows that he does not simply undergo castration: rather, "he is castration itself: that is, what remains when he loses, in the form of his eyes, one of the supports elected as object a."[28] But even as he loses his eyesight, Oedipus gains a support in the form of his daughter: Oedipus' "stick," says Lacan, is Antigone herself.[29] This is a reference to a recurring motif in the play, the characterization of Antigone and Ismene as the crutches of their aged father. Oedipus repeatedly apostrophizes his daughters as the "props of my age!," to which Antigone responds: "So sorrow sorrow props."

How then does the sorrow or suffering of the daughter "prop" the father? And what is the face of the father she supports? The "stick" is an allusion to the third part of the Sphinx's riddle (*What walks on four legs in the morning, two legs at noon, and three legs in the evening?*), and evokes the cane that supports a man in his old age. As such, it both compensates and underscores a fundamental deficiency. The same ambiguity marks the way Antigone "supports Oedipus in his blindness." On the one hand, she supports Oedipus because he is blind, lending her eyes to make up for his loss. But on the other, she supports Oedipus *in his blindness*, sustaining and upholding him there where he is blind. If Oedipus *is* castration, then Antigone is the support of *castration itself.*

In a departure from Freud's treatment of the Oedipus myth, Lacan's reading suggests that the father at issue in the tragic story is not Laius, but Oedipus: not the murdered father, that is, but the *castrated* father blinded by the truth he cannot access. As a myth, the story of Oedipus concerns what it means to *be* a father, not to be subject to the father's prohibition or wish him dead so as to enjoy the mother. As Lacan puts it, "if the essence of the master's position is to be castrated, does this not mean that succession proceeds from castration? If castration strikes the son, is it not what makes him accede to the function of the father?"[30] Lacan implies that Freud dissimulates the castration of the father with the "idealized" form of this truth, the myth of the all-powerful father. He keeps the father's potency alive by having him murdered, which allows him to become the foundation of an entire order through the love he inspires in his sons. In "idealizing" or dissimulating this castration as *murder*, Lacan suggests, Freud also forecloses its true potential – a potential glimpsed by the hysteric.

In drawing this parallel between Dora and Antigone, I believe Lacan is claiming not that Antigone is a hysteric, but that she sustains and supports what is only implicit or veiled in the hysterical symptom: the interdependence of desire and castration that the symbolic father sustains.

Dora is well aware that her father is a castrated man with respect to his sexual potency, an aging man afflicted with syphilis.[31] But what is clear in the Dora case, as in every case of hysteria, is that the potency that sustains the father's position for the hysteric is neither a sexual potency nor omnipotence, but what Lacan calls a "potency of creation":

> In all the cases, from *Studies on Hysteria* onward, the father is constituted of symbolic appreciation … The word *father* implies something that is always potentially creative … Insofar as the father plays this major, pivotal role in the discourse of the hysteric, it is precisely this potency of creation that sustains his position with respect to the woman, even if he is out of action. This is what characterizes the function from which the hysteric's relation to the father emerges.[32]

Earlier I suggested that Dora's unconscious question might be summarized as follows: *what good is a man in a woman's relation to the jouissance for which language renders all objects inadequate?* As we have seen, Dora's father is at once a "man of means" (a rich man) and "a man without means" (sexually impotent). Lacan's reading departs from Freud's in construing this ambiguity not merely as ironic, but as an insight into his true function. If Frau K manages to be satisfied by this "man without means," then what interests Dora is to know what it is she gets from him. In emphasizing the creative potential implied in the *word* father, Lacan suggests that the "potency of creation" that sustains the idealized father is linked to the signifier and the knowledge it supports. It is thus directly related to the lack in the Other, and not to some plenitude or power.

Apollon writes that the object of the girl's desire with respect to her father is neither the coveted penis nor the baby that would function as its substitute, but a certain quality of love: more precisely, "*words* of love ... addressed to her alone in the intimacy of a unique relationship with her father."³³ The love a girl expects from her father therefore differs not only from the love the sons feel for the murdered father of the horde, but also from the love Freud diagnoses in the attitude of the believer, who sees in God an all-powerful protector. For Apollon, the girl's expectation posits her father as a "man of the signifier," revealing that his love entails "the *gift* of a word," a word that addresses her singularity as a subject: "This word is seen, at the limit, as a love of something that only has meaning for her, since she and her father are the only ones able to grasp its true signification." He hypothesizes that "one dimension of paternity – to be the father of a girl – depends on this gift of the signifier, through which the girl recognizes, thanks to her father, the 'man of the signifier,' and thus another savoir [or knowledge] about what constitutes love."³⁴

Dora's dreams transmit a knowledge about the symbolic father, the hysterical knowledge Lacan identifies as the pillar on which psychoanalysis is built. But her knowledge is an *unconscious* knowledge, which does not know itself. This symbolic father is simultaneously revealed and obscured by the symptom of bedwetting, which posits the father both as the source of her woes and as a potential savior. Dora sees herself as the victim of a crime, and this allows her to repress her own unconscious desire. To put it another way, she clings to the idea that there is a truth to be revealed, a crime to be unearthed, and therefore a possible "knowledge about the truth"³⁵: a wish that remains internal to the fantasy of seduction.

For Lacan, the way Dora terminates the analysis proves that Freud was unable to support the transference as a love for knowledge. Observing that Freud is not satisfied with the outcome of the analysis as concerns Dora's "destiny as a woman,"³⁶ and consistently overstates the value of

Herr K's marriage proposal, Lacan implies that Freud derails the transference by emphasizing the problematic of the object (the object of desire he takes Herr K to be) over the stakes of "truth" in its relation with castration. This misplaced emphasis finds expression in the clinic of the symptom in particular. At this moment in his practice, Freud is satisfied merely to clear up the patient's symptoms; as a result, Lacan contends, he actually silences the subject of the unconscious to which the symptom leads.

The proof is that by the time Freud next sees her, Dora "has gotten everyone to recognize the truth which, as truthful as it may be, she nevertheless knows does not constitute the final truth."[37] Dora ends the analysis because she is satisfied with making everyone recognize the truth that Freud helps her discover: everything the others wanted to bury about Herr K's conduct, her father's relation to Frau K, and so forth. This imposed recognition allows her to "put a dignified end to the analysis"[38] by establishing the truthfulness of her accusations. The "whole truth," however, is that there is no whole truth: that while these individual claims may indeed be true, they are not adequate to the truth of the unconscious. Dora, like every hysteric, uses "the truth" as a weapon to validate her own complaints, to expose the hypocrisy of her social world and thereby disavow her complicity in the seduction fantasy – precisely so that it can continue to function for her. In clinging to her complaints, Dora retreats into the jouissance of the symptom. She glimpses the father's castration only to retreat from it, and therefore refuses the opening on to desire it represents.

The second dream shows that the signifying articulation has led Dora to the point where she glimpses something of the truth of castration, a truth she flees. How then could Freud have supported her desire to know? Lacan's implicit argument is that while the hysteric is satisfied with the truth, the analyst must assume that this "love of truth" is – or can become – an embrace of castration, *even if the hysteric does not know it*. Even if she is interested only in truth, that is (and especially in forcing others to recognize the truthfulness of her complaints), the aim of the analytic maneuver is to redirect this love of truth toward the unconscious knowledge the transference sustains, so that it can become a love of what that truth is calculated to hide.

As Lacan puts it, the aim of the analytic maneuver is to drive the analysand to the realization that "the love of truth is the love of this weakness whose veil we have raised; it is the love of what the truth hides, which is called castration."[39] In other words, the love of truth that supports the hysteric's relation to the idealized father – who Dora appeals to as the source of a "knowledge about the truth" – ultimately leads to an "empty locus without communication": that is, to castration as the principle of the master signifier[40]

The Empty Locus of the Father's Desire

We might imagine Antigone pronouncing the same complaint about her father to which Dora gives voice, but she does not. Antigone too is the heir of her father's crime, but she relates to it differently. If Dora says, in essence, "I have been defiled by my father's *jouissance*" (a complaint that allows her to repress her own desire), Antigone's assumption of her fate suggests that she has been *marked by the father's desire*, and that his castration will be upheld as the basis of her own ethics.

Immediately following her father's dramatic death at the end of *Oedipus at Colonus*, Antigone tells her sister that she wants to "return to that place," the unmarked site where the earth opens up to receive him. This desire finds its elaboration in the tragic action of *Antigone*, where she accedes to "that place" by entering the tomb Creon has prepared for her. After she reads the edict forbidding the burial of Polynices, and resolves to commit the act anyway, Antigone speaks to Ismene of her certain punishment as a "fate that comes down to us through our father." "Fate" here must be understood not merely as something that "befalls" her as a passive victim, but as desire (which is always "desire of the Other"). Antigone's desire is the desire that comes down from her father, whose desire to know drives him all the way to castration.

Dora does not actually enter the arena to which her second dream gives access, the "empty locus" opened up by the father's death, but Antigone does enter it. In this "empty locus without communication," it is impossible not to hear an echo of Antigone's tomb. In its juxtaposition with the Dora case, however, it also functions as an image of the symbolic itself in its non-communication with the "truth."

Lacan observes that while the Oedipus myth is supposed to show that the father's murder allows for the jouissance of the mother, Oedipus actually accedes to this jouissance not by killing the father, but by answering the Sphinx's riddle. In thus "becoming the master," however, he also exposes himself to the castration that is the structural condition of the master's discourse. Oedipus can answer the riddle, but he has no idea that "his answer will end up anticipating his own drama," nor of the "extent to which, through his making a choice, this answer perhaps falls into the trap of truth."[41] The castration Antigone props is the castration at stake in the riddle itself, which concerns the split between knowledge and truth, or the impossibility of knowing – and so mastering or controlling – the truth of the jouissance that operates outside of consciousness. "Becoming the master" does not lead to the promised jouissance, that is (understood in its most imaginary guise as the ultimate enjoyment), but rather to a state of being caught between two registers: knowledge (the order of the signifier) and truth (jouissance).

When Oedipus reveals his identity to the men of Athens who make up the chorus, they beg him to give an account of himself. When he protests that they surely know his story already, they respond by saying, in essence, "yes, we know all about your story – but what we want to know is *the truth*." His answer concerns the crime of incest: not as an act or deed, however, but as a failure of nomination. These girls you see before you, he says of Antigone and Ismene, are at once my daughters and my sisters. Daughter *and* sister, father *and* brother, both and neither: the "dictionary" can tell us nothing about the truth, because it appears here only as an unspeakable. For Antigone this appears not only as an extra-symbolic truth, but as a truth about the symbolic itself. Truth is not jouissance, that is, but something that cannot be said, that cannot pass through the signifier; it is thus an *excluded* jouissance.

Dora and Antigone reveal what might be called a "feminine Oedipus": not an Oedipus complex particular to the feminine subject, but a feminine take on Oedipus as the castrated father rather than the murderous son. If we were to consider Antigone as the subject in whose unconscious we encounter the tragedy of Oedipus, and not the male child who fantasizes about killing the father so as to enjoy the mother, the result might be a decentering of the obsessional view of the father that tends to dominate in Freud's cultural writings.[42] *Oedipus at Colonus* can be read on at least one level as a confrontation between two competing ideas of paternity: the totemic or "Oedipal" view in which the brothers banish the father and struggle for the privilege of taking his place, and a feminine perspective in which the daughters are the supports of their blind father.

The hysteric's revelation of the symbolic father changes the stakes of castration by showing that it is not a matter of submitting to the law, but a structural fact of the signifying articulation in response to which one must construct an ethics. The father is the one who does not know, who cannot help, but whose love is also an initiation into the confrontation with the "lack in the Other" or "unfoundedness" of the symbolic, something that allows it to be born.

Notes

1 Jacques Lacan, *The Seminar of Jacques Lacan Book XVII: The Other Side of Psychoanalysis*, ed. Jacques-Alain Miller, tr. Russell Grigg (New York: W. W. Norton, 2007), 99.
2 For a diverse range of scholarly and clinical approaches to the Dora case, see Bernheimer and Kahane's edited collection Charles Bernheimer and Claire Kahane. *In Dora's Case: Freud – Hysteria – Feminism*. New York: Columbia University Press, 1963.
3 Sigmund Freud. *Dora: An Analysis of a Case of Hysteria*, ed. Philip Rieff (New York: Simon and Schuster, 1963), 108.
4 Jacques Lacan, *Écrits*, tr. Bruce Fink (New York: W. W. Norton, 2006), 182.
5 Ibid., 180.
6 Lacan, *The Other Side of Psychoanalysis*, 52.
7 Willy Apollon, "Four Seasons in Femininity, or Four Men in a Woman's Life," *Topoi* 12 (1993), 101–115, 101.
8 Jacques Lacan, *The Seminar of Jacques Lacan Book XX: On Feminine Sexuality, the Limits of Love and Knowledge, 1972–1973*, ed. Jacques-Alain Miller, tr. Bruce Fink (New York: W. W. Norton, 1998), 72.
9 Ibid., 63.
10 Freud, *Dora*, 40.
11 Ibid., 83.
12 Ibid., 82.
13 Ibid., 77–78.
14 Ibid., 78.
15 Ibid., 81.
16 Ibid., 66.
17 Ibid., 66–67.
18 Ibid., 74.
19 Ibid., 91.
20 Lacan, *Écrits*, 180.
21 Ibid., 97.
22 Ibid., 130.
23 Ibid., 129.
24 Ibid., 101.
25 Ibid., 97.
26 Ibid., 99.
27 Ibid., 96 (translation modified).
28 Lacan, *The Other Side of Psychoanalysis*, 121.
29 Ibid.
30 Ibid.
31 Ibid., 95.
32 Ibid., 95.
33 Apollon, "Four Seasons in Femininity," 103.
34 Ibid., 103.
35 Lacan, *The Other Side of Psychoanalysis*, 130.

36 Ibid., 36.
37 Lacan, *Écrits*, 183.
38 Lacan, *The Other Side of Psychoanalysis*, 96–97.
39 Ibid., 52.
40 Ibid., 124.
41 Lacan, *The Other Side of Psychoanalysis*, 120.
42 In the legendary chronology of the house of Laius, the events recounted in *Oedipus the King* come first, followed by the events of *Oedipus at Colonus*, and finally the story of Antigone's defiance of Creon's law and untimely death. But this is not the order in which Sophocles approaches the legendary material: he begins at the end, with Antigone. Historically we know that *Antigone* was the first of the three plays Sophocles wrote, and *Oedipus at Colonus* the last, as if he were trying to figure out what kind of father produced this daughter, Antigone.

CHAPTER 4

Psychoanalysis as Poetry in Lacan's Clinical Paradigm*

Dany Nobus

Introduction

To write about psychoanalysis as poetry is risky; it might even be considered inappropriate, reckless, and outright dangerous. To be clear, I do not intend to write about how psychoanalysis might be employed to interpret poetry, about how certain poets have taken inspiration from psychoanalysis, about the creative dialogue between psychoanalysts and poets, or about the healing power of poetry, but about how psychoanalytic theory and practice, and especially its Lacanian modalities, are inflected and refracted by poetry. My argument is that in the Lacanian tradition, the psychoanalyst is expected to embrace the richly evocative playfulness of the *ars poetica*, which celebrates the polyphonic musicality of language whilst simultaneously adhering to specific formal structures and metrical patterns, in order to stay attuned to the uniquely human subjective truth from which the discipline derives its *raison d'être*.

Developing such an argument appears to be in flagrant violation of Freud's lifelong aspiration to secure the formal recognition of psychoanalysis as a proper science. In fact, it may even be perceived as jeopardizing contemporary attempts at rehabilitating the clinical practice of psychoanalysis as an effective, evidence-based treatment for various mental health problems. It will, no doubt, also play into the hands of all those who have been claiming for years that psychoanalysis firmly belongs in the arts and

* Preliminary versions of this chapter were presented at Duquesne University, Edinburgh Napier University, the University of Essex, the California Institute for Integral Studies, Dublin City University, the University of Ghent, the State University of New York–Buffalo, and the Centre for Freudian Analysis and Research in London. I would like to thank all the participants at these seminars for their constructive criticisms and insightful comments, and in particular those people who invited me to speak: Bruce Fink, Dan Collins, Calum Neill, Jochem Willemsen, Matt ffytche, Raul Moncayo, Marcelo Estrada, Carol Owens, Gerry Moore, Paul Verhaeghe, Eline Trenson, Steven Miller, Ewa Ziarek, Pat Blackett, and Darian Leader.

humanities, and that psychoanalysts (Freud included) are first and foremost creative writers, argonauts of the literary mind, dreamers with an eye for a show.

The danger is not imaginary: in fact, the risk is real. Nevertheless, it is my conviction that by ignoring the poetic dimension of their work, psychoanalysts stand to lose more than their scientific credibility or their professional legitimacy. In failing to appreciate how much their discipline owes to literary craft and poetic artistry, they risk rendering psychoanalysis soulless. Moreover, to acknowledge the poetic quality of psychoanalysis does not *de facto* imply that the discipline becomes completely devoid of scientific respectability. Even scientists bent on rigorous empirical verification occasionally admit that science and poetry are not strictly incompatible, that science contains poetic elements, and that unverified "poetic" theories may over time become validated scientific principles.[1]

Lacan's New Signifier

On May 17, 1977, at the very end of his twenty-fourth public seminar, which was delivered under the rather bizarre title of *L'insu que sait de l'une-bévue s'aile à mourre*, Lacan disclosed to his audience that he did not consider himself to be enough of a poet, to be "poet-enough." In the only version of this session of the seminar that is currently available in an official format, Lacan's sentences are rendered as: "Je ne suis pas assez poète. Je ne suis pas poâte-assez" (I am not enough of a poet. I am not *poâte*-enough).[2] Other, unofficial transcripts of the seminar mention the sentences in a number of alternative forms: "Je ne suis pas assez poîte. Je ne suis pas poâte-assez," "Je ne suis pas assez poâte. Je ne suis pas poâtassé," "Je ne suis pas assez pohâte. Je ne suis pas pohâtassé," "Je ne suis pas assez pouate. Je ne suis pas pouate assez." The main reason as to why there are so many different textual versions of Lacan's words is that his pronunciation of the French word *poète* (poet) was distinctly odd, so much so that the sound of his signifier does not really allow for a single transcription that would do full justice to its composite sonority and strange resonances.[3] Phonetically, the signifier is pronounced by Lacan as *pwat*, which does not correspond to a single common word in French. Any transcription of Lacan's words, any reduction of the signifier to the letter, thus narrows down the semantic spectrum to one or more options, or indeed to a single neologism. In a sense, the issue of capturing meaning through writing, here, is the opposite of what is required with James Joyce's *Finnegans Wake*, in which the writing requires the signifier for the text to become meaningful and legible. The most famous example of this, which Lacan quoted in his 1975 lecture on Joyce, is no doubt Joyce's sentence "Who ails tongue coddeau, aspace of dumbillsilly," which needs to be verbalized, in French, as "Où est ton cadeau espèce d'imbécile" ("Where's your present, you imbecile?"), for it to become comprehensible.[4] However, Lacan's signifier *pwat* definitely deserves more detailed exploration, if only because he repeated it no fewer than ten times in the space of a few minutes, whilst his concurrent admission of failure – "I am not enough of a poet" – is also very evocative.

What are we to make of Lacan's signifier, then? In 1923, the French poet and essayist Léon-Paul Fargue published a small collection of short, humorous poems entitled *Ludions* (Cartesian water devils), which were subsequently set to music by his friend Erik Satie. The shortest of the poems was entitled "Air du poète" (Poet's Tune). In it, Fargue played on the near homophony between the French word for poetry (*poésie*) and the French name of Papua New Guinea (*Papouasie-Nouvelle-Guinée*), in order to mock poor, mediocre, and silly poetry, whilst the form of this critique was also clearly poetic:

> Air du poète
> Au pays de Papouasie
> J'ai caressé la Pouasie …
> La grâce que je vous souhaite
> C'est de n'être pas Papouète.[5]

> [Poet's Tune
> In the land of Papua
> I touched upon Papuatry
> The grace I wish to you
> Is that you are not a Papoet[6]]

Lacan was familiar with these verses, since he alluded to them in a "conversation" (*entretien*) at the chapel of the Sainte-Anne Hospital in Paris on January 6, 1972.[7] Exemplifying the lightheartedness (*gaieté*) with which he had always approached the foundations of psychoanalytic theory and practice, Lacan reminded his audience of a poem, by Antoine Tudal, that he had chosen as an epigraph for the third section of his 1953 "Rome Discourse," and which he claimed to have culled from an almanac entitled *Paris en l'an 2000* (Paris in the Year 2000):

> Entre l'homme et l'amour,
> Il y a la femme.
> Entre l'homme et la femme,

Il y a un monde.
Entre l'homme et le monde,
Il y a un mur.[8]

[Between man and love,
There is woman.
Between man and woman,
There is a world.
Between man and the world,
There is a wall.]

Thought-provoking as the content of these verses may be, as poetry they are of fairly poor quality. At Sainte-Anne, Lacan stated that they were "not lacking in talent," but he nonetheless called them "poésie proverbiale" and "vers de mirliton," that is, what would be designated in English as doggerel.[9] It is therefore no coincidence that Lacan alluded to Fargue's "Air du poète" in the context of a discussion of the style, tone, and overall value of a mediocre poem taken from an almanac: "It's a matter now of seeing what will come next. How can it be written? What will there be between man, that is, him the pouet [*le pouète*] – the pouet of *Pouasie* as dear Léon-Paul Fargue once said – and love?"[10] In addition, Fargue's *Pouasie*, and the sorry *Papouète* who produces it, reflect the poet's own humorous take on the pejorative French word *poâte*. Although this word is archaic and rare, it refers to a flawed lyrical poet, a peddler of mediocre verses, in short a rhymester, versifier, or poetaster, much like the inimitable William McGonagall or like the equally famous bard Cacofonix in the comic books of Asterix and Obelix, who terrorizes the little village of indomitable Gauls with his unbearable musical drivel.[11] Lacan's signifier at the end of Seminar XXIV may thus be rendered more judiciously in writing as "Je ne suis pas assez poâte. Je ne suis Papouète assez."[12] Or, in accordance with some of the paranomasias that appeared in Lacan's paper "Lituraterre" – those familiar with the text will recall how he included the words *papeludun* (for *pas-plus-d'un*) and *hun-en-peluce* (for *un-en-plus*) – I would even suggest that the signifiers in the last sentence are rendered, here, as *papouètassé*.[13]

Although it does not seem to make immediate sense, "Je ne suis papouètassé" clearly incorporates an admission of failure – the failure being that Lacan considered himself to be not enough of a "mediocre poet," of the kind that produces doggerel. Of course, this admission is in itself quite ambiguous. If Lacan lamented the fact that he was not enough of a mediocre poet, does this imply that he effectively regarded himself as a highly accomplished poet? Or does it merely mark his aspiration to be *more* of a mediocre poet, to become better and more prolific at producing mediocre poetry, and thus more successful at failing to be a good poet? If so, would not a successful attempt at "failing more" still be a failure in its own right, despite the fact that the goal has been achieved? The paradox is similar to that of the student who is determined not to pass an exam: if they succeed in failing, does this imply that they have properly failed or rather that they have been successful after all? Be that as it may, Lacan's admission of failure (of *insuccès*) here constitutes the point where he inscribed himself in the title of his own seminar – *l'insu que sait* (the knowing unknown) is homophonic in French with *insuccès* (failure). At this point, Lacan thus allowed the title of his seminar to become a placeholder for his own position, as a practicing psychoanalyst and a teacher of psychoanalysis. The clearly discernible overtones of failure (dissatisfaction, disappointment, and frustration) that characterize this last session of Lacan's Seminar XXIV are also reminiscent of the pessimism that pervaded Freud's late paper "Analysis Terminable and Interminable," in which the founder of psychoanalysis designated his own invention as an impossible profession, with the small comfort that the same applies to education and government.[14]

When Lacan confessed to "not being poetaster-enough," the pronouncement is as intriguing as it is surprising, as puzzling as it is provocative. As is so often the case with the "later Lacan," the statement is apodictic, declarative, and assertive, rather than the logical outcome of a carefully constructed argument. If there is an argument to support and justify the point, we are left with the task of having to construct it for ourselves. In what follows, then, I will demonstrate that, despite its fanciful, frivolous character, "not being poetaster-enough" reopens some fundamental issues concerning the "function of speech" and the "field of language" in psychoanalysis, and also raises important questions regarding the "function of interpretation" and the "field of meaning" in the direction of the treatment.

As a first approximation of this argument, it should be noted that Lacan's lament occurred as part of a series of reflections on how psychoanalysis operates, on the target, impact, and effect of psychoanalytic interpretations, and, more specifically, on how a psychoanalyst may escape spurious "effects of meaning" each time the patient is being offered an interpretation. This in itself indicates how Lacan's signifier *papouètassé* encapsulated a clinical and theoretical concern for the direction of the psychoanalytic treatment. It needs to be situated at the end of Lacan's lifelong quest for a type of psychoanalytic interpretation that might avoid the clinical pitfalls of a patient's being provided with additional, even alienating, sources of meaning. As he had already put it in Seminar VIII:

> [B]y interpreting, you [as a psychoanalyst] give the subject something speech can feed on . . . Thus, every time you introduce metaphor . . . you remain on the very path that gives the [patient's] symptom consistency. It is no doubt a more simplified symptom, but it is still a symptom, in relation, in any case, to the desire that must be brought out.[15]

Whereas during the 1950s, Lacan had adhered to a conception of interpretation as decipherment, he had gradually come to the realization that this hermeneutic, "meaning-generating" approach merely replaced one system of meaning (the patient's) with another (the analyst's). As such, it did not succeed in moving beyond the boundaries of the symbolic network of signifiers in which the patient's symptoms are embedded. This had brought him to the formulation of an alternative modality of psychoanalytic interpretation, focusing on oracular or apophantic interventions, such as enigmas and citations, which would have the advantage of being non-suggestive, of not adding new meaning to the patient's discourse, and of reaching out toward what he called the real – the point where all symbolization fails.[16]

In Seminar XXIV, Lacan at one stage reminded his audience of his definition of the signifier: the signifier represents the subject for another signifier. Lacan emphasized that the subject (despite considering himself to be God, especially in his "scientific" pursuits) cannot actually justify why and how "signifier" is being produced, and even less why and how this signifier represents him for another signifier.[17] Yet, since all effects of meaning (*effets de sens*) have to pass through this process, it results in their being "blocked up" (*se bouchent*), which effectively constitutes an impasse. If this sounds obscure, then we should no doubt assume, here, that the effects of meaning become blocked up, because these effects endlessly proliferate as "fictional" corollaries of the symbolic, without ever succeeding in capturing the real. Lacan continued by saying that man's shrewdness (*l'astuce de l'homme*) is to stuff all of this – the inherent deadlock of the effects of meaning – with poetry, which remains in itself an effect of meaning (*effet de sens*), but also an effect of the hole (*effet de trou*). "It is only poetry," he added, "that allows for interpretation . . . That's why in my technique I can no longer get it [interpretation] to hold up."[18] The point is that poetry does not just generate meaning, or that good poetry, apart from generating meaning, also makes space for meaning not to be reduced to one single strand of semantics. Put differently, any kind of meaning that is associated with (good) poetry is immediately undone by the fact that it should be balanced against other meanings, and against the musicality and the rhythm of language, so that poetry effectively creates a hole in the field of meaning, which allows for limitless semantic configurations and permutations to take place. In Lacan's late conception of psychoanalytic interpretation, poetry thus becomes a staple of the analytic act, and psychoanalysts are being given the duty and responsibility to safeguard the poetic quality of their words, as new signifiers that do not immediately enter a known symbolic circuit, and whose meaning is therefore not instantly recognizable. Does this imply that the best analyst is also a good poet? Why did Lacan say, then, that he was not enough of a poetaster, and that he no longer managed to get interpretation to hold up? Why, at this point, would he have expressed a desire to be more mediocre at producing poetry?

A Born Poem

As I mentioned earlier, in conceding to being *papouètassé*, and thus admitting to his own failure, Lacan inscribed himself in the title of the seminar he was delivering, which was announced as a series of lessons on the failure of a blunder (*l'insuccès de l'une-bévue*), and which also conjured up the failure (and the knowing unknown) of the unconscious (*l'insu que sait de l'Unbewußte*).[19] Who or what is failing here? And what is the status of this failure, if its object is always already in itself some type of failed (disrupted and disruptive) accomplishment, be it the unconscious or, indeed, mediocre poetry? What does it mean for Lacan to have been a failed poetaster?

In 1933, the budding psychoanalyst – he had started his training analysis with Rudolph Loewenstein just the year before – published a sonnet entitled "Hiatus Irrationalis" in the final (double) issue of the short-lived and largely forgotten surrealist journal *Le Phare de Neuilly*, which was edited at the time by Lise Deharme (née Anne-Marie Hirtz), the mysterious "lady with the sky-blue gloves" in André Breton's *Nadja*.[20] The poem was dated August 1929, and would therefore have been composed around the time Lacan completed his clinical training in psychiatry at Gatian de Clérambault's Infirmerie Spéciale de la Préfecture de Police, and just before he embarked on a new two-year internship at the Hôpital Henri-Rousselle, which was attached to the Sainte-Anne Hospital in Paris. A close reading of Lacan's poem reveals that, in all likelihood, the inspiration for it came from Alexandre Koyré's monumental 1929 treatise on the philosophy of Jakob Böhme – a German cordwainer *cum* Christian theologian and mystic, to whose theory of the "signature of things" (*signatura rerum*) Lacan would later return on a regular basis – and that it also adopted the style of the French writer and poet Pierre Jean Jouve, who was married to the psychoanalyst Blanche Reverchon at the time.[21]

Lacan does not seem to have referred to his youthful poetic production in any of his subsequent writings and seminars, despite the fact that its title as published, "Hiatus Irrationalis," may very well be regarded as an early anticipation of his later concept of the real.[22] Insofar as the poem recalled Böhme's theory of signatures, in which the German theologian posited that the signature supersedes the sign as the decisive and superior operator of knowledge, it could even be argued that in his poem, Lacan attempted to convey the significance of symbolic representations for the revelation of the true meaning of "things" – a project which would keep him busy for fifty odd years. However, I am not particularly concerned, here, with the intellectual and artistic sources that could have prompted Lacan to compose his poem, even less with the meaning and importance of the poem for Lacan's subsequent theoretical and clinical trajectory. In a sense, the question that concerns me is much simpler, although no doubt much more difficult to answer than any question concerning sources of inspiration and intellectual significance. Was Lacan a good poet? Did he consider himself a good poet?

In the summer of 1929, at the age of twenty-eight, Lacan wrote a poem which he sent to a dear friend yet which, for some reason, he did not decide to publish until four years later, and under a different title, when his psychiatric training was coming to an end, and his clinical training as a psychoanalyst started. In 1929, Lacan clearly believed he could be a poet, yet maybe not enough of a proper poet or too much of a mediocre poet (*papouète*) to push himself to release the poem into the public domain, only sending it to a friend and maybe sharing it with a loved one. In 1933, shortly after starting his analysis, when he submitted his poem to *Le Phare de Neuilly*, things had clearly changed, insofar as something prompted Lacan to stop keeping his poem to himself. He no longer considered himself enough of a mediocre poet, thought of himself as "not that bad a poet" or "not bad poet enough" (*papouètassé*) to publish his poem and expose it to external commentary and interpretation. Not being enough of a poetaster, not being poetaster enough is thus, one could say, what encouraged Lacan to submit his poem to *Le Phare de Neuilly*. Once Lacan was a poet, once he considered himself a poet – a good enough poet to share his poem with others, notably the discerning readership of a trendy surrealist magazine. Over and above his own considerations regarding the artistic value of his verses, the question could be raised as to whether Lacan's poem actually constituted "good poetry." What, for that matter, is good poetry? When Lacan, in January 1972, referred to Antoine Tudal's verses as doggerel, what authorized him to make this claim? To all intents and purposes, Lacan's "Hiatus Irrationalis" is probably "not too bad," inasmuch as it was composed in proper alexandrines, with consistent metrical structures, in accordance with the Petrarchan, lyrical form of the sonnet (four stanzas, including two quatrains and two tercets), with careful attention to the musicality of the words, and with a perfect tail rhyme that even included his own surname. Compared with, say, the verses of William McGonagall, Lacan's poem is of a decent standard, but then again he was not a psychoanalyst yet, and he had not started bemoaning his failure to be a good poetaster.

Until something over ten years ago, I remained convinced that "Hiatus Irrationalis" was the only "philosophical" poem Lacan had ever committed to writing. Yet on June 30, 2006, I was privileged to attend a public auction at the sumptuous Hôtel Marcel Dassault on the Champs-Elysées in Paris, during which 117 graphic designs and unpublished manuscripts by Lacan were put up for sale. The owner of this extraordinary cache of papers was Jean-Michel Vappereau, a psychoanalyst and mathematician with whom Lacan had worked during the 1970s on various intricate elaborations of his infamous knot theory. Amongst the documents sold – this one for no less than €3,000 – was an undated and untitled hologram of twenty-three lines, written in violet ink, with corrections by Lacan in black, and the caption "A lire après" (to be read afterwards).[23] The opening lines of the text read as follows: "Comme je suis 'né' poème et papouète, je dirai que le plus court étant le meilleur, il se dit: 'Etre où?' Ce qui s'écrit de plus d'une façon, à l'occasion: étrou. Le refuser pour que l'étrou vaille ..., tient le coup quoiqu'en suspens. C'est un poème signé: Là-quand ..., parce que ça a l'air d'y répondre, naturel ment." I shall hopefully be forgiven for not attempting a full translation of these lines here. Suffice it to say that the word *étrou* – although it exists in the dialect of the Anjou region in France, where it stands for an oarlock on the side of a rowing boat – does not correspond to any known French noun, and is another typically Lacanian paranomasia, in this case of the phrase "être où" (being where), which in itself contains a critical allusion to the French rendition of Heidegger's term *Dasein* (literally: being there), as "être-là", in Rudolf Boehm and Alphonse de Waelhens's seminal translation of the first section of Heidegger's *Sein und Zeit*.[24]

For all I know, Lacan never actually read this text at his seminar, or anywhere else for that matter, despite his own reminder at the top of the page. Maybe he changed his mind about it, maybe he gave the text to Vappereau (intentionally or accidentally) before reading it out and then forgot about it; maybe it was not intended to be read in public in the first place, but rather at a more intimate, private, and personal occasion.[25] Whatever the circumstances may be, the text is important for at least two reasons. Firstly, Lacan's use of the term "papouète", here, indicates again that his wordplay on *poète* in the session of May 17, 1977 of his Seminar XXIV was not just a momentary flight of fancy, a sudden eruption of seemingly nonsensical lyricism, but indeed a deliberate evocation of the last line of Leon-Paul Fargue's "Air du poète," much like he had done at Sainte-Anne on January 6, 1972.[26] We need to be careful, therefore, not to immediately ascribe the status of neologism to words used by Lacan that do not always make "immediate sense," insofar as they are sometimes taken from specific literary sources (*papouète*) or the broader cultural realm of language (*poâte*). Secondly, in the unpublished manuscript which he gave to Jean-Michel Vappereau, Lacan describes himself not only as a *papouète*, but also, and quite crucially, as a *poem*: "je suis 'né' poème et papouète" (I am "born" a poem and not poet). Lacan may have decided to give the poem to Vappereau in response to his collaborator's own musings on poetry, mathematics, and topology, or in order to invite critical comments and stimulate further reflection, or simply as a present which he later seemed to have forgotten about – echoing Joyce, one might say "Où est ton cadeau espèce d'imbécile?" (Where's your present, you imbecile?) – yet in the poem he also designates himself as a poem. The statement, here, echoes a paragraph from Lacan's preface to the English edition of Seminar XI, which was dated May 17, 1976, roughly one week after Lacan delivered the last session of Seminar XXIII.[27] In French, the paragraph reads: "Quelle hiérarchie pourrait lui [l'analyste] confirmer d'être analyste, lui en donner le tampon? Ce qu'un Cht me disait, c'est que je l'étais, né. Je répudie ce certificat: je ne suis pas un poète, mais un poème. Et qui s'écrit, malgré qu'il ait l'air d'être sujet."[28] In his official English translation of Seminar XI, Alan Sheridan renders these lines as: "What hierarchy could confirm him as an analyst, give him the rubber-stamp? A certificate tells me that I was born. I repudiate this certificate: I am not a poet but a poem. A poem that is being written, even if it looks like a subject."[29] Unfortunately, this translation is quite flawed in a number of places, and I would therefore suggest the following alternative: "Which hierarchy could confirm to him [the analyst] that he is an analyst, could give him the seal of approval for it? What a northerner told me is that I always was one, born as such. I repudiate this certificate: I am not a poet but a poem. And which is being written, despite the fact that it looks like being a subject.'"

Needless to say, even in a more accurate translation, these sentences remain rather cryptic, and therefore warrant an explanatory paraphrase. In short, Lacan argued that the psychoanalyst can now be counted (as a new professional position) amongst those who provide treatment. Without Freud, the psychoanalyst would have had no social status, because Freud is the one who invented the name "psychoanalyst." It is important for us to remember, here, that Lacan did not believe that any-one should be entitled to nominate someone as "psychoanalyst." By way of an alternative, Lacan proposed that psychoanalysts derive their authori-zation qua analysts exclusively from their own analysis, and therefore from themselves, regardless of the fact that this may subsequently be confirmed by a specific body within an institutional hierarchy, such as a training committee.[30] Disclosing how someone from the north had once told him that he was a "born analyst," Lacan explicitly repudiated this kind of "certificate" on the grounds that he did not consider himself to be a born poet, but rather a poem – and a poem that is being written for that mat-ter, however much it may give the impression that it is a subject.[31]

What could it possibly mean for Lacan to claim, here, that he was not a born analyst *cum* poet, but rather a born poem? And doesn't this pas-sage contradict the manuscript that ended up in the possession of Jean-Michel Vappereau, in which he wrote: "je suis 'né' poème et papouète"? I think we need to read Lacan's *papouète* from "À lire après" as "pas poète," and thus as born "not a poet," or indeed as born "not a proper poet" – perhaps born a mediocre poet, or a poetaster, but definitely not a poet who is truly deserving of that name. Furthermore, it is impor-tant to recognize that the statement "je suis 'né' poème et papouète" in the Vappereau manuscript is in itself part of a poem, which probably would have gone unrecognized were it not for the fact that, much like an epigraph, Lacan placed it at the beginning of his text – thus setting it apart not only graphically, but also stylistically and semantically from the rest – and also explicitly identified it as such: "C'est un poème" (It's a poem). Hence, the *papouète* as it appears in the untitled poem which opens the untitled manuscript is Lacan's own poetic take on the "pas poète," whereby he once again appropriated the word from Fargue's "Air du poète." Yet whereas in Fargue's poem the *Papouète* is what the poet recognizes in exotic others, hoping that his reader will not commit any form of *Pouasie*, Lacan acknowledged the *papouète* in himself, which sug-gests that the untitled poem may not actually be a proper poem at all, or at least not a poem that is instantly recognizable, or even deserves to be recognized as such, and which may explain why Lacan felt the need to identify it as poetry himself. The matter is also made more complicated by the fact that we cannot reasonably assume that the "je" (the "I") in "je suis 'né' poème et papouète," i.e. the subject of the statement, coincides with the enunciating, or in this case the writing subject, that is, Lacan. The "I" in the poem looks like it is, has the air of being the same subject as the one who writes the poem, yet one cannot be sure. We can only be sure that the poem is being written, or has been written, and that the subject is somewhere in the act of writing. What we cannot be sure of, is whether the subject is equally present in the written text. For this reason, and also because of Lacan's own suggestion in the aforementioned paragraph of his introduction to the English edition of Seminar XI, and as a tribute to Léon-Paul Fargue, I propose to entitle the poem that features as the epigraph of the Vappereau manuscript as "Air d'être sujet," which would then constitute, after "Hiatus Irrationalis," a second "philosophical" poem stemming from the pen of Jacques Lacan.

> Air d'être sujet
> Comme je suis "né" poème et papouète,
> je dirai que le plus court étant le meilleur, il se dit: "Etre où?"
> Ce qui s'écrit de plus d'une façon, à l'occasion: étrou.
> Le refuser pour que l'étrou vaille …, tient le coup quoiqu'en suspens
> Là-quand

> [Being Subject's Tune
> Since I am "born" a poem and not poet,
> I'll say that the shortest is the best, and called: "Being where?"
> Which can be written in more than one way, on occasion: outhole
> To refuse it for the outhole to be valid . . ., is holding on although in suspense
> Là-quand]

How are we supposed to interpret – in this poem, as well as in the distinctly unpoetic text of his introduction to the English edition of Seminar XI – Lacan's admission that he was not a born analyst *cum* poet, but rather a born poem? To answer this question, we need to focus on Lacan's signature, not so much the way in which he signed his letters in general, but on the peculiar play on the sound of his own name that he offered as a signature to the poem that from now on I will refer to as "Air d'être sujet." The subject writing the poem was born as Jacques Lacan – as it happens, he was born as Jacques-Marie Lacan – or, in short, Lacan. This Lacan does not feel very strongly about being called a born poet, let alone a born analyst, yet he believes he is a born poem, because the name (the proper name) does not make "immediate sense"; it does not have an instantaneous *"effet de sens,"* and if it elicits interpretation, this "reading" of the name will not contribute anything to a better understanding of it, let alone of the subject who carries it. This, for Lacan, is the key characteristic of (good) poetry: meaning is evacuated to the point where only "signification" remains. Put differently, (good) poetry is poetry whose meaning is not immediately clear, whose words evoke both more and less than what they mean in common parlance, and which therefore requires interpretation, although without this interpretive act generating a single meaning, however much interpretation is being exercised.[32] At that precise point, poetry coincides with the given name, the name one is given at birth. For if the given name is interpreted and recuperated within the symbolic structure of signifiers (as Lacan does by signing his poem *Là-quand*, i.e. literally "There-when"), this is a purely fictional attempt at "translation," which has no bearing on the real of the subject who is covered by this name.

In "Air d'être sujet," it is written, then, that the shortest poem is the best, and that it is called: "Etre où" (Being where). This is followed by a wordplay, whereby the sound of "Etre où" is written down differently as *étrou*. It can be written in many different ways, the poem suggests, so *étrou* is but one amongst many options. Other alternatives may be *êtreou, êtrou,* or even *untrou. Étrou* does not mean anything as such in standard French, yet the preposition *é* generally refers to "taking out," "extracting," "allowing to be removed," as in *évacuer, évasion,* or *émigration,* etc. Were the verb to exist, *étrouer* could mean "carving out a hole." The play on words, here, resonates with what Lacan had averred earlier in the final session of Seminar XXIV, namely that poetry constitutes an effect of the hole, *un effet de trou.*

Conclusion

Toward the end of his career, Lacan did not consider himself enough of a poetaster to ensure that his psychoanalytic interpretations would remain effective. I do not think that this confession should be interpreted as an unequivocal expression of regret, that is to say as Lacan merely wishing that he had been *more* of a bad poet. On the contrary, as we saw with "Hiatus Irrationalis," and in a sense also with the poem he "donated" to Jean-Michel Vappereau, probably some time during the spring/summer of 1976, the fact that he considered himself "not enough of a bad poet" may have prompted him to share his verses with others, to release them into the public domain, or present them to a collaborator. Sharing a poem implies that the author does not regard him- or herself as bad enough to keep the work to themselves. In the act of giving (to Vappereau), the object of the gift (the poem) would have been *de facto* turned into a "good object," especially if the gift-giving had occurred as an act of love – spontaneously, courageously, and riskily, like the morra game (*le jeu de la mourre*) – and if it had been driven by the "failure/knowing unknown" of the unconscious.[33] Indeed, Lacan's title of Seminar XXIV should be read, here, not as the unconscious having failed, but as failure (the knowing unknown) being the hallmark of the unconscious – of the unconscious being synonymous with failure, of failure being the name of the unconscious, and of this failure being the condition for love, in all its contingencies.

Bad poetry is poetry that does not require interpretation, because its meaning is obvious to anyone who reads it. Vice versa, the more the poetry is truly poetic, the more the interpretation will be challenging and limitless, to the point of it never resulting in any kind of fixed meaning. As Lacan said in Seminar XXIV, (good) poetry may have an effect of meaning, but it definitely also has a hole-effect, which implies that it does not provide the interpreter with any clear indication as to its signifieds, irrespective of the seductive play of the signifier. As such, the most radical poem would be the one which brings its reader to the conclusion that interpretation is futile, that the meaning of the poem will never become clear, that the poem's meaning is irrelevant compared with its other non-semantic aspects, i.e. its soundscape, its sonority, rhythm, meter, intonation, timbre, tempo, and musicality. At that particular point, the poem is indeed reduced to the quality of a personal name (and so Lacan referred to himself as a born poem) which, although it can carry a meaning (*Là quand*), is not to be read as a signifier representing the subject for another signifier, and thus generating effects of meaning.

What Lacan really complained about at the very end of his career, when he confessed to not being *papouètassé*, is that he had become too much of a professional bad poet. Partly owing to his public success, partly because of his firmly established reputation as a psychoanalyst, his words did not require interpretation anymore, because they had become saturated with meaning, so much so that as soon as he said something his signifier would acquire a specific meaning. What Lacan complained about, as a teacher as well as a psychoanalyst, is that his words were no longer being questioned, probed, dismantled – neither by his audience nor by his patients. He had become the supreme interpreter of maladies, an intellectual sorcerer whose words served the exclusive purpose of

turning nonsense into meaning, of making sense of gibberish, of unlock-
ing hermetic seals. Paradoxically, this is precisely why he could claim
that he no longer succeeded in making interpretation work. Lacan had
spent his life looking for a psychoanalytic hermeneutics that would not
just generate meaning, and here he felt trapped more than ever before in
the realm of semantics. The upshot is that psychoanalytic interpretation
should no longer be seen, here, as being situated exclusively on the side
of the analyst. It is the analysand, as the recipient of the analyst's words,
whose primary task it should be (and for which the analyst should create
the circumstances) to interpret, to decipher, to explore meaning, and to
balance one meaning against another. At the very end of his career, Lacan
was therefore working toward the invention and articulation of a new,
truly poetic signifier for psychoanalysis, a signifier approximating the
real, which no longer carried any meaning, but which was pure sonority,
pure invocation, a polyphonic soundscape of infinite resonance, in short
a signifier of love. When Lacan considered the psychoanalyst's interpretations as "amateur good poetry," and "amateur good poetry" as the means
to generate interpretation on the side of the analysand, it is because he
did not wish for the psychoanalyst to become stuck in a self-absorbed,
arrogant process of deciphering. Rather than being solely interpreting, he
wanted the analyst's words to be interpreted in their own right.

Of course, if good poetry invites interpretation, and interpretation
is always a form of translation, this process is most likely to generate
loss, insofar as it could never do justice to the original, all the less so as
the poetry celebrates the polyphony of language in its play on rhythm,
intonation, resonance, etc. Something will always get lost in the act of
interpretive translation. Yet what Lacan suggested in Seminar XXIV is
for this loss itself to be elevated to the dignity of the Thing, for this real
to be regarded not as an obstacle, but as the most valuable, effective, and
productive element of the equation – one that is initiated and maintained
by the analyst during the course of an analytic treatment.[34] Poetry, as an
interpretive act in Lacan's late clinical paradigm, thus needs to be
reevaluated in relation to the end of the psychoanalytic experience, as the
patient's acceptance of the fundamental lack, loss, and uncertainty that
governs the human condition.

Finally, in Seminar XXIV, Lacan moved from a new exploration of
topological figures such as the torus toward the "invention of a new signifier," and thus from topology to poetics, with a view to advancing not
just his own "linguis-tricks," but rather what I would call an idiosyncratic
conception of "topo-linguistrics." This new outlook was designed to turn
language inside out, to explore the elasticity of the symbolic structure,

much like topology explores the plasticity of space. Poetry added art to the science of topology, and the new hybrid form of "topo-linguistrics" was there to shake the foundations of all epistemic structures, including those of language itself. This might also explain why, in his seminar of 1977–1978, Lacan moved toward psychoanalysis as a practice of babbling (*une pratique de bavardage*).[35] Needless to say, the cardinal question Lacan leaves us with – and it is a question which is never fully articulated, but which permeates each and every corner of the later seminars – is that of psychoanalytic training. How does one train a born poem, how does one train someone to become better, or good enough, at being an amateur good poet? How does one avoid someone becoming too much of a professional bad poet?

Notes

1 See, for example, Steven Weinberg, *To Explain the World: The Discovery of Modern Science* (London: Penguin, 2016), 14.

2 Jacques Lacan, "L'insu que sait de l'une-bévue s'aile à mourre" (1977), *Ornicar?* 17/18 (1979), 22.

3 The reader can gauge the peculiar soundscape from a recording of the session that is available at http://www.valas.fr/IMG/mp3/12_insu17-05-77.mp3.

4 See James Joyce, *Finnegans Wake* (1939) (Oxford University Press, 2012), 15; Jacques Lacan, "Joyce the Symptom" (1975), in *The Seminar. Book XXIII, The Sinthome (1975–'76)*, ed. Jacques-Alain Miller, tr. Adrian R. Price (Malden, MA: Polity Press, 2016), 145.

5 Léon-Paul Fargue, "Ludions" (1923), in *Poésies: Tancrède. Ludions. Poëmes. Pour la musique* (Paris: Gallimard, 1967), 41. Unless otherwise noted, all subsequent translations of French-language sources are mine.

6 To the best of my knowledge, there is no official English translation of the poem. Two English versions, one by Peter Low and one by Christopher Goldsack, are available on the internet, yet none of these captures Fargue's play on the near homophony between the French words for "not being a poet" (*pas poète*) and an inhabitant of Papua New Guinea (*Papouète*).

7 See Jacques Lacan, *Talking to Brick Walls. A Series of Presentations in the Chapel at Sainte-Anne Hospital (1971–'72)*, tr. Adrian R. Price (Medford, MA: Polity Press, 2017), 71–103 and 95–96 in particular.

8 Jacques Lacan, "Fonction et champ de la parole et du langage en psychanalyse" (1953), in *Écrits* (Paris: Seuil, 1966), 289. For the English version, see Jacques Lacan, "The Function and Field of Speech and Language in Psychoanalysis" (1953), in *Écrits*, tr. Bruce Fink (New York : W. W. Norton, 2006), 239. It is interesting to note, here, that when he quoted Tudal's poem in his conversation at Sainte-Anne, Lacan changed the first two lines to *Entre l'homme et la femme,/Il y a l'amour. Entre l'homme et l'amour,/Il y a un monde.* (Lacan, *Talking to Brick Walls*, 92). Some small typographical errors aside, the lines included in the 'Rome Discourse' match the original,

and as tape-recordings of the conversation at Sainte-Anne evince, the text of the poem as included in the published version of Lacan's conversation does not contain a transcription error. For the almanac from which Lacan took the poem, see André Beucler and Jean Masson (eds.), *Almanach de Paris: An 2000* (Paris: Paul Dupont, 1949). Tudal's complete poem, which is entitled "Obstacles," can be found on p. 273. For an analysis of Lacan's poetic love-blunder, see Roberto Harari, "Un doble lapsus de Lacan," *Revista de Psicoterapia psicoanalítica* (Uruguay), 2 (1988), 417–430; Jean Allouch, *L'amour Lacan* (Paris: EPEL, 2009), 252–256. For a commentary on Lacan's engagement with Tudal, see Philippe Porret, "Un mur de lumière," *Le Coq-Héron* 178(2004), 139–148.

9 Lacan, *Talking to Brick Walls*, 92.

10 Ibid., 95–96. Strictly speaking, Fargue did not use the word *pouète*, nor *pouète de Pouasie* for that matter, but only *Pouasie* and *Papouète*. Hence, *pouète de Pouasie* is Lacan's own take on Fargue's *pays de Papouasie*.

11 The word *poâte* appears, for instance, in the sixth short story ("Les voies de fait") of Alphonse Daudet's *Les femmes d'artistes* (*Artists' Wives*). See Alphonse Daudet, *Les femmes d'artistes* (Paris: Alphonse Lemerre, 1874), 42; Alphonse Daudet, *Artists' Wives*, trans. Laura Ensor (London: George Routledge & Sons, 1892), 119.

12 In his intervention at the Rome Congress of the École freudienne de Paris (October 31–November 3, 1974), which was subsequently transcribed and published as "La troisième" (The Third), yet without the text having been verified by Lacan, he also seems to have played on *poète*, *po(h)âte*, and *pouète*, since the transcription (in both published versions) contains the following sentence, launched in response to the line "Je ne me sentis plus guidé par les haleurs" from Arthur Rimbaud's "Bateau ivre": "Il n'y a aucun besoin de rimbateau, ni de *poâte* ni *d'Ethiopoâte* . . ." See Jacques Lacan, "La troisième" (1974), *Lettres de l'École freudienne. Bulletin intérieur de l'École freu-dienne de Paris* 16 (1975), 196; Jacques Lacan, "La troisième" (1974), *La Cause freud-ienne* 79 (2011), 26.

13 See Jacques Lacan, "Lituraterre", tr. Dany Nobus, *Continental Philosophy Review* 46 (2013), 331.

14 See Sigmund Freud, "Analysis Terminable and Interminable (1937c)," in *The Standard Edition of the Complete Psychological Works of Sigmund Freud*, tr. James Strachey (London: Hogarth Press and the Institute of Psycho-Analysis, 1964), 248.

15 Jacques Lacan, *The Seminar. Book VIII: Transference (1960–'61)*, ed. Jacques-Alain Miller, tr. Bruce Fink (Malden, MA: Polity Press, 2015), 208.

16 On interpretation as citation and enigma, see Jacques Lacan, *The Seminar. Book XVII: The Other Side of Psychoanalysis (1969–'70)*, ed. Jacques-Alain Miller, tr. Bruce Fink (New York : W. W. Norton, 2007), 36–37. On the status of oracular speech, see Jacques Lacan, *The Seminar. Book XX: On Feminine Sexuality, the Limits of Love and Knowledge (Encore) (1972–'73)*, ed. Jacques-Alain Miller, tr. Russell Grigg (New York : W. W. Norton, 1998), 114; Jacques Lacan, "Introduction à l'édition allemande d'un premier

volume des Écrits" (1973), *Scilicet* 5 (1975), 16. On apophantic statements, see Jacques Lacan, "L'étourdit" (1972), *Scilicet* 4 (1973), 30.

17 The French reads: "Le sujet se prend pour Dieu, mais il est impuissant à justifier qu'il se produit du signifiant." The expression "qu'il se produit du signifiant" is ambiguous and may also be rendered as "that he [the subject] is being produced by the signifier", or as "that signifier can be produced." See Lacan, "L'insu que sait de l'une-bévue s'aile à mourre," 21.

18 The French "[J]e n'arrive plus, dans ma technique, à ce qu'elle [l'interprétation] tienne" could also be rendered as "In my technique, I no longer succeed in making interpretation work," or "In my technique, I am no longer successful at making effective interpretations." See ibid., 22.

19 Freud's German term *Unbewußte* is always translated in English as "the unconscious," yet given the fact that *wußte* is derived from the verb *wissen* (to know), it would not be far-fetched to consider the alternative, more literal option of "the unbeknownst."

20 See Jacques Lacan, "Hiatus Irrationalis", *Le Phare de Neuilly* 3-4 (1933), 37. The published poem differs in a number of places from the manuscript of the poem that Lacan sent to his friend Ferdinand Alquié. On Lise Deharme and *Le Phare de Neuilly*, see Marie-Claire Barnet, "To Lise Deharme's Lighthouse: *Le Phare de Neuilly*, a Forgotten Surrealist Review," *French Studies* 57 (2003), 323–334. The manuscript of the poem as sent to Ferdinand Alquié is in the archives of the Bibliothèque municipale de Carcassonne, 60817-AL QMS 34.

21 For a detailed commentary and analysis of the poem, see Annick Allaigre-Duny, "À propos du sonnet de Lacan," *L'Unebévue* 17 (2001), 27–48. See also Dany-Robert Dufour, *Lacan et le miroir sophianique de Boehme* (Paris: EPEL, 1998), 29–54. For Koyré's volume, see Alexandre Koyré, *La philosophie de Jacob Boehme* (Paris: J. Vrin, 1929).

22 The notion of "hiatus irrationalis" was coined in 1804 by the German idealist philosopher Fichte to capture the transcendental abyss, the irreducible and unbridgeable gap, that separates thought from reality. See Johann Gottlieb Fichte, *Die Wissenschaftslehre. Zweiter Vortrag im Jahre 1804* (Hamburg: Meiner, 1986), 217.

23 For a facsimile, see Jacques Lacan, *Œuvres graphiques et manuscrits* (Paris: Artcurial, 2006), 48.

24 See A.-J. Verrier and R. Orillon, *Glossaire étymologique et historique des patois et des parlers de l'Anjou*, vol. 1 (Angers: Germain & G. Grassin, 1908), 373; Martin Heidegger, *L'Être et le temps* (1927), tr. Rudolf Boehm and Alphonse de Waelhens (Paris: Gallimard, 1964), 7 note 4.

25 Lacan's instruction at the top of the page is in black ink, and thus forms part of his later corrections to the text, and it is also preceded by a large Roman letter 2 (II), yet this in itself does not prove that he himself intended to read the revised version at his seminar or at the end of a conference talk. If "à lire après" is clear as an instruction – but to whom exactly? – one is still left with the question "Après quoi?" After the first part of a presentation? After dinner? After Lacan's death?

26 As a matter of fact, the manuscript sold at auction in Paris contains the only written trace that I have been able to find of Lacan literally employing Fargue's word *papouète*, all the other texts being transcriptions of oral presentations, and therefore open to error.

27 The unpublished manuscript "A lire après" – as good a title as any that Lacan could have given it – may therefore have been composed around the same time, and may have served as a coda to Seminar XXIII.

28 Jacques Lacan, "Préface à l'édition anglaise du *Séminaire XI*", *Autres Ecrits* (Paris: Seuil, 2001), 572.

29 Jacques Lacan, "Preface to the English-Language Edition", in *The Four Fundamental Concepts of Psycho-Analysis* (1964), tr. Alan Sheridan (Harmondsworth: Penguin, 1994), xl.

30 On the controversial, and often misunderstood, principle that psychoanalysts derive their professional authorization only from themselves, see Jacques Lacan, "Proposition of 9 October 1967 on the Psychoanalyst of the School" (1967), tr. Russell Grigg, *analysis* 6 (1995), 1; Jacques Lacan, "Note italienne" (1974), *Ornicar?* 25 (1982), 7.

31 The strange word "Cht" in Lacan's text should indeed be interpreted as a pejorative reference to someone from the north of France. The more commonly used terms are *Ch'ti*, *Chti*, or *Chtimi*. See Michel Bousseyroux, *Au risque de la topologie et de la poésie. Élargir la psychanalyse* (Toulouse: Érès, 2011), 300.

32 Lacan's perspective on poetry was clearly indebted, here, to Geoffrey Hartman's deconstructionist views, which could have been transmitted to him through the work of Tzvetan Todorov, although Lacan also met Hartman in person at Yale in November 1975. See Jacques Lacan, "Conférences et entretiens dans des universités nord-américaines. Yale University – Kanzer Seminar. 24 novembre 1975" (1975), *Scilicet* 6/7 (1976), 7–31; Tzvetan Todorov, "Autour de la poésie", *Les genres du discours* (Paris: Seuil, 1978), 99–131.

33 The second part of the title of Lacan's Seminar XXIV, "s'aile à mourre" is homophonic with "c'est l'amour" (is love), and invokes the ancient morra game (*jeu de la mourre*), in an equivocation reminiscent of Apollinaire's poem "*L'Ermite*": "Les humains savent tant de jeux l'amour la mourre . . ." See Guillaume Apollinaire, "L'Ermite," in *Alcools* (1913) (Paris: Gallimard, 2009), 49.

34 In Seminar VII, Lacan defined sublimation as what "raises an object . . . to the dignity of the Thing," with the caveat that the Thing is the quality of the object that can never be reached. See Jacques Lacan, *The Seminar. Book VII: The Ethics of Psychoanalysis (1959–60)*, ed. Jacques-Alain Miller, tr. Dennis Porter (New York: W. W. Norton, 1992), 112.

35 See Jacques Lacan, "Le moment de conclure," *Ornicar?* 19 (1979), 5–9. Lacan would have known something about babbling from the works of his friend Roman Jakobson. See Roman Jakobson, *Child Language, Aphasia, and Phonological Universals (1940–42)*, tr. Allan R. Keiler (The Hague: Mouton, 1968); Daniel Heller-Roazen, *Echolalias: On the Forgetting of Language* (New York: Zone Books, 2008), 9–12.

PART II

After Lacan

CHAPTER 5

The Queer Repression of Jacques Lacan

Merrill Cole

Repressing Repression

In the 1915 essay "Repression," Sigmund Freud asserts that "the motive and purpose" of his titular term is "nothing else than the avoidance of unpleasure."[1] "[T]he essence of repression," he elaborates, "lies simply in turning something away, in keeping it at a distance, from the consciousness."[2] "Repression," I would argue, names just one of the defense mechanisms that characterize queer theory's quarter-century evasion of Lacanian psychoanalysis. The act of repressing the unconscious might seem entirely different from the decision to reject the psychoanalytic theory of the unconscious. Yet, as Freud writes in the 1925 "Negation," "[a] negative judgement is the intellectual substitute for repression; its 'no' is the hallmark of repression, a certificate of origin."[3] Defense mechanisms defend against unconscious desire, which, Freud tell us, "would be pleasurable," if it weren't for "other claims and intentions."[4] Unconscious desire, or libido, frustrates both the claims and intentions of the conscious self, and the claims and intentions of theoretical discourse. This happens not only with speaking beings, but also in writing – even in discourses, like queer theory, which strive to delegitimize identity. Professedly non- and anti-identitarian writing risks reinforcing the very self to which it objects when it fails to take unconscious desire into account.

In spite of several Lacanian interventions in queer theory, most notably Tim Dean's 2000 *Beyond Sexuality*, queer theory continues, by and large, to avoid Jacques Lacan, when it doesn't badly misconstrue the Lacanian text.[5] While it is crucial to critique Lacan's lapses into sexism and heterosexism, as well as his tendency to make all meaning depend on the phallus, when such a critical stance justifies sweeping dismissal, we might suspect it serves as an alibi to fend off something altogether more repulsive than a phantom appendage: unconscious desire.

It is my argument in this chapter that one of the concepts of Lacanian theory that queer theory finds inadmissible is repression. Indeed, repression has been somewhat of a bugaboo since queer theory's inception. Eve Kosofky Sedgwick's 1990 *Epistemology of the Closet* adopts Michel Foucault's argument against the "repressive hypothesis," which he articulates in the 1976 *The History of Sexuality, An Introduction.*[6] Foucault doesn't claim that repression has ceased to operate, but rather, that other power mechanisms have superseded it.[7] Many of his followers, like Sedgwick, proceed as if he did away with the concept. The word "repression" is mobilized repeatedly in Judith Butler's 1990 *Gender Trouble* to critique psychoanalytic theory, when, for instance, Butler accuses Julia Kristeva of "delivering a psychoanalytic truth about repression."[8] In the 1993 follow-up to *Gender Trouble, Bodies that Matter*, Butler faults Foucault for not addressing "the ways in which 'repression' operates as a modality of productive power."[9] The scare-quotes are significant, for Butler's version of repression isn't Freud's or Lacan's. In a long footnote arguing that Foucault "fails to take account of the generative effects of the law [of desire] in Lacan,"[10] she insists that the law's repetition marks not only "that subjectivication has in some sense *failed* to occur, but that it is itself a further instance of that failing."[11] Albeit that the failures of subjectification are crucial to Lacanian theory, Butler refashions "repression" in terms of identification in order to fit her theory of the failure of reiterative gender norms, whereby it operates in accordance with Foucault's theory of "regulatory power." Butler's "repression" involves the repetitive performance of identifications that fail, rather than engaging the unconscious desire that causes the failure.[12]

When queer theory rejects repression as an explanatory mechanism, or reduces repression to a function of the ego, it also rejects unconscious desire. And it may not be only on the conceptual level that queer theory is repressed. As early as 1996, Leo Bersani pointed out that "gay critiques of homosexual identity have generally been *desexualizing* discourses."[13] Today, according to Dean's 2015 "No Sex Please, We're American," "there is an open secret about sex: most queer theorists don't like it."[14] With important exceptions, queer theory doesn't like to talk about sexual desires, sexual acts, and erotic fantasies.[15]

Commodify Your Repression

Lacan states in *Seminar III: The Psychoses* that "repression and the return of the repressed are one and the same thing."[16] Repression keeps working, which also means it keeps not working. *Repression always stops not being written.*[17] An anti-identity tends to consolidate into an identity, as the historical permutations of the word "queer" illustrate. This word is perhaps an example of what Lacan terms "quilting points," a signifier that "hooks on, creates a discourse."[18] In the 1990s, queer theorists attempted to re-signify a homophobic slur – the nastiest *you are this!* – as the sexy catchword of the questioning of any stable identity.[19] Recently, though, "queer" has often regressed into designating one substantive identity among others – how nice, *you are this* – which is made clear in acronyms like "LGBTQ." Paul B. Preciado argues that "*queer* has been recodified by the dominant discourses."[20]

Likewise, the better part of recent queer activism – by whatever name or acronym[21] – has retreated from the call to revolutionize capitalist society, which was proclaimed after Stonewall in the 1970s.[22] Instead, the queer mainstream, if I may term it thus, has mostly limited itself, since the end of the AIDS crisis, to identity politics, as exemplified in the push for affirmative mainstream media representation and the struggle for the right to marriage.[23] Such politics do not contest contemporary capitalism, but accept it as the frame of political possibility. To confirm a "queer" identity, image, or relationship is to normalize it, allowing assimilation into unquestioned social and economic institutions that are then slightly modified. Capitalism easily commodifies such sanctioned identity, enjoining it to package its pleasure for sale and to purchase its happiness repeatedly, under consumerism's indictment to enjoy.[24]

In her 2000 *Profit and Pleasure*, Rosemary Hennessy asserts that "[a]s postmodernism is fast becoming the cultural common sense of postindustrial capitalism, it brings in its wake porous, gender-flexible, and playful subjects, subjects more adequate to the complexities of multinational commodity exchange." Queer theory, instead of addressing this development, has repressed "the links between sexual identity and [economic] exploitation."[25] However, if we claim that sexual ambivalence is *always* the effect of class inequality, it only follows that achieving class equality would resolve all of our sexual problems. Dismissing the divided subject of Lacanian psychoanalysis, Hennessy discovers no ambivalence that is not ultimately determined by class antagonism. Behind this determination, it seems to me, is the unarticulated utopia of a society and a subjectivity beyond alienation, wherein sex could belong to a seamless human continuity. I agree with Hennessy that capitalism "relies on and continually reproduces ways of knowing and feeling that conceal the exploitative human relations that the accumulation of profit requires."[26] Yet I question whether "exploitation," any more than "repression," can provide the sole explanation of human relations.

   In the wake of the Brexit vote in the UK and Donald Trump's election in the USA, to continue to claim that the "queer" has been successfully commodified, or fully assimilated into the dominant cultural discourses, seems ill-advised. Queer populations find themselves suddenly under greater threat, the extent of the danger unclear. The current situation, though, makes Hennessy's argument all the more pressing. Diagnosing "the drift in cultural studies toward making representation, identities, and the politics of subjectivity its main concerns while leaving the structures of capitalism invisible," Hennessy insists that "capitalism relies on and continually reproduces ways of knowing and feeling that conceal the exploitative human relations that the accumulation of profit requires." Queer theory and queer politics need to extend beyond the cultural purview of identity politics to address what she terms "capital's commodification of consciousness."[27] *Profit and Pleasure* repeatedly brings the language of repression into play to explain how such commodification operates, but it unfortunately does not attempt a rapprochement between Marxism and psychoanalysis. My chapter will conclude with brief speculations on a more capacious queer theory that could consider the two together.

Keeping the Subject Open

What, specifically, does classical psychoanalysis have to say about queerness? The discussion starts with Freud's *Three Essays on the Theory of Sexuality*.[28] There is a major contradiction in this text, as Leo Bersani shows, between a conservative ideology upholding heteronormativity and radical insights undermining it.[29] Freud rejects degeneracy theory and the pathologizing of what he terms "inversion."[30] Presenting heterosexuality as a problem, rather than as natural or pregiven, he indicates (in footnotes added later) that both homosexuality and heterosexuality result from repression.[31] *Three Essays* enables us to interpret genital heterosexuality as repression, fixation, or even perversion.[32] However, in his "Summary," Freud returns to the importance of genital heterosexuality and the development of the mature heterosexual ego: "We were thus led to regard any established aberration from normal sexuality as an instance of developmental inhibition and infantilism."[33] In Freud's best outcome, the subject represses not only homosexual object-choice, but also inappropriate objects (like shoes or excrement) and the over-titillation of inappropriate areas of the body.

Repression, arguably, is at work in Freud's writing of the theory of repression. His regressions into the conservative ideology of his day, however, aren't necessary to, or constitutive of, psychoanalysis.[34] Jacques Lacan takes up what in Freud's writing most challenges the privileged positioning of the ego, including "philosophical 'consciousnesses'" that "have no other function than to suture [the] cleavage of the subject."[35] Repression functions differently – more queerly – in the Lacanian text. In his seminars and *Écrits*, Lacan mimes the workings of the unconscious, so that repression plays out in the reading process. His stylistic difficulty infuriates, repels readers permanently, or impels them to impose more intelligible meaning. In opposition to Anglo-American ego psychology, Lacan argues against the idea that psychoanalysis ought to help individuals – *including his listeners and readers* – fortify their egos, so as to fit into society as it is. He objects to using psychoanalysis as "the exercise of power."[36] In *The Other Side of Psychoanalysis*, Lacan criticizes the French student radicals of 1968 for limiting revolution to replacing one master with another. He asserts that psychoanalysis is not a discourse that "wants to master," but one calling into question "the function in society of a certain form of knowledge" that assumes it "can make a whole."[37] The self or society that would make itself whole, that would eliminate all contradiction, is a fantasy Lacan demystifies throughout his oeuvre. Yet despite his disapproval of psychoanalysis as a politics, his writing has lent itself to politically motivated theory, especially that concerning fantasies of social wholeness.[38]

There Is No Language of Desire

In *Beyond Sexuality*, Tim Dean argues that the "constitutive resistance to closure" in Lacan's writing "bears witness to a fundamental antimony between the unconscious and all techniques of normalization."[39] The Lacanian subject is barred, split, unfixed by the action of the signifier on its body, which leaves a remainder. Lacanian psychoanalysis provides the framework that most rigorously avoids the traps of identity, locating the cause of desire not in gendered bodies, but in part objects or remainders, what Lacan calls the *objets petit a*, "little o objects," many of them ungendered.[40] They include "the lips, 'the enclosure of the teeth,' the rim of the anus, the penile groove, the vagina, not to mention the hollow of the ear," "the mamilla, the feces, the phallus (as an imaginary object), and the urinary flow. An unthinkable list, unless we add, as I do, the phoneme, the gaze, the voice . . . and the nothing."[41] Dean asserts that "we misconstrue sexuality's functioning when we begin our analysis of it from the point of view of men and women, rather than from the perspective of language and its effects." We could develop a different queer theory that in "conceiving of desire in terms of multiple, partial, not necessarily gendered, not necessarily genital objects [would] most fully [extricate] a model of desire from heterosexual assumptions."[42]

Dean writes that Lacan's theory of language "takes account of the resistance or negation *within* language, which Lacan terms the real."[43] Lacan's *real* does not refer to a world of objects existing independently of human subjectivity, but to that which subjectivity cannot approach directly, evading linguistic capture.[44] What we conventionally designate as "reality," Lacan reads as social fantasy; that is to say, the fictions – or symbolic realities – in which we are enmeshed as signifying beings. Three different kinds of other emerge from Lacanian theory. The imaginary other is another person, someone I might imitate or rival, my mirrored opposite. The symbolic Other is the signifying system, often mistaken for God or some other master signifier. The real other is the *petit objet a*, "the object of unconscious fantasy," the remainder escaping "the imaginary and the domain of the ego."[45] For Lacan, one of the correlates of the real is *jouissance*, a colloquial French word for orgasm that he resignifies, taking Freud's "unpleasure" (*Unlust*) in a new direction. In Seminar VII Lacan calls jouissance "evil."[46] Lacanian jouissance is a pleasure so intense as to push past the point of bearability. Žižek explains in *The Sublime Object of Ideology* that "*jouissance* does not exist, it is impossible."[47] However, as Dean elaborates, "the real represents the condition of possibility for both the subject and discourse, insofar as the real is what must be excluded for the subject as a speaking being to constitute itself."[48]

To "be excluded" is to undergo repression: there is no speaking being without repressed desire, which insists on returning, troubling the coherence of the ego, as well as the symbolic. Dean explains that "although desire is 'in' language, *desire is not itself linguistic*.": "desire originates from negative instances and is therefore not a product of positive linguistic or rhetorical constructions."[49] Desire is not articulated. It does not speak, but comes through in the jouissance where articulation breaks down. Because it is impossible for *objets petit a* to be articulated in language and consciousness, "the objects of desire we picture are merely substitutes."[50] Desire in Lacanian psychoanalysis emerges not with identification, but with the failure of identification; that is to say, where language fails to articulate the self and its desire.[51] Other people can only inadequately stand in for objects we relinquish when we enter symbolic networks.[52] Dean concludes that "once sexuality is grasped impersonally – that is,

in terms of the unconscious rather than the self – then we may find ourselves inhabiting a different deployment of sexuality."[53]

Serial Evasion

Beyond Sexuality critiques queer, non-Lacanian readings of sexuality at the
end of the twentieth century for their reliance on the ego. Judith Butler,
Dean charges, writes "about lesbian and gay egos," treating "subjectivity
and sexuality as if these dimensions of social life were a function of one's
self-image rather than, as psychoanalysis insists, a function of the unconscious."[54] "[T]heories of mimesis or imitation" like Butler's "represent the
wrong approach to gender altogether, because formulating questions of
gender and sexuality" in these terms makes them a function of the ego and
its identifications.[55] Lacanian psychoanalysis has an extradiscursive dimension absent in Butler's Foucauldian theory: the real. Without it, she creates
a "one-dimensional theory of sexed subject formation, in which discourse
comprehends everything and knows no logical limit."[56] Read through
the lens of Lacanian theory, such perfectly self-enclosed discourse is a
mirage of wholeness existing only in the imaginary. In *Bodies that Matter*,
Butler insists on reading "social content" into the real, refusing to allow
that anything escapes discursive capture.[57] *Bodies that Matter* systematically and perhaps symptomatically misreads the Lacanian text: "Trivial in
themselves," Dean writes, "the cumulative effect of [her] parapraxes is
serious."[58] Butler's writing "is peppered with terminological slips and conceptual slippages."[59] Her theory seems troubled by what keeps escaping it.

In "On the Eve of a Queer Future," Dean criticizes Sedgwick, the
other foundational voice in queer theory. In dismissing psychoanalysis in
Epistemology of the Closet, Dean charges that Sedgwick brings back a "normative, ego-based model of subjectivity."[60] Her treatment of homophobia
exemplifies this. Sedgwick suggests that if we don't take what people tell
us about their sexuality at face value, we are homophobes:

> To alienate conclusively, *definitionally*, from anyone on any theoretical
> ground the authority to describe and name their own sexual desire is a
> terribly consequential seizure. In this century, in which sexuality has been
> made expressive of the essence of both identity and knowledge, it may
> represent the most intimate violence possible . . . It is, of course, central to
> the modern history of homophobic oppression.[61]

While Sedgwick carefully avoids naïvely positing that we know the truth
about our sexuality and can articulate it fully, she rules out as homophobic any theory that would bring the coherence and authority of the

self into question. Of course, one such theory is Lacanian psycho-analysis, which speaks of the subversion of the self by unconscious desire. Sedgwick, without making her exact position clear, circles closely around the model of sexuality that Foucault warns against, wherein sex is "consti-tuted as a problem of truth."[62] Conceiving male homophobia as a "defi-nitional crisis" involving men's *conscious desire* not to appear homosexual to other men, Sedgwick represses repression, forestalls the possibility that a man might keep from himself knowledge of his homosexual desire and react violently to anyone eliciting it.[63] I am unconvinced that we can understand the intimate violence of gay-bashing, with its blood and base-ball bats, in terms of a reaction to perceived images and stereotypes.

Sedgwick's "endless catalogues of variables and listlike [sic] sentences" and "ungainly" articulations involve more than what Dean calls a "resist-ance to generalization":[64] such rhetoric registers as serial evasion. Dean writes elsewhere, in reference to Lauren Berlant and Lee Edelman's *Sex, or the Unbearable*, that "[a]bstraction enables the maintenance of a hygienic distance from the messiness of embodied desire. Hatred of sex likewise manifests itself in the form of a preoccupation with affect."[65] The same "hygienic distance" registers in Sedgwick's style. Disdaining psycho-analysis, Sedgwick, Dean contends, is compelled "to *reinvent* fundamental psychoanalytic concepts, such as the unconscious," albeit not reinstating the concept's psychoanalytic complexity.[66] In her 2003 *Touching Feeling*, Sedgwick disparages Lacanian psychoanalysis as a paranoid reading prac-tice.[67] *Touching Feeling* has helped launch affect theory as an important, if not the hegemonic, articulation of queer theory in the present day.[68] Much of affect theory follows Sedgwick in avoiding Lacan.

Keeping It Real

Since *Beyond Sexuality* appeared, the most controversial attempt to bring Lacan into queer theory has been Lee Edelman's 2004 *No Future*.[69] Following Bersani, Edelman uses the male homosexual's anti-sociality to theorize a queer agenda of negativity; yet unlike Bersani, Edelman abso-lutizes anti-sociality in order to dismiss the future and any politics that might engage it. He writes that the attempt "to produce a more desirable social order" calls forth the fantasy "image of the Child" that "*invari-ably* shapes the logic within which the political itself must be thought."[70] Edelman insists that "queerness can never define an identity; it can only ever disturb one." Queerness, for Edelman, should involve not "an oppo-sitional political identity," but "opposition to politics as the governing fantasy" of imaginary closure.[71] It is perhaps only from a privileged social position that one could dismiss politics as fantasy, for however unreal politics may seem, it directly affects people's lives and well-being. Rather than holding itself aloof, I argue that queerness should engage in the struggle to change people's lives for the better.

In "The Unpredictable Future of Fantasy's Traversal," Chris Coffman presents a brilliant Lacanian critique of *No Future*. She writes, "Edelman's refusal of all modes of addressing the future is a problem, because it downplays the transformative aims of the [Lacanian] theory of 'traversing the fantasy' upon which he relies." Traversing the final fantasy is the endpoint of Lacanian psychoanalysis, where we dispossess ourselves of the unconscious fantasies structuring our reality, an evacuation that, as Coffman argues, "clears the ground for a future that could be lived otherwise." Clinical Lacanian psychoanalysis aims at radical change: "'traversing the fantasy' is futurally oriented."[72] The real, contrary to Edelman's claim, is not a place that queers or anyone else could occupy. As Coffman puts it, there is no "permanent state of *jouissance*."[73] That would be, in Žižek's terms, impossible. Possibility resides in political efforts to shape the world around us differently.[74]

Lauren Berlant's 2011 *Cruel Optimism* makes the sweeping claim that "[a]ll attachments are optimistic." In defining optimism as "the force that moves you out of yourself and into the world in order to bring closer [a] satisfying *something*," she limits attachment to the operations of the pleasure principle.[75] Restricting attachment in this way excludes from critical inquiry the ruthless attachments having nothing to do with optimism, attachments (or fixations) offering no purchase on fantasies of what she designates "the good life."[76] In the 1920 *Beyond the Pleasure Principle*, the observed phenomena of self-destructive and harmful attachments lead Freud, psychoanalyzing victims of war trauma in the aftermath of the First World War, to formulate the death drive as "a compulsion to repeat which overrides the pleasure principle."[77] If Berlant's sophisticated analyses of the social symbolic owe a debt to psychoanalytic theory, she excludes, in the effort to redefine trauma, the death drive and its Lacanian cognate, the real. I will argue, however, that trauma becomes tractable only when the dimension of the real disappears.

Closing off the extimacy of the real – at once its radical interiority and its radical outsidedness – Berlant moves repeatedly in *Cruel Optimism* to circumscribe trauma in "crisis ordinariness."[78] Because crisis has become so banal and unremitting in the contemporary world, she no longer finds trauma a useful analytic concept. Berlant contends that "a logic of adjustment within the historical scene makes more sense than a claim that merges the intense with the exceptional and the extraordinary."[79] My counterclaim to "crisis ordinariness" is that by foreclosing the real – which is the intense, the exceptional, and the extraordinary – Berlant ultimately rules out the possibility of radical social transformation. When reality, "that porous domain of hyperexploitative entrepreneurial atomism that has been variously dubbed globalization, liberal sovereignty, late capitalism, post-Fordism, or neoliberalism," is conceptualized as external and pregiven, all that seems left for the political subject are meek affective adjustments.[80] At the same time that she registers the crisis of contemporary capitalism, Berlant closes off the means to resist it. She defines affect as "a metapsychological category spanning what's internal and external to subjectivity," but the externality she references lacks Lacanian dynamism. If we instead conceive the utmost exteriority as also radically inside – that is to say, if we consider "extimacy," as defined in *The Ethics of Psychoanalysis* – we might bypass or trespass what she calls "the impasse of the present."[81]

Berlant's engagement with what Lacan terms "social fantasy" has much to offer. Yet without the category of the real, which disrupts social fantasy, her theorization of adversarial art narrows down to subjective orchestration, reducing the oppositional to that which provides affective support for already left-politicized publics. She suggests that "perhaps reinforcing intimate binding is the main function of avant-garde counternormative political work."[82] *Cruel Optimism* ends up on a dichotomy that seems to me not completely thought through. On the one side, there is art, or symbolic expression, that can intimately bind us, but can effect no consequential change in the governing, external hegemonies of the symbolic. On the other side, there are referents ambiguously hailed as "genres of direct action,"[83] which, even though framed in literary critical terms, seem oddly bracketed from symbolic articulation. That direct action and art can bear intimate relation, however, is abundantly evident in the history of ACT-UP, on which Berlant has written elsewhere,[84] and we can also find it in more recent political movements, such as Occupy Wall Street and #BlackLivesMatter.

According to Berlant, "[t]he utility of thinking about 'crisis ordinariness' as that which is incited by the traumatic event is in its focus on the spreading of symbolizations and other inexpressive but life-extending actions throughout the ordinary and its situations of living on."[85] "Crisis ordinariness" appears here to exclude political action. Berlant unfortunately rephrases "the compulsion to repeat" as "the compulsion to repeat

optimism," which she claims "is another definition of desire."[86] This definition writes over, or represses, unconscious desire. When she claims that
the logic of trauma, as understood by psychoanalysis, is "fundamentally
ahistoricizing,"[87] she seems to forget what Fredric Jameson (whom she
lauds in *Cruel Optimism*) has to say about the absent cause of history in
The Political Unconscious: "[H]istory is *not* a text, not a narrative, master
or otherwise, but . . . an absent cause . . . inaccessible to us except in textual form."[88] The absent cause of history, which is the real, will never find
its way into any historicizing account of the present. In a Lacanian phra-
seology, such historicizing misses what is in history more than history, in
the present more than the present. In *Read My Desire: Lacan against the
Historicists*, Joan Copjec contends that when historicism collapses society
into its constituent relations, it fails to register that which disrupts the
self-reflexive closure of the system, "the pockets of empty, inarticulable
desire that bear the burden of proof of society's externality to itself."[89]
What is "inarticulable" is not what Berlant terms "inexpressive," for the
"inarticulable" can never find its way back into crisis ordinariness.

In the context of analyzing William Gibson's novel *Pattern
Recognition*,[90] Berlant asserts, "[m]eanwhile, the impasse of the present
that is controlled structurally by transnational capital with all its force of
direct and indirect violence and coercion – that hasn't changed."[91] Here
again, we find art on one side and external reality on the other. *Cruel
Optimism*, in the examination of contemporary artworks, privileges "a
politics and an aesthetics that is genuinely dedramatized and embedded
in the new ordinariness, which is organized by a postspectacular articulation of banality, catastrophe, and structural crisis."[92] Berlant opposes
the extraordinary qualities of modernist formalism to an aesthetic of the
ordinary that does not, like some modern art, attempt to intervene in the
structural contradictions of capital. I would ask whether this attenuated,
postmodern version of the avant-garde is not ultimately a capitulation
to the capitalist ever-same, the favoring of artworks that, like Edelman's
queers, "wander the zone of the body politics without referring or recom-
mitting to the project of civil society."[93]

The Technoego

In marvelous contradistinction to *Cruel Optimism*'s hesitant austerity,
Paul B. Preciado's *Testo Junkie*, originally published in Spanish in 2008
and republished in English translation in 2013, is lusty, hyperbolic,
and explosive. Part postqueer, trans-feminist manifesto, part record of a

cis-female's illicit experimentation with testosterone, part explicit fuck-
ing, we can't complain that "intellectual respectability" edges out "bodily
desire" in this book.[94] *Testo Junkie*'s greatest innovation, the retheorization
of Foucauldian biopower, is also, however, its point of limitation. Preciado
argues that the twenty-first-century *pharmacopornographic* regime utilizes "biomolecular (pharmaco) and semiotic-technical (pornographic)"
processes to produce and control "sexual subjectivity" and gender.[95] This
new regime moves beyond Foucault's "orthopedic politics and disciplinary
exoskeletons," an emerging "system of knowledge-power," in which "[t]he
body no longer inhabits disciplinary spaces but is inhabited by them."[96]

Championing "a micropolitics of disidentification" that would bypass
the self and its identifications, Preciado doesn't consider the Lacanian
micro-objects eluding the grasp of every identification, the *objets petit a*.
Testo Junkie is introduced as "a somatopolitical fiction, a theory of the
self."[97] Replacing the unconscious with pharmacopornographic biocodes – hormone shots or money shots – the politics that Preciado advocates
risks reification into what we might call the *technoego*. *Testo Junkie* makes
no space for the Lacanian real, that which jams every coding mechanism.
Without the real, the modes of resistance Preciado proposes remain confined within Judith Butler's hermetically sealed discursive universe. Even
while innovating on Butler's formulations, bringing into consideration the
techniques through which drugs and visual technologies fabricate our sub-
jectivities at microlevels, *Testo Junkie* never gets beyond the Foucauldian
binary loop, in which we are repeatedly "subjected to new forms of political control but also able to develop new forms of resistance."[98]

I agree with Dean that *Testo Junkie* is a trailblazing queer theoretical
work maximizing "the conceptual resources of Continental philosophy."[99] Yet *Testo Junkie* is also symptomatic of queer theory's avoidance
of Lacanian psychoanalysis. At one point, Preciado reads Freud as a drug
self-experimenter whose "new techniques of the self" get sabotaged by
the "institutionalization" of psychoanalysis.[100] Ten pages later, Preciado
redefines psychoanalysis as narcotic intoxication translated into linguistic practice: Freud uses "memory, imagination, and free association to
induce a psychic impact that is comparable to the ingestion of poison-
ous chemicals in small quantities."[101] Curiously, albeit discussing a wide
range of contemporary continental and North American theory, *Testo
Junkie* is completely silent on Jacques Lacan. We might follow Foucault
in considering that "[t]here is not one but many silences, and they are an
integral part of the strategies that underline and permeate discourses."[102]
In Preciado's interpretation, psychoanalysis has either been coopted by

a "disciplinary modernity" that pathologizes "intoxication," or is an institution that creates viable verbal substitutes for drug intoxication.[103] Mutually exclusive interpretations of Freud and the omission of Lacan read easily as an elaborate defense strategy against the unconscious.

In the *Three Essays*, Freud is interested in what Preciado terms "the biochemical transformation of feeling,"[104] and he foresees in 1905 that once the science improves, a biochemical understanding of sexuality will be integrated into psychoanalysis. "You are now," Lacan tells his 1973 audience in *Seminar XX: On Feminine Sexuality: The Limits of Love and Knowledge*, "infinitely more than you think, subject of instruments that, from the microscope right down to the radiotelevision, are becoming elements of your existence."[105] Lacan anticipates here, I think, the implantation of which Preciado speaks. For Preciado, the self is subject to internal colonization, inhabited by disciplinary spaces. However, from a psychoanalytic perspective, that colonization – whether familial, architectural, or microprosthetic – is never completely successful. The rigorous narrative of disidentification offered by Lacanian psychoanalysis doesn't fall back into fictions of the self, for it insists on the self's failure. The symbolic likewise fails, but this processual and non-teleological model of subjectivity is what makes Lacanian psychoanalysis so promising for queer theory.

Really Queer

I share Dean's interest in "a different deployment of sexuality," but I am not convinced this goes far enough. Queer theory should, at the same time it employs Lacanian psychoanalysis, engage Marxism, with the consideration that ideology represses its material basis in a more or less parallel manner to the way in which the self represses unconscious desire. "Commodity fetishism," Hennessy writes, "entails the misrecognition of the structural effects of certain social relations as an immediate property of one of an object, as if this property belonged to it outside of its social history."[106] Reified sexual identities, like "gay" and "straight," are ways of knowing oneself "that shore up the logic of commodity exchange on which capitalism is based."[107] According to Lacan, the ego is formed though a series of misrecognitions, yet he does not connect such misrecognitions to the material contradictions of capital. I am not suggesting that we collapse the unconscious into material contradictions, but that the relation between unconscious desire and exploitation deserves a lot more critical scrutiny.

Another possible new direction for queer psychoanalytic theory involves reconceptualizing the Lacanian real. The real, for Lacan, insists in the compulsive repetitions of trauma. It often seems an obdurate staying-in-place at antipodes to revolution, though there are hints pointing otherwise in *Seminar XI: The Four Fundamental Concepts of Psychoanalysis*. In the 1988 *Being and Event*, Alain Badiou reconfigures the Lacanian real as "the event." The event, he writes, is "always that which makes a hole in a knowledge."[108] This "hole" is not simply a gap or tear, but an opening for what has not yet come to be. "The paradox of the evental-site," Badiou asserts, "is that it can only be recognized on the basis of what it does not present in the situation in which it is presented."[109] That is to say, we can only register the real by what is not there in the ordinary, not readable in the biocodes, not manufactured in the mode of production, not yet spelled out in a symbolic system.

There is little sense in Badiou's philosophy, though, of the possible queerness of the event, even as he is careful to make room for same-sex couples in his recent *In Praise of Love*.[110] This essay's binding of homo-eroticism to the heterosexual ideality of the couple strikes me as unfortunate. Badiou's assimilationist model disallows consideration of how the queer event might rupture the commodified homonormative, heteronormative, and cis-gender continuums of the present. And at the same time that he opens "the real" and "the unconscious" to the possibilities of revolution, Badiou seems almost to empty these concepts of sexual reference.

Without collapsing the event *that is the real* into the queer, queer theory could reembody it, not in the terms of substance and essence that Badiou rightly abjures, but in the psychoanalytic sense that there is no human happening, not even a phantom dance of which we are unconscious, that escapes desire. This would neither evacuate the word "queer" of non-normative erotic specificity, nor repress the non-substantiality of the event, its unsymbolizable jouissance. What interests me are those sites at which the event and the queer concur, collude, or collide, where the sexy strangeness of language, image, code, or chemical shakes us out of ourselves, opens us to arrival. Let revolution stop not being written. Beyond affective readjustment to structures of domination misunderstood as external or prefabricated, and outside the Foucauldian do-si-do of power and resistance, the queer event might lead us to articulate the symbolic order differently, providing an opening – to borrow a phrase from Djuna Barnes's *Nightwood* – for "something not yet in history" to emerge.[111]

Notes

1 Sigmund Freud, "Repression" (1915), in *The Standard Edition of Complete Psychological Works of Sigmund Freud (SE)*, vol. XIV, tr. James Strachey (London: The Hogarth Press, 1962), 146–158, 153.

2 Ibid., 147, italics in original.

3 Sigmund Freud, "Negation" (1925), in *The Standard Edition of Complete Psychological Works of Sigmund Freud (SE)*, vol. XIX, tr. James Strachey (London: The Hogarth Press, 1962), 235–239, 236.

4 Ibid., 147.

5 Tim Dean, *Beyond Sexuality* (University of Chicago Press, 2000). Other Lacanian interventions include Christine Coffman, *Insane Passions: Lesbianism and Psychosis in Literature and Film* (Middletown, CT: Wesleyan University Press, 2006); Merrill Cole, *The Other Orpheus: A Poetics of Modern Homosexuality* (New York: Routledge, 2003); James Penney, *The World of Perversion: Psychoanalysis and the Impossible Absolute of Desire* (Albany, NY: SUNY Press, 2006); James Penney, *The Structures of Love: Art and Politics beyond the Transference* (Albany, NY: SUNY Press, 2012); Calvin Thomas, *Masculinity, Psychoanalysis, Straight Queer Theory: Essays in Abjection in Literature, Mass Culture, and Film* (New York: Palgrave Macmillan, 2008); Mikko Tuhkanan, *The American Optic: Psychoanalysis, Critical Race Theory, and Richard Wright* (Albany, NY: SUNY Press, 2009).

6 Academia started using the term, "queer theory" around 1990, at the time that the first related programs were being established. Eve Kosofsky Sedgwick, *Epistemology of the Closet*, 2nd edn (Los Angeles: University of California Press, 2008; first published 1990); Michel Foucault, *The History of Sexuality, volume i: An Introduction*, tr. Robert Hurley (New York: Random House, 1990; first published 1976), 10.

7 Foucault asks, "[d]o the workings of power, and in particular those mechanisms that are brought into play in societies such as ours, really belong *primarily* to the category of repression? Are prohibition, censorship, and denial truly the forms through which power is exercised *in a general way?*" (*The History of Sexuality*, 10, italics mine) His answer is that "the 'putting into discourse of sex,' far from undergoing a process of restriction, on the contrary has been subjected to the mechanism of increasing incitement; that the techniques of power exercised over sex have not obeyed a principle of rigorous selection, but rather one of dissemination and implantation" (ibid., 12). The repression against which Foucault argues is, it should be pointed out, not the one that Lacan articulates.

8 Judith Butler, *Gender Trouble: Feminism and the Subversion of Identity* (New York: Routledge, 1990), 87.

9 Judith Butler, *Bodies that Matter: On the Discursive Limits of Sex* (New York: Routledge, 1993), 22.

10 Ibid., 248 n. 19.

11 Ibid., 249 n. 19, italics in original.

12 Ibid., 22.

13 Leo Bersani, *Homos* (Cambridge, MA: Harvard University Press, 1996), 5, italics in original.

14 Tim Dean, "No Sex Please, We're American," *American Literary History* 27, 3 (Fall 2015), 614–624, 614.

15 In "No Sex Please, We're American," Dean discusses Lauren Berlant and Lee Edelman's *Sex, or the Unbearable* (Durham, NC: Duke University Press, 2013), alongside Benjamin Kahan's, *Celibacies: American Modernism and Sexual Life* (Durham, NC: Duke University Press, 2013). The latter text, Dean writes, "wants to claim that not having sex is, in fact, the queerest sex of all" (Dean, "No Sex," 616, italics in original). In the influential *Cruising Utopia*, José Esteban Muñoz casts opprobrium on queer theory's "scenes of jouissance, which are always described as shattering orgasmic ruptures often associated with gay male sexual abandon or self-styled risky behavior" (José Esteban Muñoz, *Cruising Utopia: The Then and There of Queer Futurity* (New York: New York University Press, 2009), 14). "The mode of 'Cruising,' for which this book calls is not only or even primarily 'cruising for sex,'" he writes. Where queer sex appears in *Cruising Utopia*, it is haunted by the gay past before the AIDS crisis, as the title of the second chapter, "Ghosts of Public Sex," indicates. What *Cruising Utopia* designates as the "utopian impulse" most often does not relate directly to sex (ibid., 26). While we can criticize the androcentric focus of male theorists like Bersani and Edelman, for psychoanalysis, starting with Freud, sexual self-shattering (by whatever name) is not gender-exclusive. In 1990, Catherine Clément brilliantly theorized abandon from a psychoanalytically informed, French feminist perspective (Catherine Clément, *Syncope: The Philosophy of Rapture*, tr. Sally O'Driscoll (Minneapolis: University of Minnesota Press, 1994); first published 1990.

16 Jacques Lacan, *The Seminar of Jacques Lacan, Book III: The Psychoses, 1955–56*, ed. Jacques-Alain Miller, tr. Russell Grigg (New York: W. W. Norton, 1993), 60.

17 In Seminar XX, Lacan characterizes the phallus as that which "stops not being written (cesse de ne pas s'écrire)." With desire, the phallus "turns out to be mere contingency" Jacques Lacan, *The Seminar of Jacques Lacan, Book XX, Encore: On Feminine Sexuality, The Limits of Love and Knowledge, 1972–1973*, ed. Jacques-Alain Miller, tr. Bruce Fink (New York: Norton, 1999), 94.

18 Jacques Lacan, *The Seminar of Jacques Lacan, Book XVII: The Other Side of Psychoanalysis, 1969–1970*, ed. Jacques-Alain Miller, tr Russell Grigg (New York: W. W. Norton, 2007), 189.

19 This was also a motive behind the early 1990s direct action movement, Queer Nation.

20 Paul B. Preciado, *Testo Junkie: Sex, Drugs, and Biopolitics in the Pharmacopornographic Era*, tr. Bruce Benderson (New York: The Feminist Press, 2013; first published 2008), 341, italics in original.

21 "Queer" is not a favored term for many activists.

22 Among relevant texts from the 1970s are the Gay Liberation Front *Manifesto* (London, 1971, 1978, accessed through Internet History Sourcebook, Fordham University, https://sourcebooks.fordham.edu/pwh/glf-london.asp, July 7, 2016) and Guy Hocquenghem, *Homosexual Desire*, tr. Daniella Dangoor (Durham, NC: Duke University Press, 1993; first published 1972).

23 See, for instance, Michael Warner, *The Trouble with Normal: Sex, Politics, and the Ethics of Queer Life* (Cambridge, MA: Harvard University Press, 1999).

24 Slavoj Žižek argues that today's capitalism commands us to enjoy Slavoj Žižek, *The Sublime Object of Ideology*. The Essential Žižek (London: Verso, 2008; first published 1989); Lacan states in Seminar XX that "[t]he superego is the imperative of jouissance – Enjoy!" (*Encore: On Feminine Sexuality*, 3).

25 Rosemary Hennessy, *Profit and Pleasure: Sexual Identities in Late Capitalism* (New York: Routledge, 2000), 68.

26 Ibid., 6.

27 Ibid., 33, 6, 106.

28 Sigmund Freud, *Three Essays on the Theory of Sexuality*, tr. James Strachey (New York: Basic Books, 2000; first published 1905).

29 Leo Bersani, *The Freudian Body: Psychoanalysis and Art* (New York: Columbia University Press, 1986). Cf. also Arnold I. Davidson, "How to Do the History of Psychoanalysis: A Reading of Freud's Three Essays on the Theory of Sexuality," in *The Trial(s) of Psychoanalysis*, ed. Françoise Meltzer (University of Chicago Press, 1988), 39–64; Tim Dean discusses both this essay and *The Freudian Body* in *Beyond Sexuality*.

30 Freud, *Three Essays*, 2. "Inversion" suggests men trapped in female bodies and vice versa. Reading homosexuality as a reversed heterosexuality, inversion rules out same-sex desire. Freud uses the word "inversion" throughout the *Three Essays*, with and without quotation marks, even though he contests the inversion model: "Inversion is found in people who exhibit no other serious deviations from the normal" (ibid., 4); "inversion and somatic hermaphroditism are on the whole independent of each other"; and "character inversion" doesn't always occur (ibid., 8).

31 Freud suggests that inverts "may have repressed the evidence of their heterosexual feelings from their memory" (*Three Essays*, 3 n. 2) and asserts that "all human beings are capable of making a homosexual object choice and have in fact made one in their unconscious" (ibid., 11 n. 1).

32 See Freud, *Beyond the Pleasure Principle*, 232–240.

33 Freud, *Three Essays*, 97.

34 In *The Freudian Body*, Leo Bersani deconstructs *Three Essays* as "a kind of resistance to, or denial of, the work's failure to define sexuality" (*The Freudian* Body, 4, italics in original). I would agree, with the caveat that without ceasing to fail defining sexuality, we don't have to fail the same way as Freud.

35　Jacques Lacan, *Television: A Challenge to the Psychoanalytic Establishment*, ed. Joan Copjec, tr. Jeffrey Mehlman (New York: W. W. Norton, 1990; first published 1974), 108.

36　Jacques Lacan, *Écrits*, tr. Bruce Fink (New York: W. W. Norton, 2005), 511.

37　Lacan, *The Other Side of Psychoanalysis*, 79, 198, 31.

38　This includes much of the work of Slavoj Žižek and Joan Copjec, as well as Renata Salecl, *The Spoils of Freedom: Psychoanalysis and Feminism after the Fall of Socialism* (New York: Routledge, 1994).

39　Dean, *Beyond Sexuality*, 17. By "antimony," I understand Dean to mean an irreconcilable opposition.

40　The "a" stands for the French "autre," which translates into English as "other." For this reason, I have chosen to translate the term with a small "o."

41　Lacan, *Écrits*, 692, 693, ellipsis in original.

42　Dean, *Beyond Sexuality*, 18, 201.

43　Ibid., 18, italics in original.

44　Cf. Merrill Cole, "Backwards Ventriloquy: The Historical Uncanny in Djuna Barnes's Nightwood," *Twentieth-Century Literature* 52, 4 (Winter 2006), 391–412 for a more comprehensive reading of the Lacanian real.

45　Dean, *Beyond Sexuality*, 34.

46　Lacan, *The Ethics of Psychoanalysis*, 184.

47　Žižek, *The Sublime Object of Ideology*, 164.

48　Dean, *Beyond Sexuality*, 88. An incomparable source for understanding the relationship between the real, jouissance, and the uncanny is Mladen Dolar, "'I Shall Be with You on Your Wedding-Night': Lacan and the Uncanny," *October* 58 (Fall 1991), 5–23.

49　Dean, *Beyond Sexuality*, 178, 186, italics in original.

50　Ibid., 58.

51　Ibid., 187.

52　In "The Subversion of the Self and the Dialectic of Desire," Lacan asserts that "castration is what regulates desire" (*Écrits*, 700). Even if we call this "symbolic castration," I would argue that we can't help but call forth the physical penis.

53　Dean, *Beyond Sexuality*, 272.

54　Ibid., 190–191.

55　Ibid., 71. Dean critiques Lee Edelman, *Homographesis: Essays in Gay Literary and Cultural Theory* (New York: Routledge, 1994) on similar grounds.

56　Dean, *Beyond Sexuality*, 77.

57　Butler, *Bodies that Matter*, 189.

58　Dean, *Beyond Sexuality*, 208 n. 38.

59　Ibid., 183 n. 15.

60　Tim Dean, "On the Eve of a Queer Future," *Raritan* 15, 1 (Summer 1995), 116–134, 122.

61　Sedgwick, *Epistemology of the Closet*, quoted in Dean, "Eve," 121–1222, italics in original.

62　Foucault, *History of Sexuality*, 56.

63 Sedgwick, *Epistemology*, 20.

64 Dean, "Eve," 120.

65 Dean, "No Sex Please," 621.

66 Dean, "Eve," 122, italics in original.

67 Eve Kosofsky Sedgwick, *Touching Feeling: Affect, Pedagogy, Performativity* (Durham, NC: Duke University Press, 2003).

68 In *Cruel Optimism* (Durham, NC: Duke University Press, 2011, 123), which I discuss below, Lauren Berlant spells out her debt to Sedgwick's "reparative criticism," one of the operative terms in *Touching Feeling*. Reparative criticism opposes, for Sedgwick, paranoid reading practices like Lacanian interpretation. There are numerous articles speaking in praise of Sedgwick, including an issue of the journal *Criticism* (vol. 52, 2, spring 2010), published shortly after her death.

69 Lee Edelman, *No Future: Queer Theory and the Death Drive* (Durham, NC: Duke University Press, 2004).

70 Ibid., 2; italics mine.

71 Ibid., 17.

72 Christine Coffman, "The Unpredictable Future of Fantasy's Traversal," *Angelaki* 18, 4 (December 2013), 43–60, 45.

73 Ibid., 49.

74 For more on the *No Future* controversy, the reader might consult Robert L. Caserio, Lee Edelman, Judith Halberstam, José Esteban Muñoz, and Tim Dean, "Forum: Conference Debates: The Antisocial Thesis in Queer Theory," *Publications of the Modern Language Association of America (PMLA)* 121, 3 (May 2006), 819–828, on "The Antisocial Thesis in Queer Theory" and Dean's "No Sex Please, We're American."

75 Berlant, *Cruel Optimism*, 23, 1–2, italics in original.

76 Ibid., 2.

77 Freud, *Beyond the Pleasure Principle*, 24.

78 Berlant, *Cruel Optimism*, 10 passim.

79 Ibid., 10.

80 Ibid., 167.

81 Ibid., 16, 85 passim.

82 Ibid., 238.

83 Ibid., 249.

84 See Lauren Berlant and Elizabeth Freedman, "Queer Nationality," in *Fear of a Queer Planet: Queer Politics and Social Theory*, ed. Michael Warner (Minneapolis: University of Minnesota Press, 1993), 193–229.

85 Berlant, *Cruel Optimism*, 81.

86 Ibid., 121.

87 Ibid., 10.

88 Fredric Jameson, *The Political Unconscious: Narrative as Socially Symbolic Act* (Ithaca: Cornell University Press, 1981), 35, italics in original.

89 Joan Copjec, *Read My Desire: Lacan against the Historicists* (Cambridge, MA: MIT Press, 1994), 14.

90 Wilson Gibson, *Pattern Recognition* (New York: Putnam, 2003).

91 Berlant, *Cruel Optimism*, 85.

92 Ibid., 232.

93 Ibid.

94 Dean, "No Sex Please," 616. "Postqueer" is Preciado's term for modes of sexual embodiment that go beyond the queer anti-identity of the 1990s, such as the body at the center of *Testo Junkie*.

95 Preciado, *Testo Junkie*, 33–34.

96 Ibid., 76, 77, 79.

97 Ibid., 398, 11.

98 Ibid., 98.

99 Tim Dean, "Mediated Intimacies," *Sexualities* 18, 1–2 (2015), 224–246, 237.

100 Preciado, *Testo Junkie*, 351.

101 Ibid., 361.

102 Foucault, *History of Sexuality*, 27.

103 Preciado, *Testo Junkie*, 351.

104 Ibid., 12.

105 Lacan, *On Feminine Sexuality*, 82.

106 Hennessy, *Profit and Pleasure*, 129.

107 Ibid., 106.

108 Alain Badiou, *Being and Event*, tr. Oliver Feltham (New York: Continuum, 2012; first published 1988), 337.

109 Ibid., 109.

110 Alain Badiou, with Nicholas Truong, *In Praise of Love*, tr. Peter Bush (New York: The New Press, 2012; first published 2011).

111 Djuna Barnes, *Nightwood* (New York: New Directions, 1937). Readers outside the United States may not be familiar with the "do-si-do," a country square dance in which the dancers pass around each other back to back and return to their starting positions. The name is an Americanization of the French *dos-à-dos*.

CHAPTER 6

Cinema after Lacan

Todd McGowan

The Art of the Gaze

The concept of the gaze represents Jacques Lacan's most important contribution to film theory. The gaze, first developed by Lacan in his *Seminar XI* entitled *The Four Fundamental Concepts of Psychoanalysis*, is not the look of the subject but the way that look manifests itself as an object within the visual field.[1] As Lacan puts it, "I am not simply ... located at the geometral point from which the perspective is grasped. No doubt, in the depths of my eye, the picture is painted. The picture, certainly, is in my eye. But I am in the picture."[2] That is to say, the gaze marks the point in the visual field where this field takes the subject's look into account, the point at which the subject's desire deforms the structure of this field. Because the gaze marks the point at which the subject's desire manifests itself visually, it has the ability to disrupt the subject's look and make clear that the subject is part of the world that it assumes to be purely external. The importance of recognizing the gaze for the subject implies directly the importance of cinema for the subject's political emancipation.

Though a plea for the political importance of cinema seems out of place given its clear role in the propagation of ideological fantasies, film marshals the gaze in its political radicality more than any other artistic medium. When it succumbs to ideological fantasies owing to commercial or other pressures, cinema betrays its inherent allegiance to the gaze. Other visual arts, such as painting or sculpture, can deploy the gaze, but they cannot facilitate the spectator's encounter with it through a fantasmatic narrative, a narrative that creates a structure through which desire can relate to its object. Though many leftist filmmakers and theorists see fantasmatic narrative as cinema's capitulation to ideology, it is actually fantasmatic narrative that enables cinema to produce an encounter with the gaze.

Neither painting nor sculpture utilizes narrative to the extent that cinema does, so the encounter with the gaze in these forms necessarily works in a haphazard way. The artist cannot establish a precise moment for the encounter because it is utterly dependent on the whims of the spectator who decides when and where to look. Consciousness plays too much of a role in the viewing of painting or sculpture for these arts to privilege the encounter with the gaze in the way that cinema does. The fantasmatic narrative of cinema speaks directly to the spectator's unconscious. The spectator can encounter the gaze because cinema controls the look.

Theater is a visual art that employs narrative, but it lacks the fantasmatic quality of the filmic narrative. The lack of realism in theater sets – one must imagine the existence of the house around the room that one sees on the stage, for instance – is in fact a deficit on the level of fantasy, not on the level of realism. Theater's demand that spectators use their imagination testifies to the limited role that fantasy plays in the theater. Film, in contrast, bathes the spectator in fantasy throughout the viewing experience.[3] One does not require a great imagination to watch a film because the film supplies the entire fantasy for the spectator. This separates it from the other traditional arts (though not from video games, which deploy the gaze in related but different ways than cinema).

When Lacan first explained the gaze, he had recourse to a painting rather than a film, and he never turned to cinema to explicate it, perhaps because he wanted to leave this fecund territory open for future psychoanalytic theorists. The painting that Lacan uses to illustrate the effect of the gaze is Hans Holbein's *The Ambassadors*. Through the process of anamorphosis, the painting undergoes a change when the spectator looks at it from a sharp angle. The distended blot in the bottom front of the painting becomes visible as a skull. Though the painting takes the spectator's movement into account, it cannot precipitate that movement in the way that a film might, which represents a limitation in the deployment of the gaze in a painting.

One of Lacan's most influential explicators, Slavoj Žižek, has explored the possibility of recognizing the gaze in cinema as much as anyone else. When he clarifies the concept of the gaze, he almost always finds a cinematic example. One of his favorites comes from Alfred Hitchcock's *Psycho* (1960), when Norman Bates (Anthony Perkins) attempts to sink the car of Marion Crane (Janet Leigh) into the swamp behind the Bates Motel in order to cover up her murder. As the car descends into the swamp, it suddenly stops sinking, and Hitchcock cuts back from the car conspicuously protruding from the swamp to a nervous look on

Norman's face. At this point, Hitchcock activates the gaze by revealing the spectator's desire for the car to sink and the cover-up of the crime to be successful. The relief that the spectator experiences as the car sinks into the obscurity of the murky swamp signals the spectator's connection to a criminal desire.[4] We want the car to sink even though we recognize that this will leave a murderer on the loose. Such a sequence is only possible in cinema, where the editing can manipulate the narrative sequence to implicate the spectator in what she or he sees.

Recognizing that one is implicated in the visual field – recognizing that the visual field is not a neutral representation but rather given to be seen – is the basis for any politics at all. This recognition enables subjects to gain a sense of the role that their own desire plays in what they see. It is only on this basis that one conceives of oneself as a political actor with the ability to intervene in the visual field. As long as this field appears as a given, there is nothing that subjects can do. But film has the ability to make us aware of the role that our desire plays in constituting what we see.

This does not mean that film is the most radical art. On the contrary, the central role that the gaze plays in film transforms most cinema into an ideological vortex designed to protect the spectator from the threat of the gaze immanent in filmic art. Popular cinema has largely taken it upon itself to shelter spectators from the trauma of the gaze and to assure them that they can enjoy a film without encountering any manifestation of their own desire. If the essence of cinema involves the confrontation with the gaze, the betrayal of this essence constitutes the most common filmic practice.

The Impossible Look

The gaze marks the point at which filmic art draws attention to the fact the spectator's look is not neutral but replete with a desire that distorts the image. Of course, the spectator's look doesn't physically transform the film that the spectator sees. By looking at a film, the spectator is not reshooting or reediting it. The spectator's desire manifests itself through the emergence of an absence in the filmic image, an absence indicating that the film has taken the spectator's desire into account. There is no film that doesn't deploy the gaze since there is no film that doesn't appeal to the spectator's desire (even if the point is to display indifference toward that desire), but most films obscure the gaze by creating a sense of a filmic reality complete unto itself that enables the spectator to watch from a safe distance. The gaze prevents the spectator from watching the

film from a safe distance because it indicates the inclusion of the spectator in what she or he sees.

The possibility for the encounter with the gaze is the political kernel
of cinema despite the relative rarity of this encounter in popular cinema.
The gaze does not just make the spectator aware of looking in a reflexive
way – by depicting the camera in the shot, for instance – but reveals
that spectator's desire is included within the image in the form of the
image's distortion. The gaze means that there is no neutral image, no
image not deformed by how it would be seen. No subject can recognize
its unconscious desire directly, which is why film has such an important
status for the dissemination of psychoanalytic theory. The medium of the
filmic image provides a site for recognizing one's desire as a distortion in
the field of vision. Film guides the spectator along by appealing to the
unconscious rather than to consciousness. While watching a film, one
cannot look at oneself looking, but one can see the gaze.

Lacan has no commensurate words in French to distinguish between
the look and the gaze. The same term translates both English words – *le
regard*. But he does distinguish them conceptually. When Lacan develops
the concept of the gaze, he moves away from the emphasis on identification in looking that he had conceived decades earlier. Lacan formulates
the association of vision with identification in his best-known essay, "The
Mirror Stage as Formative of the *I* Function." Here, he conceives of
the subject's look in terms of a mirage that produces an imaginary ego.
In the mirror stage essay, Lacan emphasizes the illusory status of the
subject's look. It gives the image of what the subject's doesn't possess.
Lacan states, "For the total form of his body, by which the subject anticipates the maturation of his power in a mirage, is given to him only as a
gestalt."[5] The look of the subject in the mirror creates coherence out of
fragments, but this coherence exists only as an image. The subject establishes an ego through looking, but at this point in his intellectual career,
Lacan does not theorize a disruption of the look. That comes when he
conceives of the gaze as a version of the *objet a*, the object that causes the
subject's desire.

Lacan uses the term objet a in order to distinguish the object that
causes desire from the object of desire.[6] While objects of desire exist
empirically through the subject's field of experience, the objet a does not.
It is what doesn't fit within the subject's field of experience that serves to
arouse the subject to desire the empirical objects of desire. Lacan provides
his most detailed elaboration of the gaze as the version of the objet a in
the visual field in *Seminar XI*. He states,

> the gaze [is] the most characteristic term for apprehending the proper function of the *objet a*. This *a* is presented precisely, in the field of the mirage of the narcissistic function of desire, as the object that cannot be swallowed, as it were, which remains stuck in the gullet of the signifier. It is at this point of lack that the subject has to recognize himself.[7]

The gaze as objet a is an absence that indicates the subject's distortion of the visual field. As the object that causes the subject's desire, the gaze marks the effect of the subject on the terrain of the visible.

Without an objet a as an absent cause, no present object would appear desirable to the subject. The subject desires objects within its field of experience insofar as they appear to incarnate the objet a. This is why acquiring an object is always fundamentally disappointing: having the object of desire reveals that it is not the objet a but just an ordinary object. Thus, the objet a defines the subject through its intractable absence. It accompanies the subject throughout the subject's experience, but it is never present within that experience.

The objet a marks a traumatic lack in the structure of subjectivity. As a result, the subject cannot consciously decide to encounter it. But it embodies the subject's capacity for politicizing itself, for recognizing itself as a divided subject and for recognizing the Other as divided. Without this recognition, the subject remains within the demand laid out by the Other, and it gains freedom from this demand only through the encounter with the objet a. The trauma of the encounter stems from what it reveals to the subject. As Lacan notes, "the objet a is not tranquil, or rather, one must say, it could be that it doesn't leave us tranquil."[8] This lack of tranquility is traumatic, as it confirms that symbolic identity cannot fully define and contain subjectivity.

What stands out in the cinema is that spectators enjoy the possibility of the traumatic encounter with the gaze. In order for it to attract the desire of the spectator, every film must include the objet a, an object that is lacking, a gap in the form of the film. The gaze is not optional. The spectator engages the film because she or he experiences an absence in the film or a deformation in its structure. This is true of even the most ideological film, like Damien Chazelle's *La La Land* (2016). Though the film portrays an America in which there are no real barriers to realizing one's dreams, it nevertheless relies on moments of interruption when the spectator sees the failures that lurk behind the realized dreams. A film that lacks nothing would be absolutely closed in on itself and inaccessible to the spectator. The way in which a film deploys its lack is at the same time the way it shows its gaze as objet a.

One must be looking in order to see the gaze. But the gaze interrupts the look. The gaze is both a product of the subject's look and a disruption of it. When one looks, most often one sees only images, a visual field that seems coherent and self-contained. In this sense, the look is fundamentally deceptive. It is only when the gaze emerges as a disruption of the visual field that the subject becomes aware of the incoherence of this field and its reliance on the subject who sees it. Every film depicts a confrontation between the gaze and the image, though typically the image obscures the gaze to the point of unrecognizability. Typically, but not always.

A Vertiginous Necklace

Encounters with the gaze are the high points in the history of cinema, though most often Hollywood cinema obscures the gaze to the point of its unrecognizability. Cinema can't do without the gaze: it arouses the desire of spectators to watch the film. However, the gaze threatens both spectators and filmmakers with the trauma of this desire. As a result, cinema constantly walks a fine line between depicting the gaze and obscuring it within the image. It is impossible to create a film that deploys the gaze without any recourse to the image. The image is the necessary terrain through which the gaze must manifest itself.[9] It is my argument that the great films in cinematic history are the ones that reveal the gaze while still managing to create an image that engages the spectator. For this reason, the aesthetic high points of cinema are also its political high points, points at which cinema forced spectators to recognize their involvement in what they see and thereby abandon their everyday pose of neutrality relative to the visual field.

If we take, for instance, the three films named the greatest of all time in the prestigious poll conducted by *Sight and Sound* in 2012, we can see this coincidence of aesthetics and politics. For some inexplicable reason, the voters demoted *Citizen Kane* (Orson Welles, 1941) from the top spot and replaced it with Alfred Hitchcock's *Vertigo* (1958). After *Citizen Kane* in second, they selected Yasujiro Ozu's *Tokyo Story* (1953) for the third place. These three films depict fleeting encounters with the gaze throughout, but each has a key moment when the encounter becomes unavoidable for the spectator.

This moment comes in *Vertigo* when Scottie (James Stewart) discovers that the woman he has fallen in love with never existed. Scottie trails a woman he believes to be Madeleine Elster, the spouse of his old friend Gavin Elster (Tom Helmore), but who is actually Judy (Kim Novak), hired by Gavin to play Madeleine. Gavin warns Scottie that Madeleine appears possessed by the spirit of Carlotta Valdez, her great-grandmother who committed suicide, and he says he fears that Madeleine will repeat the act of self-harm. After Scottie and Madeleine fall in love in the wake of a first staged suicide attempt, she apparently kills herself by jumping from a bell tower. In fact, Gavin has thrown the real Madeleine from the tower as Judy arrived at the top. Gavin staged everything, including Scottie's desire for Madeleine, in order to do away with his wife. At this point, Scottie, not aware of the plot, feels devastated at the loss of what he considers his great love.

Later, Scottie spots Judy on the street and notices her remarkable resemblance to Madeleine. They begin seeing each other. When he has her change her appearance to more fully approximate the lost Madeleine, he finds this new version satisfying until he notices her putting on the necklace of Carlotta Valdez, the ancestor who purportedly fascinated Madeleine. The discovery of this necklace is the encounter with the gaze for the spectator, even though the fact that Madeleine was Judy does not catch the spectator by surprise. This seems like an encounter with the gaze for Scottie rather than for the spectator. Scottie learns that his lost object never existed – the Madeleine he loved was just Judy dressing up as Madeleine – and this reveals the definitive separation of the objet a from his object of desire. But he is just a character in the film. We, the spectators, watch his encounter with the gaze but do not encounter it the way that he does.

The difference between Scottie and the spectator at the moment when he sees the necklace is that the spectator has already seen a flashback, which reveals just how Judy has acted the part of Madeleine. Thus, for the spectator, the revelation is no revelation at all. Some critics view the flashback as an error on Hitchcock's part, as a diminution of the power of Scottie's discovery of the necklace for the spectator. But the flashback has the effect of aligning the spectator with Judy at this pivotal point in the film. Our knowledge as spectators is on a par with Judy's knowledge in the film, not with Scottie's, unlike earlier in the film, when our ignorance about the identity of Madeleine paralleled Scottie's.

Hitchcock structures the spectator's knowledge in the way that he does in order to facilitate the spectator's encounter with the gaze as the stripping away of the fantasmatic possibility of a complete enjoyment. As a result of the flashback, the spectator experiences the discovery of Carlotta's necklace not as the recognition that the objet a never actually existed – what happens to Scottie – but as the destruction of Scottie's apparently complete enjoyment in having the object. In this key scene, it is Scottie, not Judy, who is shrouded in the fantasy of complete enjoyment. Just before Judy comes out of the bathroom and puts on the necklace, Hitchcock includes a shot of Scottie sitting in a chair in Judy's apartment, surrounded by a halo of luminous green light from the neon signs outside the window behind him. Hitchcock includes this shot to indicate that at this moment in the film Scottie is immersed in a fantasy space that the subsequent realization that Judy was Madeleine destroys, as it deprives him of his lost object.

The revelation occurs in a shot of Scottie hooking the clasp of the necklace for Judy. Hitchcock shows Scottie seeing the necklace in the mirror and immediately thinking back to the portrait of Carlotta in the museum that Madeleine used to spend hours staring at. Before the film reveals the identity of the necklace, it shows Scottie's shocked reaction. He leans back away from Judy as the camera tracks toward him. The look on his face registers that the enjoyment of a few moments earlier has disintegrated as the illusory status of Madeleine becomes evident to him. It is Scottie's face in this scene that incarnates the gaze.

Hitchcock focuses on Scottie at the moment of the revelation because he has become the fantasmatic object for the spectator. When his enjoyment collapses, his status in the film undergoes a dramatic transformation. The encounter with the gaze exposes not only how the subject's desire shapes the nature of all reality – and that Gavin and Judy created Madeleine to trap Scottie's desire – but also the dependence of this reality on our belief in a naïve Other who has complete faith in the reality he inhabits (and the accessibility of the objet a). By giving the spectator knowledge that Scottie doesn't have through the flashback, Hitchcock establishes Scottie as this naïve Other, whom the spectator imagines can be protected from the devastating knowledge about Madeleine's non-existence. This protection fails when Scottie recognizes the necklace. At this moment, the gaze strips away the naïve Other from the spectator, thereby cutting off the spectator's ability to believe in the possibility of a complete enjoyment through this (naïve) Other.

This scene in which Scottie recognizes the necklace and the spectator encounters the gaze is the highlight of *Vertigo*. It comes quickly on the heels of a scene in the apartment when Judy fully remakes herself again as Madeleine for Scottie. We see them kissing bathed in the neon green light through a 360-degree tracking shot that evinces Scottie's unlimited enjoyment that the film invites the spectator to partake in. Hitchcock gives the spectator the image of complete enjoyment only to subsequently take it away and expose its illusoriness. That is to say, enjoyment depends on a naïve Other that the encounter with the gaze strips away.

Appointment with Nothingness

The gaze proliferates in *Citizen Kane*, but just as in *Vertigo*, the encounter with it becomes unavoidable at the moment of the film's most important revelation. The film begins with the final word of Charles Foster Kane (Orson Welles). This word, "Rosebud," engenders a search by the reporter Jerry Thompson (William Alland) for its significance and thus for the secret of Kane's desire. Thompson interviews several of Kane's closest friends and associates, and the film shows their recollections as flashbacks that depict Kane's life in a fragmentary form. Despite the abundance of information that Thompson discovers about Kane, he doesn't find the significance of "Rosebud." He ends up telling himself that we can never know someone's secret, that no one is reducible to a single word. Many viewers of the film accept Thompson's skepticism about the other's desire, but doing so requires walking out of the theater prior to the scene that follows this statement.

Just after Thompson proclaims the unknowability of anyone's desire, the film concludes with a worker at the Kane mansion throwing Kane's childhood sled into a fire. In a shot of fire consuming the sled, the name "Rosebud" comes clearly into view. The film presents the sled as the solution to Kane's desire, the object that corresponds to the signifier that begins the film. But the sled is also just an ordinary object, indicating a desire for a childhood that is valuable only insofar as it is lost. The point is definitely not that if Kane had simply remained with his parents in Colorado instead of moving to New York to become important, he would have led a genuinely satisfying existence. Instead the sled indicates Kane's desire for what can never be re-found.

By structuring the film around the search for an object to attach to the signifier "Rosebud," Welles associates the object with the promise of realizing the spectator's desire. The object remains absent within the film's visual field throughout the running time and only appears when the film ends. But even when it appears, the way that Welles shoots it makes clear that the sled cannot realize our desire as spectators or Kane's desire as a subject. Welles shows the insignificance of the sled by juxtaposing it with thousands of other objects that Kane accumulated. While watching it burn, the spectator experiences the object's failure to do what the signifier promises.

In this sense, the sled incarnates the gaze for the spectator, and the disappointed exclamation, "it's just a sled," would be entirely appropriate at this point. Though "Rosebud" initially suggests a great past love or some other sublimity to the spectator and to the investigator Thompson, it turns out to be nothing but a sled, which is why it functions as the gaze. The gaze is the point of an excessive nothing within the plenitude of the image. When the spectator sees it and recognizes it as the solution to Kane's desire, the emptiness of this desire becomes readily apparent.

No one within the diegesis of the film recognizes the sled as Rosebud. As it burns, the spectator loses the hope that someone might genuinely recognize Kane, that Thompson might figure out the reference of his dying word. Like Hitchcock, Welles creates a divide between the spectator's knowledge and that of the characters within the diegetic reality of the film, and he does so in order to facilitate an encounter with the gaze. When no one recognizes the sled, the spectator must confront the absence of any ultimate record of subjectivity within the symbolic order. Even in the case of a subject as important as Kane, his desire simply disappears without anyone noticing.

Through this depiction, *Citizen Kane* extends the political significance of the encounter with the gaze. If the spectator grasps what's at stake in this display of the gaze, it opens up a radical freedom for the subject because it reveals that the Other cannot see the subject and ultimately doesn't care about it. Welles focuses on a rich and powerful man to show that even in this case, the Other treats the subject with disregard. The Other's demand for the proper orientation of the subject's desire, as manifested in *Citizen Kane*, conceals a profound indifference to this desire. The gaze is the point of this disregard, the point at which the subject shatters the illusion of the Other's omniscience.

Unconscious Desire vs Conscious Wish

In *Tokyo Story*, the gaze is much more a constant force throughout the film than in *Vertigo* or *Citizen Kane*. The film shows an elderly couple, Shūkichi Hirayama (Chishū Ryū) and Tomi Hirayama (Chieko Higashiyama), visiting their son, daughter, and daughter-in-law in Tokyo. Ozu sustains the gaze by establishing the couple as an intrusion not just on their children's lives but also on the spectator's experience. Because the couple evinces no desire of their own, they occupy the field of the visible in the film without contributing to it.

As we watch Shūkichi and Tomi interact with their children, we see the way that the son Kōichi (Yo Yamamura) and the daughter Shige (Haruko Sugimura) desperately want to get rid of them and safely ignore them. The film forces us to experience the couple in exactly the same way. We view the couple not as subjects worthy of compassion, but from the perspective of the children who no longer want anything to do with them. Herein lies the film's exceptionality. Through Ozu's depiction of the elderly couple as a constant presence disturbing the visual field occupied by the children, he doesn't permit the spectator simply to feel sorry for the elderly couple. The desire of the spectator makes itself known in what the spectator knows that she or he shouldn't want.

Ozu does not leave the spectator in this situation but provides a final twist in the decisive scene in which the impact of the gaze becomes even more prominent. The daughter-in-law of the couple, Noriko (Setsuko Hara), displays much more kindness to them than do their own children, even though her husband, another son of the couple, is dead. At the end of the film, Noriko comes to visit Shūkichi – his wife Tomi has died – at his home to tell him that she must return to Tokyo. Shūkichi quickly launches into apparently heartfelt praise of Noriko's care for them, which he contrasts with that of his children. When Noriko protests that she is no better than the children, Shūkichi insists even more, interpreting her protestations as a sign of her humility.

But the spectator cannot interpret the protestations in the same positive light. As in both *Vertigo* and *Citizen Kane*, it is a question of knowledge distributed to the spectator that the character lacks, and again, the film uses this uneven distribution of knowledge to produce an effect of the gaze. In the scene just prior to the conversation between Shūkichi and Noriko, we have seen Noriko confess to Shūkichi's youngest daughter, Kyōko (Kyōko Kagawa), that she too experiences the elderly couple as a burden and sympathizes with the children who ignored them. By including this scene, Ozu prepares the spectator to encounter the gaze during the subsequent conversation with Noriko. Though Kyōko vows never to become like her siblings, she acknowledges that life is disappointing and disillusioning, as she sees even the most dedicated relative finally express an absence of connection with the couple.

In the next scene, Ozu focuses on Shūkichi's repeated praise of Noriko, praise that he amplifies after each denial by Noriko. The shots of Shūkichi juxtaposed with shots of Noriko's embarrassment facilitate the spectator's embarrassment as well. The spectator experiences the image of Shūkichi praising Noriko as a disruption within the film's visual field. This praise confronts the spectator with the consequences of her or his desire, which is the gaze.

The result of the encounter with the gaze in *Tokyo Story* varies from the encounter in *Citizen Kane*. Whereas the gaze in Welles's film highlights the absence of recognition from the Other, Ozu employs the gaze to indicate the spectator's responsibility for the structuring of the visual field. In this way, he challenges the basic form of cinematic spectatorship. What we see in the cinema seems completely removed from us. Unless we work for a production company or movie studio, we have no hands-on involvement in the filmmaking process. But as spectators, we are responsible for what we see. Our spectatorship is not only what enables films to be made but also the driving force in their production. But this is not just an insight confined to the act of watching a film.

In everyday life, we experience the external world as external to our desire. Perhaps it presents a terrain on which we can realize our desire, but it is not organized around this desire. As a result, we are not responsible for it (unless of course we dump toxic waste in a reservoir or something equally drastic). The gaze in Ozu's film gives the lie to this pseudo-distance from the external world. Though we haven't created the external world, it nonetheless bears the structural imprint of our desire: we miss such an encounter in our everyday experience only to find it in the cinematic one.

Ozu's film seems to suggest that our desire plays a key role in how others act toward us. No one acts the same way toward all others but rather acts in response to the desire she or he expects. In this way, we encounter a world organized around our desire, even though this organization remains invisible to us outside of the cinema. The gaze in *Tokyo Story* shows that while the world resists our conscious wishes – putting up barriers to our dreams of making millions or finding an extremely attractive lover – it bears throughout the impact of our unconscious desire. The encounter with this gaze reveals our involvement in the external world and cuts off any illusion we may have maintained of a critical distance from it.

Aesthetics and Politics

The problem with film as an art form is that *Vertigo*, *Citizen Kane*, and *Tokyo Story* are exceptions.[10] Even with these films, though critics universally acknowledge their aesthetic greatness, few see the link between their aesthetic breakthrough and their political one, a link that is necessary for understanding what constitutes a political film, a film that would

encourage spectators to become politically engaged subjects. Leftist critics have historically struggled with the question of the relation between
aesthetics and politics. This was the source of vigorous disputes between
Theodor Adorno and Jean-Paul Sartre as well as those between Bertolt
Brecht and Georg Lukács. Adorno mocked Sartre's call for a politically
engaged art, while Brecht ridiculed Lukács's rejection of modern literature for its lack of historical situatedness. Theorists have been unable to
reconcile the call for a politicized art with the aesthetic demands of artistic form without lapsing into dogmatism or aestheticism. Lukács would
be an instance of the former, while Adorno represents the latter.

Lacan's theory of the gaze has the great virtue of answering the question
of the relation between aesthetics and politics in the cinema. Through the
manner in which a film deploys or obscures the gaze, its aesthetic significance and its political engagement come together. The power of cinema to
precipitate a politicized subjectivity does not reside in its content, in the
ability to depict the horrors of capitalist production or the formation of
a proletarian class consciousness. It lies rather in the formal capacity that
cinema acquires through the role that the gaze has in cinematic art. The
spectator's encounter with the gaze is a formal encounter, but its importance outstrips whatever revelation cinema can make in its content.

In 1968, Jean-Luc Godard proclaimed an end to narrative cinema. It
was, for him, nothing but an ideological trap for spectators, and his subsequent career has been a chronicle of its abandonment in favor of a radical
juxtaposition of images. But the fantasmatic narrative that Hollywood
employs to lure eager spectators into its ideological betrayal of the gaze
is not necessarily ideological. Fantasmatic narrative is the political battle-
ground of cinema. Alfred Hitchcock, Orson Welles, and Yasujiro Ozu show
that a politically engaged subjectivity can emerge from this narrative form.

It is always the site of the greatest political potential that gives birth to
the most extreme ideological manipulation. This is how we must consider
the cinema. The unique relationship that cinema has to the gaze creates
a political opening that ideological forces work tirelessly to obscure. But
ultimately, this opening remains visible. The task for the psychoanalytic
film theorist is one of seeing the gaze even amid the most sustained
efforts to hide it.

Notes

1 Psychoanalytic film theory begins with a misinterpretation of Lacan's concept of the gaze, taking it as the subject's look rather than an object encountered. Joan Copjec provides the first Lacanian corrective to this film theory
in *Read My Desire*, where she points out that "film theory operated a kind of

'Foucauldinization' of Lacanian theory." Joan Copjec, *Read My Desire: Lacan against the Historicists* (Cambridge, MA: MIT Press, 1994), 19. Copjec argues that the temptation of interpreting the gaze as the manifestation of the all-seeing subject leads theorists to miss its status as what obstructs vision and stains the visual field. By transforming the Lacanian gaze into the panoptic look, psychoanalytic film theory deprived cinema of any potential radicality and reduced it to an ideological apparatus.

2 Jacques Lacan, *The Seminar of Jacques Lacan, Book XI: The Four Fundamental Concepts of Psychoanalysis*, ed. Jacques-Alain Miller, tr. Alan Sheridan (New York: W. W. Norton, 1978), 96 (translation corrected). Sheridan's translation of *Seminar XI* indicates the exact opposite of what Lacan says in French. The last line of the paragraph in French reads, "Mais moi je suis dans le tableau." Sheridan translates this as: "But I am not in the picture."

3 The inherently fantasmatic dimension of the cinematic experience leads Christian Metz to locate this experience in a nether region between wakefulness and sleep (which often leads to sleep). In *The Imaginary Signifier*, he writes, "the filmic state as induced by traditional fiction films ... is marked by a general tendency to lower wakefulness, to take a step in the direction of sleep and dreaming. When one has not had enough sleep, dozing off is usually more a danger during the projection of a film than before or even afterwards." Christian Metz, *The Imaginary Signifier: Psychoanalysis and Cinema*, tr. Celia Britton, Annwyl Williams, Ben Brewster, and Alfred Guzzetti (Bloomington: Indiana University Press, 1982), 106–107.

4 Žižek analyzes this scene multiple times in his work. For one instance of this analysis, see Slavoj Žižek, "'In His Bold Gaze My Ruin Is Writ Large,'" in *Everything You Always Wanted to Know about Lacan (But Were Afraid to Ask Hitchcock)*, ed. Slavoj Žižek (New York: Verso, 1992), 210–272.

5 Jacques Lacan, "The Mirror Stage as Formative of the *I* Function," in *Écrits: The First Complete Edition in English*, tr. Bruce Fink (New York: W. W. Norton, 2006), 76.

6 Lacan first conceives of the objet a in *Seminar X* on anxiety, but then develops it further in his subsequent seminars. See Jacques Lacan, *The Seminar of Jacques Lacan, Book X: Anxiety*, ed. Jacques-Alain Miller, tr. A. R. Price (Malden, MA: Polity Press, 2014) and Lacan, *Four Fundamental Concepts*.

7 Lacan, *Four Fundamental Concepts*, 270.

8 Jacques Lacan, "Le Séminaire XIII: L'objet de la psychanalyse, 1965–1966, " unpublished seminar session of December 1, 1965.

9 Richard Boothby captures perfectly this paradox of fantasy. Though it occurs through images, it points to what exceeds the image altogether. He states, "phantasy is always a picturing, an imaginal figuration, yet also aims toward something unimagable. What is most deeply sought by desire in the phantasy cannot be given in the register of the image." Richard Boothby, *Freud as Philosopher: Metapsychology after Lacan* (New York: Routledge, 2001), 275.

10 It is tempting to mock polls like the one commissioned by *Sight and Sound* to establish the greatest films of all time, but looking at just the top three (and disregarding the order), it seems as if they got something right.

CHAPTER 7

Lacan and Politics

Jodi Dean

Many on the Left think that the party is an outmoded political form. For them, what 1968 inspired and 1989 ostensibly confirmed is the conviction that radical left politics necessarily exceeds the constraints of the political party. Often voiced as a criticism of specific parties, the conviction that the party is useless for the Left overlooks a host of historical particulars. The rejected communist party is not simply the ossified bureaucracy of the Communist Party of the Soviet Union and the other ruling party-states of the former East. It is neither China's Communist Party, unable to free itself from its inner bourgeoisie, nor France's and Italy's compromised and complicit parties. It's the party form as such. Specific parties are rejected for errors singular or aggregate. They pushed for revolution at the cost of unnecessary violence and loss of life. They pulled back from revolution, selling out the working class and setting back the communist cause. These specific errors are offered as evidence of the hierarchy, exclusion, and discipline irrevocably staining the party form as such, preventing it from being responsive to our changing times. Criticism of specific parties for the betrayals accompanying their acquiring of or participation in state power merges with a more general critique of the party as an ultimately authoritarian political association. The party is reduced to the actuality of its mistakes, its role as concentrator of collective aspirations and affects diminished, if not forgotten.[1]

This chapter turns to Lacan for help in confronting these rejections of the party form. It enlists Lacan in the service of a theory of the party that emphasizes the psycho-dynamics of collectivity, the ways that collectivity works back on us to make us more than many. In contemporary left discussions, criticisms of the party for its centralism and authoritarianism are voiced as if they were new insights born of recent experience. They aren't. They were present already in the early years of working-class political movement. I focus on the most thorough version of the critique of the party as it appears in the work of Robert Michels. Michels's famous "iron law of oligarchy" applies not just to socialist parties. He extends it to democratic and anarchistic political formations as well. Political organization of *any* sort entails a gap between the few and the many, a point contemporary left critics of the party form omit. Rather than attending to the weakness of socialism or the party form, then, Michels's analysis highlights the enabling conditions of political collectivity. It thereby opens up a way to understand the effects of collectivity on the collective. No party, class, or collectivity is identical with itself. Each is ruptured by an irreducible gap. Lacan lets us theorize this gap as a social link or space. By attending to the relation of transference, we can see the dynamic features concentrated in the space of the Other. I close by illustrating my Lacanian account of the party with examples from the Communist Party of the United States in the 1930s. My goal in using Lacan to theorize the party is to dissolve the hold that criticism of the party form still has on the Left so that we can accept again the responsibility of political organization.

The Iron Law of Oligarchy

Some current rejections of the party say its time has passed.[2] Maybe at one time such a political form made sense for radical politics, some concede, but now is not that time. This rejection errs when it proceeds as if the critique of the party were something new, a response to objective changes in the mode and relations of production. The mistake is one of omission: left criticism of the party form is in fact coextensive with the emergence of working-class political movement in the nineteenth century. As debates between Marx and Bakunin, Bolsheviks and Mensheviks, and Lenin and Luxemburg repeatedly demonstrated, socialists worried about their organizations becoming centralized and authoritarian, and hence alienated from actual proletarian struggle. Repeated today, the charges of centralism and authoritarianism, the domination of the many by the few, are damning, striking at the very heart of people's struggle. If the few dominate the many, then working-class struggle merely replaces one set of oppressors with another. The very organization indispensable to people's political struggle stifles and deforms it.

Charges of centralism and authoritarianism, however, have not been confined to socialist and communist parties or even to the party form as such. Already at the beginning of the twentieth century, Michels leveled these charges against democratic political participation most broadly: democracy itself leads to oligarchy. The conditions that make democracy possible also make it impossible, whether one is talking about a polity, a party, a union, or a council (syndicate or soviet). Michels's analysis reminds us that critiques of centralism and authoritarianism have been attacks on mass, democratic, and people's politics more generally.

Michels's *Political Parties* was originally published in 1911.[3] A student of Max Weber's, Michels taught in Germany, Italy, and Switzerland; he was a member of the German Social Democratic Party, the Italian Socialist Party, and, later, Mussolini's Fascist Party.[4] Social science treats *Political Parties* as a classic, even "one of the twentieth century's most influential books."[5] The book set out an "iron law of oligarchy" or rule of the few. Unlike ancient Greek visions of democracy as the *response* of the people against oligarchy's owners of property, Michels construes oligarchy as *intrinsic* to democracy. Democracy, *of any kind*, tends to oligarchy.[6] So while *Political Parties* concentrates primarily on socialist parties, Michels's argument is broader, a political version of the Pareto principle or 80/20 rule: in any human association, the few will have more – whether this "more" is of goods, influence, or power – than the many.[7] Parties one might most expect to incorporate rule by the workers in their basic structure, organizations animated by ideals of democratic participation, even groups with aspirations to anarchism, all ultimately take on a whole slew of oligarchical characteristics. Rule by the few is unavoidable. Michels surmises: "the appearance of oligarchical phenomena in the very bosom of the revolutionary parties is a conclusive proof of the existence of immanent oligarchical tendencies in every kind of human organization which strives for the attainment of definite ends."[8] Socialist parties and working-class organizations are not unique. They are representative, clear instances where oligarchical tendencies can be isolated and observed precisely because they conflict with party ideology. If democracy means rule by the many, democracy is impossible.

Michels presents tendencies to oligarchy as technical and psychological. Technical tendencies concern the indispensability of leadership in groups. Psychological tendencies involve people's responses to leadership. They are effects of the fact of leaders back on the people. Both tendencies are matters of number: the problem and force of many, the complexity of mass organization and the prestige accompanying that to which many adhere.[9]

Michels orients his account of the inevitability of oligarchy in a theory of the crowd reminiscent of Gustav Le Bon's. The crowd is suggestible, incapable of serious discussion or thoughtful deliberation, and susceptible to the influence of orators. Michels finds evidence of the crowd's incapacity in the fact that most people avoid going to meetings unless the event promises some kind of spectacle or someone famous is speaking. Conversely, the crowd may be politically indifferent, hard to arouse, and a barrier to action. Number itself undermines direct democracy: thirty-four million people cannot "carry on their affairs without accepting what the pettiest man of business finds necessary, the intermediation of representatives."[10] Considerations of space, amplification, and the time, duration, and frequency of meetings, not to mention preparing the agenda and carrying out decisions, point to the unavoidability of delegation.[11] The crowd's very nature makes it vulnerable to oligarchy. Not only can it not protect itself from bold power-seekers, but it relies on them. It needs leaders to get things done. It even enjoys them.

Michels narrates the slide into oligarchy as an ersatz "story of the Fall" as technical tendencies to oligarchy come to dominance in a group. This story applies to "every organization," whether party, union, or other kind of association. From an initial equality, wherein delegates are chosen by lot or rotation, gradual change sets in as delegates' responsibilities become more complicated. Demands arise for "a sort of official consecration for the leaders." Leaders need to be vetted and trained, their expertise established. A system of examinations, courses, and schools emerges. Michels concludes, "Without wishing it, there is thus effected a continuous enlargement of the gulf which divides the leaders from the masses."[12] Even leaders originating from the masses become separated from them in the course of their acquisition of expertise, validation, responsibility, and experience.

The larger the organization, the more powerful the leaders. For Michels, this is in part a technical tendency toward oligarchy, the challenge of organizing many. But it includes a corresponding psychological tendency as well, the psychic effects on collectivities of the fact of leadership. In larger organizations, tasks become increasingly differentiated. Seeing the "big picture" becomes harder and harder. At the same time, voluntary organizations like unions and parties encounter constant turnover among their members. Most people have what feel to them better things to do than spend their free time in political struggle. But not all: some, for varying reasons, attach themselves to organizational work. These who are more constant and attached start to function as leaders. Unlike those only sporadically engaged, these more permanent members know what the organization has done and is doing. They are the repository of organizational history, practice, and knowledge. Leadership can be a matter less of office than of the influence exercised by the regulars.

As leaders emerge, the rank and file become less able to conduct or supervise the organization's affairs. They have to trust those to whom they've delegated the various tasks, perhaps instructing them to provide reports on the work of the group. Generally speaking, most people like it that way. "Though it grumbles occasionally," Michels writes, "the majority is really delighted to find persons who will take the trouble to look after its affairs."[13] This delight is an affective response, the pleasure that arises from pawning tasks on to others. What matters for my argument here is the flow from the technical to the psychological tendency to oligarchy. Michels argues that the majority revere or even adore their leaders. Accompanying the crowd's need for direction and guidance is "a genuine cult for the leaders, who are regarded as heroes." So not only does the crowd need leaders for technical reasons, it is also affectively attached to them.

A decade before Freud, Michels anticipates key elements of Freud's crowd psychology: primitive love, gratitude to and reverence for leaders, dynamics associated with prestige, identification, and imitation or "imitative mania." Michels invokes Tarde, noting the way fame impresses with the number of admirers. Prestige is like fame insofar as it incorporates the views of many. It's a matter less of talent than of the esteem held by the crowd. Even as the crowd responds enthusiastically to great orators, it responds even more to the enthusiasm of others, to others' feelings and responses. People adhere with and to others in common admiration. One admires the leader because others do. When celebrity influences us, Michels explains with a quote from Tarde, "it is with the collaboration of many other minds through whom we see it, and whose opinion, without our knowledge, is reflected in our own."[14] Unconsciously, we see through others. We take the perspective of the many. Our seeing is collective.

This seeing through others manifests in "imitative mania." The object being imitated is not a specific person but prestige itself, the press and presence of the many, crowd, or mass. Lacan reminds us, "Whenever we are dealing with imitation, we should be careful not to think too quickly of the other who is being imitated."[15] Imitating a leader or celebrity, the many act for each other, showing themselves in their admiring enthusiasm to themselves, making themselves the objects of their own collective gaze. When fans dress up as characters in a movie to attend a movie's opening (as with the *Harry Potter* or *Star Wars* movies) or when they go in costume to fan conventions, they are doing it for each other. As they see themselves seeing themselves, they demonstrate the contingency and replaceability of the revered leader: any one of those imitatively adopting the leader's characteristics is in the leader's place.

The point of imitation is not the adoration of one, of a leader or celebrity. It is that the one is a placeholder, a function enabling the many to experience its collective force. Enthusiasm arises out of this experience of collective imitation because the collective feels itself amplified, strengthened. Enthusiasm is *nothing but* this collective sense of collective power. In imitative mania, what is being imitated is not a person; it is prestige, which in itself is a reflection of the regard of the collective.

Just as the distinctions between technical and psychological tendencies to oligarchy blur into and reinforce one another, so do the distinctions between crowd and leader, mass and party. Each twists into the other. Each ruptures the other from within, preventing it from achieving self-identity. For example, Michels emphasizes the importance of detachments from the bourgeoisie aligning themselves with the proletariat and animating their class consciousness. These members of the bourgeoisie – "philosophers, economists, sociologists, and historians" – help transform instinctive, unconscious rebellion into clear, conscious aspiration. Michels writes,

> Great class movements have hitherto been initiated in history solely by the simple reflection: it is not we alone, belonging to the masses without education and without legal rights, who believe ourselves to be oppressed, but that belief as to our condition is shared by those who have a better knowledge of the social mechanism and who are therefore better able to judge; since the cultured people of the upper classes have also conceived the ideal of our emancipation, that ideal is not mere chimera.[16]

Bourgeois detachments, as a matter of fact comprising the majority of European socialist leaders, serve psychological as much as technical purposes: they enable workers to reflect on themselves; they provide a standpoint from outside the workers that workers can take toward their own condition. Michels concludes, "who says organization, says oligarchy." Political enthusiasm – the joy of self-sacrifice, the thrill of struggle – inspires the crowd, but it can't endure. The crowd disperses and people go home. Keeping the fight alive requires dedicated, professional cadre, a few who devote themselves to the cause. This very requirement separates the few from the many.

The socialist party is not identical with the working class. Workers are not automatically socialists and socialists are not necessarily workers. The party can have bourgeois and working-class members (not to mention other classes). These members may be active or not, leaders or led. The class fragments into various interests, personal as well as political. Michels writes, "The party, regarded as an entity, as a piece of mechanism, is not necessarily identifiable with the totality of its members, and still less so with the class to which these belong."[17] The party is more than the sum of the particular interests of its members. The very non-identity of class and party, the gap between few and many, produces something new.

We have hints about this "something new" in the ideas of prestige, identification, and that exterior point from which the working class can reflect back on itself. These ideas suggest that the party is a psychic space irreducible to its members and excreted out of the technical needs it fulfills. Michels recognizes this space, marking it with the party program. He writes, "A party is neither a social unity nor an economic unity. It is based upon its political program."[18] The program sets out the party's principles, ostensibly providing the missing point of unity in the "idea" of the working class. To be sure, this theoretical unity cannot eliminate the more fundamental class conflicts that express themselves in the party. The collectivity incorporated in the party will always be in excess of, never fully reconcilable with, a particular interest. A degree of alienation, of non-identity, is ineliminable. The very fact of a party – or any few carrying out some kind of organizational work – exerts a force counter to personal desire. If personal desire were enough, if it could simply be aggregated into happy outcomes, if the crowd had the capacity to know and get what it wanted, leaders wouldn't emerge. But the gap is irreducible, a repetition in the party of the antagonism rupturing society.

Mind the Gap

Psychoanalysis helps us understand this gap. It lets us see why the division between few and many should not be solidified as a division between real and ideal, pragmatic and utopian, but acknowledged instead as a constitutive, enabling split: impossibility is the condition of possibility for communist politics. The non-identity between people and party is what enables each to be more and less than what they are, for each to enable, rupture, and exceed the other. Michels specifies this gap as the crowd's missing capacity supplied by the leader and the working class's missing consciousness supplied by the bourgeois deserters. Acknowledging that these technical provisions remain incomplete, that organization is more than an instrument, he supplements them by attending to the psychological tendencies of crowds. As gratitude, prestige, imitation, and identification demonstrate, leaders are means through which the crowd can feel and enjoy itself. Michels's gestures to the unconscious provide the entry point for psychoanalysis.

Lacan associates the Freudian unconscious with a gap, a gap where something happens but remains unrealized.[19] It's not that this something is or is not there, that it exists or doesn't exist. Rather, the unrealized makes itself felt; it exerts a pressure. The communist party is a political form for the press of the unrealized struggles of the people, enabling the concentrating and directing of this press in one way rather than another.

That the subject of politics is collective means that its actions cannot be reduced to those associated with individual agency, actions like choice or decision. The collective subject impresses itself through ruptures and breaks and the retroactive attribution of these breaks to the subject they expressed. The punctuality of the subject could suggest that it is only evental, only disruptive, utterly disconnected from any given body, entity, institution, or advance and thus without substance or content. But this would ignore the persistence of the subject in the press of the unrealized. This persistence needs a body, a carrier. Without a carrier, it dissipates into the manifold of potentiality. Nevertheless, with a carrier some potentiality is diminished. Some possibility is eliminated. Some closure is effected. This loss is the subject's condition of possibility, the division constitutive of subjectivity. Political forms – parties, states, guerilla armies, even leaders – situate themselves within this division. Although they can be and often are fetishized (positioned so as to obscure the loss or perfectly remedy it), the fact of fetishization should not deflect from the prior condition of the gap or lack and its provisional occupation.

The psychoanalytic concept of "transference" depends on and expresses this gap. In clinical practice, the transference involves the relation between the analyst and the analysand. What sort of feelings and affects are mobilized in analysis and to what kind of structure do they attest? For example, does the analysand want the analyst's approval? Does she want to seduce him, fight with him, obliterate him? In *Four Fundamental Concepts of Psychoanalysis*, Lacan acknowledges multiple ways of conceiving the transference, but rejects the idea that analysis proceeds via an alliance between the analyst and the healthy part of the subject's ego (an idea found in some American versions of psychoanalysis). "This is a thesis," Lacan writes, "that subverts what it is all about, namely the bringing to awareness of this split in the subject, realized here, in fact, in presence."[20] The function of the transference in analysis is forcing the gap. Through transference, different unconscious agencies in the subject become manifest. As the analysand learns to attend to the transference, she can come to recognize and address the Other within, the way, for example, a parental or social other has configured her desire.

Transference is important for a psychoanalytic theory of the party because of its function "as a mode of access to what is hidden in the unconscious."[21] Transference registers the effects of an Other beyond the dyad of analyst and analysand: the analytic relation is not reducible to the interaction between them; it is the site of the appearance of an Other. Transference contributes to a theory of the party in this precise sense of a "mode of access to what is hidden in the unconscious." The party is a form that accesses the discharge that has ended, the crowd that has gone home, the people who are not there but exert a force nonetheless. It is a site of transferential relations.

The party is not an analytical session. Leaders and cadre are not psychoanalysts. This does not mean, however, that something like transference is not at work in the relation between crowd and party. Michels's emphasis on gratitude points to a transference effect, a love that, counterintuitively, underpins people's adherence to the leaders of an organization. Michels argues that those who have felt like no one was fighting on their behalf generally feel gratitude toward their champions. We could add here the way that people in a group are often grateful to those who step up, do the work, and take responsibility on to themselves. The feeling of gratitude makes leadership appear like a kind of gift, but one different from that which the king bestows on the people. Rather, insofar as he is focused on leadership in democracies, Michels suggests a leadership that the crowd produces contingently out of itself as a gift to itself. These are the leaders toward whom people feel gratitude. However, even a gift the crowd gives itself is not without cost. Žižek notes that for Lacan language is a dangerous gift: "it offers itself to our use free of charge, but once we accept it, it colonizes us."[22] The gift establishes a link between giver and receiver. Acceptance creates a bond. It binds the receiver to the giver. "Gratitude" signals the binding power of the link, the felt force of the relation between giver and receiver, the pressure that renders a gift more than an exchange. What matters, then, is this link that is an effect of the gift and the force that it exerts. The gift constitutes a sociality that itself makes demands on us over and above those associated with the giver.

Lacan's term for this sociality would be the Other or the symbolic. The transference reveals various components of it, unconscious processes and perspectives contained within the Other. The space of the Other is a crowded, heterogeneous space, a mix of shifting feelings, pressures, and attachments. It has structural features, dynamic features, processes that advance and recede, flow into one another and shift in importance. Multiple, different figures inhabit and en-form these structures and processes.

Constitutive features of this Other space that Lacan highlights include the ideal ego, the ego ideal, and the superego. As Žižek explains, Lacan gives a very precise inflection to these Freudian terms:

> "ideal" ego stands for the idealized self-image of the subject (the way I would like to be, the way I would like others to see me); Ego-Ideal is the agency whose gaze I try to impress with my ego image, the big Other who watches over me and impels me to give my best, the ideal I try to follow and actualize; and superego is this same agency in its vengeful, sadistic, punishing aspect.[23]

The ideal ego is how the subject imagines itself. The ego ideal is the point from which the subject looks at itself. And the superego is the judge that torments the subject as it points out its inevitable, unavoidable failure to achieve either of these ideals. These three points are tied together: the ego ideal verifies the image of the subject. Since the ego ideal is supposed to provide this verification, the subject has certain investments in it. The subject needs the ego ideal for its stability or sense of autonomy. Because of this need, it is resistant to recognizing that the ego ideal is nothing but a structural effect and resentful of the ego ideal's simultaneous power and inadequacy. Moreover, in trying to live up to the expectations of the ego ideal, the subject may compromise its own desire. It may give up too much, which explains why the superego can exert such an extreme, unrelenting force: it is punishing the subject for this betrayal.[24]

While these features of the space of the Other may appear individual, this appearing is nothing but a Freudian residuum. Not only are the features common, but they attest to the workings of collectivity that Freud encloses in the individual psyche. Such features operate in all collectives. Groups compete with other groups as well as look at themselves from the perspective of other groups. Cities and nations, schools and parties all have self-conceptions formed via the processes and perspectives of the Other.

The transference that takes place in psychoanalysis reveals two additional features of the Other space: the subject supposed to know and the subject supposed to believe.[25] These elements are configuring suppositions within the subject, structural features that the subject posits as supports for its desire. The subject supposed to know is the figure that holds the secret to desire: it knows the truth. God, Socrates, and Freud as well as institutional roles such as parent, teacher, expert, and priest can function as such a locus of knowledge for and of a subject. Lacan writes, "As soon as the subject who is supposed to know exists somewhere ... there is transference."[26] Analysis depends on transference: the analyst has to function for the analysand as the subject supposed to know. The analysand starts talking about her symptoms, doing the work of analysis, because she thinks that the analyst knows the truth, when in actuality it's her work that produces the truth. Analysis can end when the subject recognizes that the analyst doesn't know after all.

Žižek introduces the subject supposed to believe as a more fundamental version of the subject supposed to know.[27] He explains:

> there is no immediate, self-present living subjectivity to whom the belief embodied in "social things" can be attributed, and who is then dispossessed of it. There are some beliefs, the most fundamental ones, which are from the very outset "decentered" beliefs of the Other; the phenomenon of the "subject supposed to believe" is thus universal and structurally necessary.[28]

The subject supposed to believe refers to this unavoidable displacement of belief on to some other. Popular examples include the maintenance of the fiction of Santa Claus for the sake of children or the positing of some ordinary person who believes in community values. Michels's description of those detachments of the bourgeoisie who join the proletariat provides another example. Through them, the proletariat believes that their situation is not just unfortunate. It is profoundly unjust.

Žižek emphasizes the asymmetry between the subject supposed to know and the subject supposed to believe. Belief is inseparable from the belief that another person believes. He writes: "'I still believe in Communism' is the equivalent of saying 'I believe there are still people who believe in Communism.'"[29] Because belief is belief in the belief of the other, one can believe through another. Someone else can believe for us. Knowledge is different. That the other knows does not mean that I know. I can only know for myself. No wonder, then, that a frequent refrain in contemporary capitalist ideology is that each should find out for herself. Capitalism relies on our separation from one another so it does its best to separate and individuate us at every turn.

Institutions are symbolic arrangements that organize and concentrate the social space. They "fix" an Other, not in the sense of immobilizing it but in the sense of putting in relation the emergent effects of sociality. This "putting in relation" substantializes the link, giving it its force, enabling it to exert its pressure. A party is an organization and concentration of sociality on behalf of a certain politics. For communists this is a politics of and for the working class, the producers, the oppressed, the people as the rest of us. "Party" knots together effects of ideal ego, ego ideal, superego, subject supposed to know, and subject supposed to believe. The particular content of any of these component effects changes over time and place even as the operations they designate remain as features of the party form.

The ideal ego in communist parties is typically imagined in terms of the good comrade. The good comrade may be a brave militant, skilled organizer, accomplished orator, or loyal functionary. In contrast, the ego ideal is the point from which comradeship is assessed: how and to what end is bravery, skill, accomplishment, and loyalty counted? The party superego incessantly charges us for failing on all fronts, *we never do enough*, even as it taunts us with the sacrifices we make for the sake of the party, *we have always done too much*. Each of these positions can be varyingly open and closed, coherent or contradictory. Insofar as the party is situated in an antagonistic field, insofar as it is not the state but is a part, other ideals and injunctions enter the mix: this is class struggle within the party, the challenge presented by capitalist consciousness. At the same time, the historical situatedness of the party means that the space it provides necessarily exerts effects beyond party members, providing images and reference points for those who might join, for allies and fellow travelers, as well as for former members or enemies.

The ideas of subject supposed to believe and know are particularly useful for thinking about these effects beyond party members. Critics of the communist party chastise the party for claiming to know, for functioning as a location of scientific or revolutionary knowledge. This ostensible expertise has been derided not only as monopolistic but also as false: the knowledge of living with, responding to, and fighting against oppressive power belongs to the people and cannot be confined in a set of iron laws of historical development. Given this critique, which came to be widely shared on the Left in the wake of '68, it's surprising that the collapse of the Soviet Union dealt such a mortal blow to communist and socialist organizing in the USA, UK, and Europe. By 1989, only a tiny few defended the Soviet Union any more. Most agreed that its bureaucracy was moribund and that it needed to institute market reforms. Why, then, did its collapse have such an effect? The "subject supposed to believe" helps make sense of this strange reaction. What was lost when the USSR fell apart was the subject on to whom belief was transposed, the subject through whom others believed. Once this believing subject was gone, it really appeared that communism was ideologically defeated. As a further example, we might consider the prototypical accounts of Communist Party officials with their dachas and privileges. These functioned less as factual exposés than as attacks on the subject supposed to believe: not even the party believes in communism. Where the attacks failed, however, is in the fact that they were waged at all. Insofar as they had a target, they affirmed its ongoing function as the subject supposed to believe. The flawed, dessicated party could still believe for us. Once it utterly collapsed, we lost the other through whom we could believe.

The *Party Organizer*

Writings from the 1930s in the *Party Organizer*, a publication of the Communist Party of the United States for the internal use of unit and district organizers, display the array of structural effects knotted together in the party. One writer vividly narrates how his CP-organized block committee fought to get food relief for a needy woman and her children. As he tells it, the workers "stood up like a solid wall, demanding food." The cowardly relief supervisor, "a capitalist tool," called the police, who rushed in and grabbed the CP organizer. "But the roar from the workers and my determination to fight back put fear into the hearts of the police." The police called for reinforcements and brought "the big fat Judge Mendriski" with them. With a heroic image of himself, workers, and party standing up to the capitalist relief supervisor, police, and judge, and fighting to keep a woman and her children from starving, the organizer recounts, "I looked right at him and said: 'What the hell are you here for, to help this serpent deny this mother with her three children? You don't care ... you with your belly packed with steak.'" The judge orders the police to lock up the organizer. But the police, "seeing the determination of the workers," are forced to let him go.[30] The workers appear as a crowd, a roaring steadfast wall. Their appearing compels the police to take the perspective of the CP and recognize that the united workers are stronger than any judge and his order.

In the early 1930s, the *Party Organizer* was filled with articles on how to recruit and retain new members. Month after month, the writers – many anonymous, many district-level organizers – express excitement about gains in new members and dismay over the party's failure to retain them. They worry that their meetings are too long, that they don't start and finish on time, that they aren't "snappy enough."[31] They advise one another on the best design for a party meeting: no more than two hours, not to exceed two and half hours, three hours at the absolute limit. District organizers are advised to pick up members at their houses and bring them to meetings. Members are reminded to talk to new recruits. The CP organizers writing in the magazine sense the "enthusiasm and

earnest desire of the workers," but blame themselves for the fact that the
workers drop out:

> The recruit comes into the average unit of the Party and finds there a
> group of strangers speaking a jargon which he does not understand. No
> one pays much attention to him and he is therefore left very much to
> himself ... enthusiasm cools, he becomes discouraged, loses his enthusiasm
> and finally drops out of the Party.[32]

Here, "jargon" is a symptom of the problem. "Jargon" means that the
people and the party are not speaking the same language. It marks a division between workers and party members, even when party members are
workers. The language that members share, the ideas that enable them to
see the world in terms other to capitalism's, enhance and hinder belonging at the same time. The very activities they pursue as communists –
reading, discussing, meeting, leafleting, organizing, training – separate
them from the workers. What makes them communists, what separates
them from capitalism's constraints as it provides them with political
capacity and conviction, inscribes a gap in the givenness of economic
belonging. They are not just economic producers. They are political producers creating not commodities but collective power.

One recommendation for overcoming this division is imagining
oneself as a comrade, not a professor.[33] Organizers are advised to speak
"not as a soap boxer or a seasoned Communist theorist" but just to "be
one of the workers, which indeed you are."[34] Other recommendations
include better development of cadres, more effort at education. Still others highlight a kind of transferential relation that can arise from "visiting
the workers at least two or three times a week, getting to know them by
name and their individual problems, and have them call you by name
and feel you are one of them."[35] Imagining oneself as a comrade, particularly when accompanied by instructions to do what one would normally
do, involves a reflexive turn on to the everyday as one looks at what one
does from the party perspective.

The same desire that leads people to join the party separates them from
the crowd. Once they have become communists, they see themselves
and the world from the perspective opened up by the party. They look
at the world differently from how they did before. Yet they also have to
continue to imagine themselves as the workers they are, bound to the
economic struggle. Hence the advice: "Little by little from the conditions
in the shops go on to the speed up, wage cuts, unemployment and then
to the need for organization. Don't appear too insistent at first."[36] The
organizer has to begin from the perspective of the worker and guide
the worker to a shift in perspective, to seeing from a different place.

The internal criticisms that the *Party Organizer* raises are unrelenting. For every success in increasing membership, there is an injunction to do more, to do better. One article will take up the ways problems are being addressed. The next will hammer home the problems that persist. The demands they place on themselves never let up: another membership drive, more focus on the trade unions, intensification of reading, more thorough reporting. They acknowledge small victories, but every victory – in true superegoic fashion – inspires yet more self-criticism. One writes, "Our influence among workers has increased ten-fold within the last few years, but the membership of our Party has remained practically stationary. Why do the workers come and leave our ranks? What is wrong with us?"[37]

The *Party Organizer* reveals a party in the process of exerting pressure on itself, of imagining itself and struggling as it produces a place from which to see itself. This place is in flux, unstable, sometimes occupied by idealized revolutionary workers and sometimes the place from which workers are idealized. The stronger the party feels itself becoming, the fiercer and more intense the demands it puts on itself. A letter from an active party comrade in Chicago expresses the pressure of the relentless injunction to do more:

> I will be criticized next Tuesday night at the organizers meeting because the unit is not larger; because I have not done more; because I did not attend some meeting or other … I do the best I can. However, no matter how much I do, I always hate to show my face because there are things I do not do that I was told to do. Directives, directives, directives. An organization letter sometimes of three pages. Hell, I could not do one tenth of it. I am getting tired. I am just as much a Communist as ever, but I am not 10 communists.[38]

Žižek observes that the symbolic space of the Other "operates like a yard-stick against which I can measure myself."[39] The communists appearing in the *Party Organizer* measure themselves against the many. The desire that expresses itself in the urgent demands they make on themselves is collective—ten communists to one—even as it is felt as an impossible superegoic command.

The Party Opening

Whereas critics of the party fault the form itself for its centralism and authoritarianism, I have demonstrated how Michels's discussion of the technical and psychological tendencies to oligarchy in *any* political group exposes the *unavoidability* of a gap between few and many. Lacan provides the concepts through which to theorize the gap as a link, a social space knotting together unconscious processes and perspectives. Inserting the party in this gap, I've shown collectivity's work back upon its members. Their very association alienates them from their setting, opening up the possibility of another perspective on it and separating them from how they are given under capitalism.

That political organization involves an inevitable gap between the many and the few does not automatically imply that the same people should be on one side or the other of it. The history of people's struggles (anti-racism, anti-sexism, anti-homophobia, etc.) demonstrates profound and ongoing mobilization on precisely this point. Likewise, that the gap is unavoidable does not imply that any given instantiation of the gap is permanent or justified. There are better and worse parties and leaders. Michels's own discussion brings out the torsion between many and few as power shifts and folds between them: what appears as an idolized leader is a refraction of the crowd's enjoyment of the power of number. Finally, that the gap between many and few is unavoidable does not mean that gaps should line up with each other: doing more work should not imply garnering more material benefit. The crucial point that follows from the unavoidable gap between few and many is that the charges of centralism and authoritarianism leveled at the communist party from its inception apply to politics in general. If we are to engage politically, we cannot avoid the effects – and affects – of numbers.

More than a decade ago, John Holloway claimed, "Whether or not it ever made sense to think of revolutionary change in terms of the 'Party,' it is no longer even open to us to pose the questions in those terms. To say now that the Party is the bearer of the class consciousness of the proletariat no longer makes any sense at all."[40] Holloway implies that there was a time when the party *was* the bearer of working-class consciousness. There was a time when people – workers, peasants, intellectuals, even capitalists – *believed* that the Communist Party was the bearer of working-class consciousness. More precisely, they believed that others *believed* that the Communist Party was the bearer of working-class consciousness. In the second half of the twentieth century, this belief collapsed. The slogan from the Cultural Revolution makes the point most powerfully: "the bourgeoisie is in the Communist Party." But notice the continuation of transference: Holloway doesn't say that the party *never* was a bearer of working-class consciousness. He believes that it was, for some, for a while. The space opened up and held by the party remains. Its form as "enigmatic subject support" persists even as the working class no longer appears as a revolutionary subject.[41] Such a support continues to exert an effect even in the claim that "the bourgeoisie is in the Communist Party." The claim is reflexive. This is to say that it is the party that opens the space for this criticism of itself. The party holds up the subject making this criticism, a point Holloway attempts to disavow but cannot not presuppose. He is right to say the party is not the bearer of working-class consciousness. In fact it never could be the bearer of such a fiction, the efforts of German Social Democracy to present it otherwise notwithstanding. The party is the support for the subject of communism. This subject has been variously figured as proletariat, peasantry, and divided people.

The party operates as the support for the subject by holding open the gap between the people and their setting in capitalism. The more the gap appears, the more we feel the need for the party. This gap, however, isn't a void, but a knot of processes that organize the persistence of the unrealized in a set of structural effects: ideal ego, ego ideal, superego, subject supposed to know and believe. The party, my chapter has argued, is the Other space delineated by Lacan. This Other space doesn't have its own interest, a correct line, or an objective science that tells it the truth of history. It is instead a rupture within the people, dividing them from their given milieu, a rupture that is, in fact, an effect of their collectivity and the way in which their belonging backfires on them.

The production of the collective space of the party as a knot of transferential effects is the way people are changed through struggle, the way they induce a gap in capitalism where another perspective becomes possible. Members look at themselves and their interactions from the perspective of the association they create through their association, the party. The communist goal of revolution lets us see the reflective dimension of the instrument of revolution in terms of its effects back on those out of whom it arises. The party affects members and opponents alike, and is exemplary in the way its knotting together of the elements of the Other consolidates the space of a politics, a place from which a collective can look at itself.

Notes

1 Gavin Walker, "The Body of Politics: On the Concept of the Party," *Theory and Event* 16, 4 (2013).

2 For example, Alain Badiou, *The Communist Hypothesis*, tr. David Macey and Steve Corcoran (New York: Verso, 2010) and Joshua Clover and Aaron Benanav, "Can Dialectics Break BRICS?" *South Atlantic Quarterly* 113, 4 (Fall 2014), 743–759.

3 Robert Michels, *Political Parties: A Sociological Study of the Oligarchical Tendencies of Modern Democracy*, tr. Eden Paul and Cedar Paul (Kitchener, Ontario: Batoche Books, 2001; first published 1911).

4 Juan Linz, "Robert Michels," *International Encyclopedia of the Social Sciences*, vol. x (New York: Macmillan and Free Press, 1968), 265–71. See also Juan Linz, *Robert Michels, Political Sociology, and the Future of Democracy* (London: Transaction Publishers, 2006). Equating psychology with the individual psychology of leaders, Linz overestimates the technical dimensions of organizational needs, paying little attention to group dynamics.

5 Seymour Martin Lipset, *Michels' Theory of Political Parties*, Reprint 185 (Berkeley, CA: Institute of Industrial Relations, 1962), 21–22.

6 Michels, *Political Parties*, 6.

7 Michels refers to Pareto several times in *Political Parties*, although not explicitly on this point. For an overview of debates over *Political Parties*, see Philip J. Cook, "Robert Michels's Political Parties in Perspective," *Journal of Politics* 33, 3 (August 1971), 773–796. Cook points out the mistaken tendency to read Michels as a critic of socialism when his target is actually syndicalism.

8 Michels, *Political Parties*, 13.

9 Lipset emphasizes the technical tendencies but neglects the psychological ones.

10 Michels, *Political Parties*, 39.

11 See L. A. Kauffman's critique of contemporary activist practices such as those used in Occupy Wall Street, in "The Theology of Consensus," *Berkeley Journal of Sociology* (May 26, 2015).

12 Michels, *Political Parties*, 25.

13 Ibid., 38.

14 Ibid., 47.

15 Jacques Lacan, *The Four Fundamental Concepts of Psychoanalysis*, Seminar XI, ed. Jacques-Alain Miller, tr. Alan Sheridan (New York: W. W. Norton, 1998), 100.

16 Michels, *Political Parties*, 143.

17 Ibid., 232.

18 Ibid., 231.

19 Lacan, *Four Fundamental Concepts*, 22.

20 Ibid., 131.

21 Ibid., 143.

22 Slavoj Žižek, *How to Read Lacan* (New York: W. W. Norton, 2006), 11–12.

23 Ibid., 80.

24 Ibid., 81. See also my discussion in chapter 5 of Jodi Dean, *The Communist Horizon* (London: Verso, 2012).

25 Žižek, *How to Read Lacan*, 28–29.

26 Lacan, *Four Fundamental Concepts*, 232.

27 Slavoj Žižek, *The Sublime Object of Ideology* (London: Verso, 1989), 185. Elsewhere Žižek treats the subject supposed to believe "as the fundamental, constitutive feature of the symbolic order," *The Plague of Fantasies* (London: Verso, 1997), 106.

28 Žižek, *Plague of Fantasies*, 106.

29 Ibid., 107.

30 "Organized Struggles Defeat Police Terror," *Party Organizer* 6, 1 (January 1933), 8–11.

31 "Retaining and Developing New Members of the Party," *Party Organizer* 14, 10 (November 1931), 16–19, 18.

32 Ibid., 17.

33 Ibid., 18.

34 S. V. V., "Examine Our Factory Work," *Party Organizer* 4, 5 (June 1931), 19.

35 Sylvia Tate, "Experiences of Neighborhood Concentration," *Party Organizer* 5, 8 (August 1932), 6–7.

36 "Examine Our Factory Work," 19.

37 J. A., "The Deadly Routine Which Must Be Overcome," *Party Organizer* 6, 3–4 (March–April 1933), 22–23, 22.

38 "Give More Personal Guidance," *Party Organizer* 6, 1 (January 1933), 22.

39 Žižek, *How to Read Lacan*, 9.

40 John Holloway, *Change the World without Taking Power* (London: Pluto Press, 2002), 131.

41 For a more detailed discussion of this point, see Dean, *The Communist Horizon*, chapter 3. "Enigmatic subject support" comes from Alain Badiou, *Theory of the Subject*, trans. Bruno Bosteels (London: Continuum, 2009), 189.

CHAPTER 8

Lacan and Race

Azeen Khan

I believe that in our day and age, we could classify the mark, the scar, left by the father's disappearance under the heading and general notion of *segregation*. The common belief is that our civilization's universalism and communication standardize human relations. I, on the contrary, believe that what characterizes our century – and we cannot fail to be aware of it – is a complex, reinforced and constantly overlapping form of segregation that only manages to generate more and more barriers.

Jacques Lacan, "Note on the Father and Universalism"[1]

Obscure Cause

In his 2012 address to the Congress of the World Association of Psychoanalysis, "A Real for the 21st Century," Jacques-Alain Miller suggests that the two discourses of modernity – the discourse of science and the discourse of capitalism – have produced a fundamental change in the symbolic order, the corner-stone of which, the Name-of-the-Father, has been fractured.[2] For Miller, we are at a moment of heightened denaturalization, which alters our conception of the real itself; whereas earlier the real operated according to a law and with knowledge in it (as in nature with an ascribed order), now "the real is without law," that is, there is a severing of the connection between nature and the real.[3] Miller situates his comments in the context of *The Communist Manifesto*:

> I would say that capitalism and science have combined to make nature disappear. And what is left by the vanishing of nature is what we call the real, that is, a remainder, by structure, disordered. The real is touched on all sides by the advances of the binary capitalism-science, in a disordered way, randomly, without being able to recuperate any idea of harmony.[4]

In the lecture, Miller does not directly locate this shift within the long history of colonialism or the slave trade. But neither the history of capitalism which he references, with "primitive accumulation" as its primary repressed, nor the history of science, specifically the human sciences that take both madmen and racialized bodies, and often both together, as an object of segregative reason, can be fully accounted for without attention to the way in which the master's discourse uses forms of segregative reason as an apparatus for the formation, control, and management of social groups.

In Seminar XVII, *The Other Side of Psychoanalysis* (1969–1970), Jacques Lacan comments on the effect of the dissemination of the master's discourse – here taking the form of colonial discourse – on the status of the unconscious of three people from Togo who were in analysis with him. He says:

> Now, I was unable, in their analysis, to find any trace of their tribal customs and beliefs, which they had not forgotten, which they knew, but from the point of view of ethnography. It has to be said that everything was done to separate them from this, given what they were, these courageous little doctors who were trying to insert themselves into the medical hierarchy of the metropolis – these were still colonial days. What they knew about this, then, at the level of the ethnographic was more or less that of journalism, but their unconscious functioned according to the good old rules of Oedipus. This was the unconscious that had been sold to them along with the laws of colonization, this exotic, regressive form of the master's discourse, in the face of the capitalism called imperialism. Their unconscious was not that of their childhood memories – you could sense it – but their childhood was retroactively lived out in our *famil-ial* categories.[5]

Lacan's recognition here – that "the unconscious that had been sold to them along with the laws of colonization, this exotic regressive form of the master's discourse, in the face of the capitalism called imperialism" – suggests that a particular form of the master's discourse came to order the world. The unconscious speaks of this ordering of the world that places value on particular semblants that come to organize both the social bonds between speaking beings and the specific modes of readymade jouissance available to them through the dominant discourse.[6]

In "L'étourdit," written in 1972, Lacan comments that "[a race] is constituted according to the mode in which symbolic places are transmitted by the order of a discourse."[7] In other words, while races can be physical – attributed to visual or physical difference – races are, in effect, effects of discourse. For Lacan, racism is tied to the problematic of segregation, which is intensified as a consequence of the decline of the Name-of-the-Father in an age when the discourses of science and capitalism are bringing about fundamental shifts. In "Proposition of 9 October

1967," Lacan situates the extension of segregation in the context of Nazi Germany and the concentration camp, indicating that science rearranges social groupings at the same time as it introduces a universalizing principle that, in turn, accentuates processes of segregation:

> Let me summarize by saying that what we have seen emerge from this, to our horror, represents the reaction of precursors in relation to what will unfold as a consequence of the rearranging of social groupings by science, and, notably, of the universalization science introduces into them.
>
> Our future as common markets will be balanced by an increasingly hard-line extension of the process of segregation.[8]

On the one hand, then, there is the universalizing orientation of science (for all); on the other, the accentuation of segregation (not for all). Lacan places racism within this movement. In "Racism 2.0," Eric Laurent situates Lacan's comments in a moment of European history that had very much to do with the "delight at the prospect of integrating nations into larger ensembles that would be authorized by 'common markets.'"[9] Laurent explains that in his comments on the logic of racism, Lacan is accounting for

> the varying forms of the rejected object, distinct forms that range from pre-war anti-Semitism (which led to Nazi radicalism) to post-colonial racism directed at immigrants. Racism effectively switches its objects as the social forms undergo modification. From Lacan's perspective, however, there is always, in any human community, a rejection of an unassimilable jouissance, which forms the mainspring of a possible barbarism.[10]

Taking Laurent's comments as a point of departure, this chapter considers the specificity of the psychoanalytic intervention, developed through Sigmund Freud, Jacques Lacan, and Jacques-Alain Miller, on race and racism through the concept of segregation, taking racism as one exemplary form of social group formation.[11] Miller argues for this specificity of the psychoanalytic intervention when he says:

> Theorization of the economic, social, and geopolitical causes of racism of course covers a vast field of the phenomenon, but not everything is exclusively situated at this level. There is a remainder that one could call *the obscure causes of racism*, against which indignation is perhaps not enough ... Psychoanalysis and the teaching of Lacan could allow us to shed some light on this phenomenon, a light that I did not hesitate to call *the light of reason*. I did not say "science" for the best reason in the world, because science has its own role to play in the rise of racism.[12]

Scholars who have drawn on the teaching of Lacan for critical theory and critical race studies, for example, Slavoj Žižek, Joan Copjec, Kalpana

Sheshadri-Crooks, Hortense Spillers, and Antonio Viego, have all shown, in their different ways, the usefulness of Lacan for a study of race and racism.[13] Kalpana Sheshadri-Crooks, for example, argues that "the regime of visibility secures the investment that we make in 'race'" and explores how the logic of racial difference works on an order different from sexual difference, but comes in to fill the lack that sexuality opens for a given subject.[14] Antonio Viego develops an analytic of race that is attentive to the way in which a subject's entry into language is determinative, placing race – and processes of racial differentiation – within this movement.[15] Spillers, without directly citing Lacan, in texts like "Mama's Baby, Papa's Maybe: An American Grammar Book", seems to give race, through the concept of the "flesh," the status of the real in Lacan, but where, somewhat differently than in Lacan, flesh is presented variously as an ontological *a priori*, a historicized materiality, a spectral presence, and that which precedes sexual differentiation.[16] In this chapter, I do not directly engage or extend these analyses; instead, through Freud, Lacan, and Miller, I approach race and racism through the notion of segregation, focusing specifically on the opacity of the inassimilable jouissance of the Other as an obscure cause of racism.

Minor Differences

Sigmund Freud provides the key orientation for the field of psychoanalysis. Psychoanalytic intervention on the question of race, and of racism, can be organized around two coordinates that are not mutually exclusive. First, the problem of identification, or processes of identification, that allow for social group formation, especially of those groups that have leaders. In "Group Psychology and the Analysis of the Ego" (1921), Freud writes that social group formation can come to rely for its cohesion on the "hatred" or "intolerance" of some particularity, the exclusion of which comes to predicate the psychic cohesion of the group.[17] Loosening of particular social bonds (for example, around religious lines) opens to a reconfiguration of social bonds along other lines. And second, the problem posed by the drive as an excess that cannot be completely reined in in any system of signification or sense, as Freud formulates it in "Civilization and its Discontents" (1930).[18]

In "Group Psychology and the Analysis of the Ego," Freud emphasizes that group cohesion is allowed by libidinal ties based on the mechanism of love. Using the examples of the church and the army, he indicates that cohesion is enabled by processes of identification, such that identification is the basic unit of proximity. But he also argues that

> The evidence of psycho-analysis shows that almost every intimate emotional relation between two people which lasts for some time – marriage, friendship, the relations between parents and children – contains a sediment of feelings of aversion and hostility, which only escapes perception as a result of repression. This is less disguised in the common wrangles between business partners or in the grumbles of a subordinate at his superior. The same thing happens when men come together in larger units ... Closely related races keep one another at arm's length; the South German cannot endure the North German, the Englishman casts every kind of aspersion upon the Scot, the Spaniard despises the Portuguese. We are no longer astonished that greater differences should lead to an almost insuperable repugnance, such as the Gallic people feel for the German, the Aryan for the Semite, and the white races for the coloured.[19]

In the essay, Freud works out a logic of group formation in which race is marked as one form of social grouping, amongst others, and follows in a series of relations. It is constructed analogically, although in each specific instance the excluded object is historically contingent and marked off by, and for, a particular attribute. Analysis of racial group formation comes to be circumscribed within the same logic that governs relations with the other. This does not mean that for Freud there is no historical specificity to racism but that its specificity pertains to its object, insofar as the racist relation is precisely the relation to the object. Thus Freud considers racism alongside a series of other terms, including antisemitism. The argument put forth in "Group Psychology and Analysis of the Ego" reappears later in Freud's essay "Civilization and its Discontents," where he elaborates on the irreducibility of the drive, a topic to which he also attends in "Thoughts on the Times of War and Death" (1915) and in his exchange with Albert Einstein, "Why War?" (1933).[20]

In "Civilization and its Discontents," Freud suggests that the movement of civilization relies, ultimately, on identifications, reaction-formations, and sublimations to restrain the drive. Commenting on the position of the communists, he writes that whereas there is an assumption that the abolition of private property would allow ill will and hostility to disappear, making it possible for everyone to enjoy, this hypothesis does not concur with psychoanalytic findings, which call for attention to the drive:

> I have no concern with any economic criticisms of the communist system; I cannot enquire into whether the abolition of private property is

expedient or advantageous. But I am able to recognize that the psycho-logical premises on which the system is based are an untenable illusion. In abolishing private property we deprive the human love of aggression of one of its instruments, certainly a strong one, though certainly not the strongest ... Aggressiveness was not created by property. It reigned almost without limit in primitive times, when property was still very scanty, and it already shows itself in the nursery almost before property has given up its primal, anal form ...[21]

Freud had already written about hatred in "Character and Anal Erotism" (1908). His hypothesis here, however, is that there is a certain irreduc-ibility of the drive. Although the drive can be redirected through pro-cesses of "indirection," about which Freud writes in "Why War?", it cannot be eradicated as such. Hatred of the other, aggression toward the other, the neighbor, can thus be managed but not entirely eliminated – therefore the injunction to love thy neighbor. It is in reference to this that in "Civilization and its Discontents" Freud develops his notion of the "narcissism of minor differences":

It is clearly not easy for men to give up the satisfaction of this inclination to aggression. They do not feel comfortable without it. The advantage which a comparatively small cultural group offers of allowing this instinct an outlet in the form of hostility against intruders is not to be despised. It is always possible to bind together a considerable number of people in love, so long as there are other people left over to receive the manifesta-tions of their aggressiveness. I once discussed the phenomenon that it is precisely communities with adjoining territories, and related to each other in other ways as well, who are engaged in constant feuds and in ridiculing each other ... In this respect the Jewish people, scattered everywhere, have rendered the most useful services to the civilizations of the countries that have been their hosts, but unfortunately all the massacres of the Jews in the Middle Ages did not suffice to make that period more peaceful and secure for their Christian fellows.[22]

Freud historicizes his comments here in relation to the particular role of the Jews in Europe, of which he was quite well aware. But what he emphasizes, specifically, is that each historical moment, and each civilization as such, produces an abject population that is "left over to receive the manifestations of aggressiveness." Freud's point is that this population serves a purpose, which is to bind the drive in opposi-tion to something else. What Freud then directs us toward is that the properly psychoanalytic intervention into the question of race and racism is possible only through an attention to the processes of iden-tification that lie at the root of "identity" (given by the Other and/or self-proclaimed) and the notion of the drive, that is not without history, but that remains irreducible despite the work of civilization. Lacan, in his singular way, develops these points further.

Not-All

Although scholars in critical race studies and critical theory have extended Lacan's particular psychoanalytic framework toward an understanding of race and racism, perhaps less attention has been given to Lacan's own comments on the problematic of race. These comments are scattered throughout his teachings and are, more or less, coincident with his observations on the universalization prompted by the discourses of science and capitalism that make equivalences between subjects and posit a pure subject, prior to the division of the unconscious. Here, I develop two of Lacan's comments that touch on the question of race through the concept of segregation. In his "Address on Child Psychoses," delivered on October 22, 1967 as a conclusion to the Study Days on the same topic, Lacan says:

> The factor at stake here is the most burning issue of our times in so far as this era is the first to have to undergo the calling into question of every social structure as a result of the progress of science. This is something which we are going to be contending with, not only in our domain as psychiatrists, but in the furthest reaches of our universe, and in an ever more pressing fashion: with segregation.
>
> Mankind is entering a period that has been called "global," in which it will find out about this something that is emerging from the destruction of an old social order that I shall symbolize by the *Empire* whose shadow was long cast over a great civilization, such that something very different is replacing it, something that carries a very different meaning, the *imperialisms*, whose question runs as follows: what can we do so that human masses, which are destined to occupy the same space, not only geographically, but sometimes in a familial sense, remain separate?
>
> The problem at the level at which Oury set it out just now using the pertinent term "segregation" is therefore merely a local point, a small model of something to which we need to know what the rest of us, I mean psychoanalysts, are going to respond: segregation, which has been put on the agenda by an unprecedented subversion.[23]

In these comments, Lacan points to at least two things. First, that there is a calling into question of every social structure as a result of science because the latter, while performing an ostensibly democratizing function ("for all"), also ushers in the order of numbers, the techno-sciences, etc.

And, second, that this results in new forms of segregation – new forms of maintaining separation between human masses – which he names here "imperialisms" (not for all). Lacan thus places the question of segregation as a particular consequence of the progress of science, of "the universal mode," and of the decline of the Name-of-the-Father. The latter he comments on in "Note on the Father and Universalism": "I believe that in our day and age, we could classify the mark, the scar, left by the father's disappearance under the heading and general notion of *segregation*."[24] The intensification of racisms as segregation in our historical moment, in the aftermath of Empire and in the age of imperialisms, can be situated within these shifts and fractures, raising the question that Lacan directs at psychoanalysts: how to respond to segregation?

He follows up on these comments in 1973, in *Television: A Challenge to the Psychoanalytic Establishment*, in response to a question posed by Jacques-Alain Miller on the rise of modern racism: "From another direction, what gives you the confidence to prophesy the rise of racism? And why the devil do you have to speak of it?"[25] In response to Miller's provocation, Lacan says:

> Because it doesn't strike me as funny and yet, it's true. Without our *jouissance* going off the track, only the Other is able to mark its position, but only insofar as we are separated from this Other. Whence certain fantasies – unheard of before the melting pot.
>
> Leaving this Other to his own mode of *jouissance*, that would only be possible by not imposing our own on him, by not thinking of him as underdeveloped.
>
> Given, too, the precariousness of our own mode, which from now on takes its bearing from the ideal of an over-coming [*plus-de-jouir*], which is, in fact, no longer expressed in any other way, how can one hope that the empty forms of humanhysterianism [*humanitairerie*] disguising our extortions can continue to last?
>
> Even if God, thus newly strengthened, should end up ex-sisting, this bodes nothing better than a return of his baneful past.[26]

While his comment in "Address on Child Psychoses" situates segregation within the age of science and the decline of the Name-of-the-Father, Lacan's comment on racism here has to do with the jouissance of the Other – broached through the notion of development, or rather, the underdevelopment of the Other. There is an invocation here of the colonial paradigm, the civilizing mission, by which the jouissance of the other is organized through the jouissance-organizing categories of the master's discourse – what Lacan brings up in Seminar XVII through the example of his analysands from Togo. Lacan begins to question this paradigm (the empty forms of *humanitairerie*), indicating also the rise in the various discourses of God – forms of religious fundamentalisms that attempt to scaffold the decline of the Name-of-the-Father. Laurent points out that the logic that Lacan is developing here is as follows:

> We have no knowledge of the jouissance from which we might take our orientation. We know only how to reject the jouissance of others. With this 'melting pot,' Lacan is criticizing the twofold movement of colonialism and the will to normalize the displaced person, the immigrant, in the name of all that is supposed to be for 'his own good.'[27]

Lacan's comments, then, although only briefly explored here, situate segregation – and racism – through the shifts in the social order and in the organization of the modes of jouissance of subjects under a particular instantiation of the master's discourse. In Seminar XIX, *...ou pire,* Lacan brings out the stakes of the latter, by situating racism in and through the body and suggesting that we have not, as yet, seen its ultimate consequences:

> And when we come back to the root of the body, if we are to reassert the value of the word *brother* ... you should know that what rises up, the ultimate consequences of which have yet to be seen – which takes root in the body, in the fraternity of the body – is racism.[28]

Although I do not expand on this here, in Seminar XIX, Lacan develops hate as a passion that cannot be dialectized. For the purposes of this chapter, I follow Miller's development of Lacan's indications on segregation – the hatred of the Other – through the concept of extimacy.

Extimacy

In his seminar *Extimité* (1985–1986), delivered at the Department of Psychoanalysis, University of Paris VIII, Jacques-Alain Miller extends this Freudian and Lacanian line of thought on the relation to the Other through the concept of extimacy, where he understands extimacy to be "equivalent to the unconscious itself. In this sense, the extimacy of the subject is the Other."[29] In the seminar, Miller delineates the structure of extimacy by placing alterity – the object *a* – at the center of intimacy.[30] In doing so, Miller highlights two points that provide some guidance for understanding racism, situating racism differently than simply in relation to imaginary aggressivity. First, in response to the key question – what is the Other of the Other, or what grounds the alterity of the Other? – Miller suggests that the alterity of the Other is not grounded in the signifier which allows for substitutions and equivalences, but in jouissance – in the particular mode of jouissance of the Other. He says:

> *Jouissance* is precisely what grounds the alterity of the Other when there is no Other of the Other. It is in its relation to *jouissance* that the Other is really Other. This means that no one can ground the alterity of the Other from the signifier, since the very law of the signifier implies that one can always be substituted for the other and vice versa. The law of the signifier is indeed the very law of 1–2, and in this dimension, it is as though there is a democracy, an equality, a community, a principle of peace … In racism, for example, it is precisely a question of the relation to an Other as such, conceived in its difference. And it does not seem to me that any of the generous and universal discourses on the theme of "we are all fellow-beings" have had an effectiveness concerning this question. Why? Because racism calls into play a hatred which goes precisely toward what grounds the Other's alterity, in other words its *jouissance.*[31]

The first point thus emphasizes that racism is founded on the point of the extimacy of the Other. For Miller, racism comes to name the hatred that "aims at the real in the Other. What is it that makes this Other so Other that one can hate it in its very being? This is *the hatred of the jouissance of the Other.*"[32] The second point that Miller highlights in relation to racism has to do with the "races of discourse, i.e., traditions of subjective positions" that come to organize a mode of jouissance which is elaborated, constructed, and supported by a particular (racial) group. He says:

> Racism is founded on what one imagines about the Other's *jouissance*; it is hatred of the particular way, of the Other's own way of experiencing *jouissance* … Racist stories are always about the way in which the Other obtains a *plus-de-jouir*: either he does not work or he does not work enough, or he is useless or a little too useful, but whatever the case may be, he is always endowed with a part of *jouissance* that he does not deserve. Thus true intolerance is the intolerance of the Other's *jouissance*. Of course, we cannot deny that races do exist, but they exist in so far as they are, in Lacan's words, races of discourse, i.e., traditions of subjective positions.[33]

To attend to racism in these terms then calls for a way of thinking that takes into account the inassimilability – and in some cases the incompatibility – of the specific modes of jouissance (of each subject, of a particular racial group, etc.). In other words, what is required is very much the "recognition of oneself in the Other as subject of jouissance."[34] While the signifier offers a recourse to a universal, abstract mode of organization, it does so without touching the fact of the singularity of the jouissance of each one. Miller expands on this by pointing out how there is a devalorization of the Other of the signifier in Lacan's teaching:

> Something has been introduced in Lacan's teaching which has only been understood recently, i.e, the devalorization of the Other of the signifier. He could thus say: "The Other does not exist," which does not prevent the Other from functioning, for many things function without existing. However, the sentence, "The Other does not exist," is meaningless if it does not imply that *a*, on the contrary, exists. The Lacanian Other, the Other that functions is not real. That is what allows us to understand that *a* is real, to understand how this *a* as *plus-de-jouir* founds not only the Other's alterity but also what is real in the Symbolic Other. It is not a matter of a link of integration, of interiorization, but of an articulation of extimacy.[35]

For Miller, it is precisely this – the fact that the *a* is real, that the *a* as *plus-de-jouir* founds the Other's alterity, that *a* is the real in the Symbolic Other – that the long history of humanism, in the age of science, is not able to confront. "This humanism," he suggests,

> becomes completely disoriented when the real in the Other manifests itself as not at all the same ... It is precisely when this universal humanism asserts its ambitions that the Other has a noticeable inclination to manifest itself as not the same. This disorients the progressiveness that relies on the progress of the scientific discourse as universal to obtain a uniformisation, and above all a *uniformisation of jouissance*. To the extent that the pressure of the scientific discourse operates in the direction of uniformity, a certain deformity tends to manifest itself in a particularly grotesque and horrible manner. This is linked to what we call progress.[36]

Where humanism fails is in its positing of a uniformisation of jouissance, asserting an equivalence where there is only difference and singularity. Miller's insistence here is to point to the fact that what is universalized is the uniformisation of jouissance. What is at stake in racism is precisely this demand to uniformisation.

In "Extimate Enemies," Miller indicates how in the age of science there is, on the one hand, the desegregative move – the desire to universalize the subject – which in itself can be considered liberatory, and, on the other, the move that brings the difference of the Other (its singular mode of jouissance) to the fore, thereby intensifying segregation. Modern racism, as Miller understands it, is thus a product of the discourse of science:

> The essence of the matter is that the Other is unfairly subtracting from you of a part of your jouissance. That is the constant. The question of

tolerance or intolerance does not at all concern the subject of science. The question has to be placed at another level, which is that of the tolerance or intolerance of the jouissance of the Other – of that Other inasmuch as this Other is fundamentally the one who is robbing me of my jouissance.

For our part, we know that the fundamental status of the object is to have always been stolen by the Other. We write of this theft of jouissance ... minus phi, the matheme of castration. If the problem appears unsolvable, it is because the Other is Other in my interior. *The root of racism is the hatred of one's own jouissance.* There is no other – if the Other is in my interior in a position of extimacy, it is also hatred of myself.[37]

Extimacy then comes to name a structural relation where what is most intimate to the subject is the point of absolute alterity, the particular mode of jouissance, as extimate to the subject. Extending this logic, Miller thus positions the root of racism as the hatred of one's own jouissance – in other words, that which is extimate to the subject. Racism is segregation that marks as different subjects and groups that have elaborated, constructed, and organized a mode of jouissance incommensurable with the jouissance of another group. By drawing out the logic of extimacy, Miller locates the inassimilability of jouissance (one's own jouissance, the jouissance of the Other) at the center of the problem of racism.

A Non-Segregative Reason

Why might psychoanalysis be a privileged practice from which to consider race and racism? Can a clinic be organized around a notion of non-segregation, and what kind of work would such a clinic do? Racism, understood through Lacan as segregation, can be considered at many levels. But Miller emphasizes that psychoanalysts are in a unique position, because of the intimate kind of work they do, to comment on the fact that "the universal mode – which is the mode under which science elaborates the real – seems to have no limit, when in fact it does."[38] The work in the clinic thus proceeds in a manner that is in opposition to the "universal mode" and testifies to the singular mode of jouissance of each speaking being that is incommensurable with the subject of science, of race, of gender, of the nation, of the group, of identity, etc., though indeed these are not mutually exclusive. The Lacanian clinic, in contrast to these identity categories, attends to the bits of the real for each speaking being.

In "The Sex of the Symptom," Marie-Hélène Brousse emphasizes that identity – of whatever variety – is a defense against the Other and is, as such, organized as a fantasy. Identity, in this sense, lodges the subject more firmly into the master's discourse that "the universal mode" ostensibly dismantles. She says:

> Lacan makes masculine identification a consequence of the principle of universality: "for all x, the phallic function operates" ... Identity, which is created as a defense against the Other, is organized as a fantasy. Its function is to put a big part of sexuality under the Master's discourse, be it a religious, secular or scientific master. As such, identity is therefore a matter of both set-based and category-based approaches. In the end, one cannot escape the fact that the universal of the "for all" generates the segregations it pretends to destroy.[39]

The "for all" of universality generates segregation insofar as it leaves no room for difference; or if there is difference, it takes the form of the exception. For Brousse, the only solution out of segregation is through femininity – through the logic of the not-all that creates incomplete and inconsistent sets and points to the singular mode of jouissance of each speaking being. This non-segregative clinic works against segregation insofar as it does not orient itself through the categories of the master's discourse – for example, within the mental health field, the categories laid out in the Diagnostic and Statistical Manual of Mental Disorders (DSM), which relies heavily on classification through symptomatology. Instead, as Tom Svolos emphasizes in *Twenty-First Century Psychoanalysis*,

> in contrast to this usual dichotomy of the patriarch and the bureaucrat, we also have the position of the clinician within the discourse of the analyst, where the clinician takes on the role of the *object a* for the patient, allowing an articulation of the object cause of desire specific for each individual patient within the treatment ... and not driven by external standards.[40]

The possibility of non-segregation thus enters through the not-all.

Outside the clinic, segregation as a problematic also pushes the question of the different modalities of social group formation that would be commensurate with the non-segregative work of the clinic, which attends to the singular. In the "Turin Theory of the Subject of the School" as well as "The Concept of the School," Miller emphasizes that the Lacanian School has a non-identificatory, non-segregative logic, that places the singularity of the one-by-one at the center of group formation. But the school of psychoanalysis emerges as a particular formation that cannot necessarily – and perhaps should not – extend to the different social group formations within society. It raises, nonetheless, the very pertinent question of the various possibilities of non-segregative spatial, political, and ethical configurations that allow for the singularity (of the jouissance) of each one. In "Racism 2.0," Laurent suggests that

The founding crime is not the murder of the father, but the will to murder he who embodies the jouissance that I reject. Therefore, antiracism always has to be reinvented in keeping with each new form of the object of racism, which loses its shape with the rearrangements of social groupings.[41]

Laurent's comment here provides an orientation for an anti-racism that would follow a non-segregative reason: one that places the emphasis on the historical specificity of the object of racism and on anti-racism as a task of perpetual invention.

Notes

1 Jacques Lacan, "Note on the Father and Universalism," tr. R. Grigg, *The Lacanian Review: Hurly-Burly* no. 3 (2017), 10–11.

2 For Lacan's formulation of the Name-of-the-Father, see Jacques Lacan, *On the Names-of-the-Father*, tr. Bruce Fink (Cambridge, UK: Polity Press, 2013) and *The Seminar of Jacques Lacan, Book III: The Psychoses, 1955–1956*, ed. Jacques-Alain Miller, tr. Russell Grigg (New York: W. W. Norton, 1993). For his development of the four discourses, including the master's discourse, see Jacques Lacan, *The Seminar of Jacques Lacan, Book XVII: The Other Side of Psychoanalysis*, ed. Jacques-Alain Miller, tr. Russell Grigg (New York: W. W. Norton, 2007).

3 "The real is without law" is a formulation that Lacan gives in Jacques Lacan, *The Sinthome: The Seminar of Jacques Lacan, Book XXIII*, ed. Jacques-Alain Miller, tr. A. R. Price (Cambridge: Polity Press, 2016), 118. Miller's point here is that in an earlier epoch, "nature was the name of the real," and nature served as the guarantee of the symbolic order. It was consistent and would reappear in the same place like the annual return of the seasons and the spectacle of the skies (this is Lacan's example in Seminar III). The current epoch invalidates the supposition that there is a guarantee that supports the symbolic order; therefore, there is a severing of the relation between nature and the real – with eugenics, bioengineering, constant revolution of the instruments of production, etc. Thus Miller states in his address: "The real without law appears unthinkable. It is a limit idea that in the first instance implies that the real is without natural law. Everything, for example, that had belonged to the immutable order of reproduction is in motion, in trans-formation. Whether at the level of sexuality or of the constitution of the living human being with all the perspectives that are appearing now, in the 21st century, to improve the biology of the species" (Jacques-Alain Miller, "A Real for the 21st Century," *Scilicet: A New Lacanian School Publication* (Paris: Ecole de la Cause freudienne, 2014), 25–35, 31–32).

4 Miller, "A Real for the 21st Century," 32.

5 Jacques Lacan, *Seminar XVII: The Other Side of Psychoanalysis*, tr. R. Grigg (New York: W. W. Norton, 2007), 91–92.

6 See Samo Tomšič, *The Capitalist Unconscious: Marx and Lacan* (New York: Verso, 2015) for an elaboration of the ideological structuring of readymade jouissance.

7 Jacques Lacan, "L'étourdit," *Scilicet* 4 (1973), 5–25, 19.

8 Jacques Lacan, "Proposition of 9 October 1967 on the Psychoanalyst of the School," tr. R. Grigg, *Analysis* no. 6 (1995), 1–13, 10.

9 Eric Laurent, "Racism 2.0," tr. A. R. Price, *Hurly Burly: The International Lacanian Journal of Psychoanalysis* no. 11 (2014), 217–222, 218.

10 Ibid., 219.

11 For studies of race and racism informed by, but not necessarily from, a psychoanalytic perspective, see Paul Gilroy, *The Black Atlantic: Modernity and Double Consciousness* (Cambridge, MA: Harvard University Press, 1993); Saidiya V. Hartman, *Scenes of Subjection: Terror, Slavery, and Self-Making in Nineteenth-Century America* (Oxford University Press, 1997); David Theo Goldberg, *The Racial State* (Malden, MA: Blackwell, 2002); Achille Mbembe, *Critique of Black Reason* (Durham, NC: Duke University Press, 2017). For work at the intersection of race and psychoanalysis, though not necessarily Lacanian, see Frantz Fanon, *Black Skin, White Masks* (London: Pluto Press, 2008; first published in French 1952); Christopher Lane (ed.), *The Psychoanalysis of Race* (New York: Columbia University Press, 1998); Anne Anlin Cheng, *The Melancholy of Race* (Oxford University Press, 2001); Michelle Ann Stephens, *Skin Acts* (Durham, NC: Duke University Press, 2014).

12 Jacques-Alain Miller, "Extimate Enemies," tr. F-C Baitinger, A. Khan, and R. Litten, *The Lacanian Review: Hurly-Burly*, no. 3 (2017), 30–42, 35.

13 Also see, for example, the exchange on Lacan and race between Scott Loren and Jorg Metelmann, and W. J. T Mitchell in the *Journal of Visual Culture*. Loren and Metelmann posit a primary "real" Race in the "pre-symbolic material of bodily fluids, flesh and bone, of genetic coding" and associate racism with the Lacanian imaginary (Scott Loren and Jorg Metelmann, "What's the Matter: Race as *Res*," *Journal of Visual Culture* 10, 3 (2011), 397–405), while Mitchell locates "race at the nexus of the symbolic (the negating register) and the imaginary (the affirmative): race, in my view mediates the symbolic and imaginary, and is constituted by the interplay of words and images, the sayable and seeable" (W. J. T. Mitchell, "Playing the Race Card with Lacan," *Journal of Visual Culture* 10, 3 (2011), 405–409, 408). For Mitchell, "The question of where a particular racism comes from, what specific forms it takes, how it evolves over time, is a strictly historical issue. Where I part company with the historicists is in my theoretical claim for a general, universal character of racism as a passion, and of race as a conceptual formation that makes reflection on that passion possible" (ibid., 406).

14 Kalpana Sheshadri-Crooks, *Desiring Whiteness: A Lacanian Analysis of Race* (London: Routledge, 2000), 2.

15 Antonio Viego, *Dead Subjects: Towards a Politics of Loss in Latino Studies* (Durham, NC: Duke University Press, 2007).

16 Hortense J. Spillers, "Mama's Baby, Papa's Maybe: An American Grammar Book," *Diacritics* 17, 2 (1987), 64–81. At various points in Spillers' essay, different modalities of the flesh appear: as an ontological category ("before

the 'body' there is the flesh, that zero degree of social conceptualization that does not escape concealment under the brush of discourse," 67); as a historical materiality ("If we think of the 'flesh' as a primary narrative, then we mean its seared, divided, ripped apartness, riveted to the ship's hole, fallen, or 'escaped' overboard," 67); as a spectral presence, indicted through the sigla "/" that cuts the flesh and body distinction (68); as a commodity of exchange ("the captive female body locates precisely a moment of converging political and social vectors that mark the flesh as a prime commodity of exchange," 75).

17 Sigmund Freud, "Group Psychology and Analysis of the Ego," in *The Standard Edition of the Complete Psychological Works of Sigmund Freud, volume XVIII* (London: Hogarth Press, 1955), 67–143.

18 Sigmund Freud, "Civilization and its Discontents," in *The Standard Edition of the Complete Psychological Works of Sigmund Freud, volume XXI* (London: Hogarth Press, 1964), 64–138.

19 Freud, "Group Psychology," 101.

20 Sigmund Freud, "Thoughts for the Times on War and Death," in *The Standard Edition of the Complete Psychological Works of Sigmund Freud, volume XIV* (London: Hogarth Press, 1957), 275–300; Sigmund Freud and Albert Einstein, "Why War?" in *The Standard Edition of the Complete Psychological Works of Sigmund Freud, volume XXII* (London: Hogarth Press, 1960), 197–215.

21 Freud, "Civilization and its Discontents," 113.

22 Ibid., 114.

23 Jacques Lacan, "Address on Child Psychoses," tr. B. Khiara-Foxton and A. R. Price, *Hurly Burly: The International Lacanian Journal of Psychoanalysis* no. 8 (2012), 269–277, 270–271.

24 Lacan, "Note on the Father and Universalism," 10.

25 Jacques Lacan, *Television: A Challenge to the Psychoanalytic Establishment*, tr. D. Hollier, R. Krauss, and A. Michelson (New York: W. W. Norton, 1990), 32.

26 Ibid., 32–33.

27 Laurent, "Racism 2.0," 218.

28 Jacques Lacan, *Le Séminaire. Livre XIX: … ou pire* (Paris: Seuil, 2011), 235–236.

29 Jacques-Alain Miller, "Extimité," in *Lacanian Theory of Discourse: Subject, Structure, and Society*, ed. Mark Bracher, Marshall W. Alcorn jr, Ronald J. Corthell, and Françoise Massardier-Kenney, tr. Françoise Massardier-Kenney (New York University Press, 1994), 77. For a clarification on the small other (a) and the big Other (A) in Lacan's teaching, see Jacques-Alain Miller "The Pivot of the Desire of the Other," tr. A. R. Price, *Psychoanalytical Notebooks*, no. 18 (2009), 7–26.

30 Slavoj Žižek develops this line of argument in relation to a number of films in his essay "Love Thy Neighbor? No Thanks," in *The Psychoanalysis of Race*, ed. Christopher Lane (New York: Columbia University Press, 1998). He writes there that "One must begin with the subject's elementary relationship

to the traumatic kernel of jouissance structurally unassimilable into his or her symbolic universe. Racism confronts us with the enigma of the Other, which cannot be reduced to the partner in symbolic communication; it confronts us with the enigma of that which, in ourselves, resists the universal frame of symbolic communication" (155). He develops this further in Slavoj Žižek, *Refugees, Terror and Other Troubles with the Neighbors: Against the Double Blackmail* (Brooklyn: Melville House, 2016), see in particular 83–84.

31 Miller, "Extimité," 79.
32 Miller, "Extimate Enemies," 38.
33 Miller, "Extimité," 80.
34 Miller, "Extimate Enemies," 39.
35 Miller, "Extimité," 81.
36 Miller, "Extimate Enemies," 34.
37 Ibid., 39.
38 Ibid., 37.
39 Marie-Hélène Brousse, "The Sex of the Symptom," *The Lacanian Review: Hurly Burly* 3 (2017) 133–136, 135.
40 Tom Svolos, *Twenty-First Century Psychoanalysis* (London: Karnac, 2017), 237.
41 Laurent, "Racism 2.0," 222.

PART III

Beyond Lacan

CHAPTER 9

Lacan and Disability Studies*

Anna Mollow

When Jacques Lacan delivered his essay "The Mirror Stage as Formative of the *I* Function as Revealed in Psychoanalytic Experience" to the Sixteenth International Conference of Psychoanalysts on July 17, 1949, the disability activist and writer Connie Panzarino, whose life story is chronicled in her memoir *The Me in the Mirror*, was approximately one-and-a-half-years old. If Lacan is correct that the developmental milestone that he terms "the mirror stage" is first experienced between the ages of six and eighteen months, then Panzarino was immersed in the mirror stage at the same time that Lacan was composing his pathbreaking essay. This temporal coincidence between the lives of the authors of "The Mirror Stage" and *The Me in the Mirror* is accompanied by numerous thematic similarities between the two texts. As suggested by each title's inclusion of both the word "mirror" and a first-person pronoun, Lacan's essay and Panzarino's book each foregrounds questions about selfhood and specularity. These mutual interests may arise from yet another point of contact between the writers: Panzarino and Lacan each trained as therapists, and *The Me in the Mirror* and "The Mirror Stage" each contains insights gleaned from its author's clinical work.

But here, it would seem, the similarities end. Most obviously, Panzarino's and Lacan's texts differ in terms of tone, style, and subject position. Lacan, writing in the voice of an imperious and sometimes inscrutable continental male psychoanalyst, is known for the denseness

* In a section of her acknowledgments that I find particularly moving, in part because it resonates with my own experiences as a disabled writer, Panzarino offers thanks to the assistants who typed and transcribed her memoir. Like Panzarino, I wish to express my gratitude to the devoted and hardworking typists and transcriptionists who made it possible for me to compose this chapter: my warm thanks to Chris Dunsmore, Mellissa Rohrer, and Eden Trenor. I am also indebted to Jane Arlene Herman and Kent Puckett for the many hours that they each spent discussing Lacan, Panzarino, and disability with me; their immensely insightful feedback has greatly strengthened this chapter.

and difficulty of his language, his disdain toward "American ego psychology," and, according to some readers, his sexist and homophobic biases. By contrast, Panzarino, who identifies as a disabled woman, a lesbian, and a feminist, recounts her personal and political development, forged through a lifelong involvement in US political movements, in accessible, down-to-earth prose. The genres of "The Mirror Stage" and *The Me in the Mirror* also differ: Lacan's essay is a theoretical treatise comprising less than ten pages, while Panzarino's book is an autobiography spanning seventeen chapters. Moreover, divergent theoretical and intellectual groundings inform Lacan's and Panzarino's writings. While Lacan delineates a process of subject formation that he describes as nearly universal – "the child," "the subject," or "the little man" experiences "the mirror stage," which affords psychoanalytic knowledge about "an ontological structure of the human world" (75; 76) – Panzarino tells a story about developing a minoritized political identity; because she is disabled, female, and lesbian, Panzarino's life experiences and self-understanding depart from those of an imagined "universal" (i.e., non-disabled, heterosexual, and male) subject.[1] Finally, Panzarino and Lacan approach their topics from opposing vantage points within a paradigmatic doctor–patient relationship. Lacan, who theorizes the aggressiveness that informs transference in the psychoanalytic clinic, seeks to understand why patients often evince hostility toward their analysts. Conversely, Panzarino, who recounts being mistreated by medical providers, asks why doctors are often hostile to disabled people.

But despite – or perhaps because of – the many contrasts between "The Mirror Stage" and *The Me in the Mirror*, reading the two texts together can enhance our understanding of each. In this chapter, I juxtapose Lacan's and Panzarino's accounts of subject formation, specularity, identity, aggressiveness, disability, and sexuality. In doing so, I stage a dialogue between two fields, disability studies and psychoanalysis, that have historically unfolded separately.[2] Because psychoanalytic theory has a history of pathologizing disabled people, disability scholars have tended to avoid psychoanalysis.[3] And psychoanalytic theorists have tended to ignore disability studies, perhaps suspecting that this discipline's ties to identity-centered activism conflict with the emphasis of psychoanalysis on the instability of identity. But as we shall see, psychoanalysis and disability studies each, albeit in very different ways, radically undermines constructions of stable – or, one might say, able – egos and identities. I will argue that a collaboration between disability studies and psychoanalysis can benefit both fields.

This chapter is divided into three sections. In the first, I apply Lacan's postulation of an intrasubjective antagonism between an "ideal-I" and a "*corps morcelé*" to the terrain of disability studies, to theorize suffering as a significant aspect of many disabled people's embodied experiences. In this way, I show that Lacanian theory can complicate foundational arguments in disability studies, which maintain that disability should *not* be understood as suffering. In the second part, I perform a Lacanian analysis of Panzarino's memoir, through which I elucidate psychic dynamics that contribute to the oppression of disabled people; specifically, I argue that repression of a psychic force that I term "the disability drive" is an unrecognized cause of physical and rhetorical violence against disabled people. In the final section, I perform a Panzarinian analysis of Lacan's essay, in which I contrast Lacan's and Panzarino's representations of what I call "undocumented disabilities," that is, physical impairments for which medical professionals have not identified biological causes. I argue that Lacan's use of the diagnostic category "hysteria" buttresses the fiction of a self-sufficient ego and depicts people with undocumented disabilities as less self-aware than people without such disabilities, while Panzarino's account of her impairment undermines faith in the ego's supremacy and opens up possibilities for destigmatizing disability.

Identity, Impairment, and the Body in Pieces: Bringing Disability Studies and Psychoanalysis Together

In the final pages of *The Me in the Mirror*, Panzarino recounts a speech that she gave at the National Lesbian and Gay Pride March in Washington in 1987. Her speech concludes with a call for disability access: "It's '*nice*' that they built a ramp so I could get up here to speak to you, but why are the steps in the front and the ramp in the back? Next time I want to see that ramp out front!" (259–260). In fact, the ramp was not only at the back of the stage but also poorly designed, "so steep that it took four people to help [Panzarino] up" (250). Access barriers such as these are part of daily life for disabled people. Throughout the world, oppression of people with disabilities is enforced through discrimination in employment, education, housing, and transportation; lack of access to appropriate medical care; violence and harassment; coerced sterilization and other unwanted medical procedures; and involuntary institutionalization in nursing homes and similar facilities. In poor countries, especially in the Global South, many disabled people lack basic necessities such as wheelchairs and life-saving medications.

From the time that she was in high school until her death, at age fifty-three, in 2001, Panzarino worked to end ableism, the system of social and cultural beliefs and practices that oppresses disabled people. Her activism took shape within the disability rights movement, whose influential "social model of disability" provides the foundation for disability studies. The social model posits a fundamental distinction between two terms, "impairment" (which refers to a bodily or mental condition) and "disability" (which signifies the social oppression of people with impairments).[4] Focusing on "disability," and dismissing "impairment" as politically irrelevant, the social model challenges the culturally hegemonic "medical model." The medical model defines disability in apolitical terms, casting it as a defect or disease afflicting an unfortunate individual. Thus, a medical model account of Panzarino's life might focus on her diagnosis with Spinal Muscular Atrophy (a condition in which the spinal nerves do not communicate properly with the body's voluntary muscles, causing weakness and paralysis), while a social model analysis would highlight the cultural and political obstacles that shaped her life. Panzarino underscores the social model's distinction between medical condition and systemic oppression when she recounts being denied funding for adaptive technology that would have enabled her to feed herself: "I wasn't angry about being disabled, I was angry about not being able to get what was available to make me able to function better with my disability" (235).

The social model was politically transformative. It laid the groundwork for the 1990 Americans with Disabilities Act and other legislation (some of which Panzarino herself helped write) that dramatically improved the quality of many disabled people's lives. Yet when proponents of the social model celebrate "positive" disability identities and insist that disability not be understood in terms of "suffering, tragedy, and loss," they marginalize those disabled people for whom suffering *is* a salient aspect of impairment – for example, people with chronic illnesses, pain, and/or psychiatric disabilities. In recent years, several disability scholars have drawn attention to this problem;[5] however, disability studies is still in the early stages of formulating epistemologies for theorizing suffering. In *The Me in the Mirror*, Panzarino acknowledges suffering, portraying the pain and sadness that she feels as her disability progresses (235, 255). In part for this reason, Panzarino's narrative and other disability autobiographies hover on the margins of disability studies; many disability scholars worry that narratives depicting disabled people suffering reinforce the widespread societal misperception that our lives lack value.[6]

As disability studies thinks through this dilemma, it may be help-ful to engage Lacan's "The Mirror Stage." In Lacan's telling, the mirror stage begins when a child first glimpses the possibility of understanding itself as an autonomous subject, distinct from its external environment. Typically, this phase begins when a child is positioned in front of a mir-ror, held up by a caregiver or supported by a walker. Catching sight of its refection, the infant lunges forward, jubilant and excited, and freezes the image in its mind; at this moment, "the *I* is precipitated in a primordial form" (76). The child envisions its mirror reflection as an "ideal-I," a template of the integrated self that it might become. The process of ego formation that Lacan calls the mirror stage – which signifies not only a specific developmental phase occurring in the early months of childhood but also a structural component of subjects' self-understandings through-out our lives – is founded on a "misrecognition": no person can ever fully embody the ideal-I, as this phantasmatic image of formal integrity always coexists in reciprocal relationship to another immutable aspect of our selves, the "*corps morcelé*," or "body in pieces."

The image of a "body in pieces" is highly evocative of disability, as are the tropes that Lacan uses to describe the corporeal limitations con-straining the child who lunges toward, but can never be identical with, the ideal-I. In contrast to the picture in the mirror, which appears as a "gestalt" of "totality," the actual child remains "trapped" in "motor impo-tence and nursling dependence," limited by "malaise and motor unco-ordination of the neonatal months" and "prematurity of birth" (76, 78). Although Lacan does not refer here to any particular impairment – rather, he envisions a non-disabled child passing through a normative develop-mental process – his language evokes commonplace representations of disabled bodies. One effect of Lacan's essay, then, is to suggest that the process of ego formation is inseparable from a fantasy of transcending dis-ability. Indeed, Lacan's references to the "motor impotence" and "depend-ence" that the child experiences when contemplating its reflection resonate with Panzarino's childhood struggles with mobility impairment. "It was maddening to be so immobile," Panzarino recalls, describing the enormous energy that it took to engage in activities such as coloring with crayons or playing with a doll; her efforts often left her panting and sweating with exhaustion (22).

Taking these connections further, one can map Lacan's distinction between the ideal-I and the body in pieces on to the social model's divi-sion between disability and impairment: "disability" (or political identity) resembles Lacan's notion of the ideal-I as a totalized form of the self, while "impairment" (or bodily suffering and incapacity) is similar to Lacan's trope of the body in pieces, a disavowed side of the self against which the "armor of an alienating identity" defends (78). The social model's construction of disability identities as sources of empowerment and pride can be seen as a defense of the ideal-I, a defense bound up with a fantasy of having overcome the body in pieces. This points to a paradox: although developed to challenge ableism, the social model's fantasy of transcending the *corps morcelé* nonetheless has ableist implications. These can be further illuminated by reading Lacan's theory of the mirror stage in relation to Panzarino's story. According to Lacan, ego formation involves a fantasy of progressing from "a fragmented image of the body to ... an 'orthopedic' form of its totality" (78). Lacan's use of the word "orthopedic" is echoed in Panzarino's description of medical treatments that she underwent as a child (78). Panzarino's disability prevented her from standing or walking, and her doctors directed her parents to strap her, for an hour each day, into braces that suspended her body in a standing position. These orthopedic devices caused severe pain, but Panzarino's parents forced her to endure this, along with other medical "tortures," because the doctors promised that doing so would eventually enable her to walk (17, 46). This promise was based entirely in fantasy; braces could do nothing to alter the corporeal facts of Panzarino's impairment, which, as her doctors knew, was caused by a malfunction in the nerves of her spine. Yet Panzarino's story is not unique. As disability scholars and activists point out, a deeply rooted cultural preoccupation with curing disability has punitive effects upon disabled people, who are routinely coerced – or, as in Panzarino's story, forced – to undergo harmful, painful, and ineffective medical procedures.[7] Framing this problem in Lacanian terms, one might say that the cultural imperative to cure disability is enforced in the name of "orthopedic totality." (And tellingly, the etymology of the word "orthopedic" signifies the "correction" of a "child.") "The Mirror Stage" thus helps elucidate psychic sources of social practices that seek to cure disability at all costs: such practices arise from a profound misrecognition, a fantasy that one could leave behind the body in pieces and realize the orthopedic totality of the ideal-I.

Yet while disability studies' social model has enabled potent critiques of the medical profession's mistreatment of disabled people in the name of a *literal* orthopedic totality, the model's celebration of positive disability identities nonetheless upholds a *figurative* version of this ideal. As we have seen, the social model constructs positive identities by separating the concepts of disability and suffering; in doing so, it represses the ways in which impairment threatens to render us as bodies, and minds, in pieces. The danger of defining disability identity in opposition to impairment, or to what Lacan calls the *corps morcelé*, is that other minoritized subjects – for example, people with psychiatric disabilities, chronic illnesses, or pain, who often do suffer as a result of our impairments – will be called upon to perform the cultural labor of figuring the impaired bodymind, or the bodymind in pieces. If disability studies resists accounting for those aspects of our selves that we experience as broken, insufficient, or impaired, we risk projecting an intrinsic disablement, residing within all subjects, on to stigmatized cultural minorities, who are blamed and punished for the threat that they are imagined to pose to the integrity of selves and societies. Instead, then, of insisting that disability is only neutral human variation, and not "suffering, tragedy, or loss," a Lacanian-informed disability studies might actively amplify the ways in which disability does, and perhaps *should*, register as bodies and minds in pieces.

Aggressiveness, Sexuality, and the Disability Drive: A Lacanian Reading of Panzarino

"The Mirror Stage" and *The Me in the Mirror* both allude briefly to the Holocaust. Lacan's essay, delivered shortly after World War II, suggests that the "misrecognition" that characterizes the ego's defensive structures can, in extreme materializations, lead to a "concentration-camp form" of social relationality (80). Panzarino's book, which describes her growing up in the postwar years, has as its epigraph a poem by the author, "On Disabled Children":

> Don't rip these children
>   from their wombs
>   merely because they have no limbs
>   with which to grasp
>
> Blind eyes plead
>   not to be destroyed
>   like the broken toys
>   the Nazis cooked
>   to perfect the master race (2)

The lines, "the broken toys/the Nazis cooked/to perfect the master race" refer to German physicians' murdering of disabled people during the Third Reich. The techniques that the Nazis used to murder millions of

Jewish people in gas chambers were first developed as part of Hitler's "Euthanasia Program," in which physicians killed "incurable" patients, whose lives they deemed "not worth living."[8]

Panzarino's poem anticipates a central theme of her book: a eugenics-informed belief that doctors have the moral authority to decide whether disabled people should live or die is not unique to Nazi Germany; it also operates in contemporary US society. As a young adult, Panzarino develops a bleeding stomach ulcer; after she is diagnosed, she lies in her hospital bed listening to two doctors debating the best course of action: "The first doctor argued that [blood] transfusions and extensive treatment would be a waste of time and money, since I was disabled and going to die anyway. The second doctor argued that a transfusion really wasn't that expensive, and that antacids, jello and milk were not considered extensive treatments" (118). Fortunately, the second doctor wins the argument, and Panzarino receives the treatment that she needs. Yet she continues to encounter medical professionals who assume that disabled people's lives lack value. Later in her life, when Panzarino consults with a neurologist who specializes in her disability, he tries to persuade her to participate in a study designed to discover a way to "screen out for the gene" that causes her condition. "Wouldn't it be wonderful if a woman could have amniocentesis and avoid having a child with Spinal Muscular Atrophy?" he asks (258). Like most disability activists and scholars, Panzarino supports women's access to abortion but objects to the state's and the medical profession's promotion of *selective* abortion and coerced sterilization to prevent the birth of disabled, non-white, and poor children.[9] Sobbing to her partner after the appointment with the doctor who wants to "screen out for" her disability, Panzarino wonders, "When will they learn that eliminating life isn't the same as eliminating disability?" (258).

Lacan's "The Mirror Stage" can enhance Panzarino's social critique by illuminating psychic dynamics that lead to hostility toward disabled people. Consider, for example, Lacan's remarks about the "aggressiveness" that informs "all relations with others," even those "involving aid of the most good-Samaritan variety" (79). The doctors whom Panzarino encounters exemplify this "good-Samaritan" aggressiveness; their ostensibly benevolent actions enact violence against disabled people. Aggressiveness, Lacan suggests, arises from the misrecognition initiated in the mirror stage. The dyad of the ideal-I and the body in pieces formed during this stage is intrinsically antagonistic; the very existence of the body in pieces imperils the imagined unity of the ideal-I, which is invested in the fantasy that it is the sum total of the self. For this reason, the ideal-I seeks to destroy the body in pieces – and, because it cannot accept this fragmented body as part of itself, it misrecognizes the source of the threat, attributing it to something outside itself. Applying these insights to disability politics, one can surmise that hostility toward disabled people may result from a similar misrecognition; perhaps the dominant culture projects the *corps morcelé* on to disabled people and imagines that the ideal-I could triumph over the body in pieces if disabled people could be eliminated.

These dynamics are dramatized in a passage from Panzarino's memoir that uncannily replicates numerous elements of Lacan's theorization of the mirror stage. When she is about four years old, Panzarino is sitting in her living room, wishing that she could run and play. She looks across the room and sees an image of herself in the mirror (20). This "other Connie in the mirror" asks Panzarino, "Why don't you come over here and dance with me on my side of the mirror?" (20). When Panzarino explains that she cannot walk, the "me in the mirror" refuses to believe her. "If *I* can, *you* can," the image insists (21). The "other Connie" can be read as a figure for the ideal-I; it reminds Panzarino of birthday and Christmas photographs of her, in which her disability is not visible; her mother keeps these pictures in photo albums as idealized images of her child. In keeping with Lacan's emphasis on the aggressiveness that derives from "the alienated *I* function," Panzarino's "me in the mirror" is mean. Insisting that Panzarino could walk, it echoes the words of Panzarino's healthcare providers: "You can walk if you want to," charges one of her physical therapists, adding, "I have a little boy younger than you and he runs around and climbs stairs. He's tough" (37, 38). The physical therapist's goading shows how fortifying what Lacan calls the ego's "rigid structure" (reified by Panzarino's physical therapist as the image of a "tough" boy) can incite violence against anything or anyone (for example, a girl who is unable to walk) that threatens the fantasy of the ideal-I as a gestalt of corporeal totality.

Aggression toward disabled people plays out in several scenes in which Panzarino's mother verbally or physically attacks her. Once, when Panzarino indicates that she needs to be taken to the bathroom, her mother hits her and screams that she hates her. The abuse verges on sexual when, after taking her off the toilet, Panzarino's enraged mother begins "pinching [her] legs and [her] bottom" (31). Panzarino's narrative suggests that the sexual component of this abuse is part of a broader pattern of sexual oppression of disabled people. In another scene, Panzarino is rocking back and forth, masturbating to distract herself from discomfort in her bladder while she waits for her mother to assist her.

"I know what you're doing, you stop that business," her mother snaps (22). Although reprimanding children for masturbating was common in the 1950s, Panzarino faced far more constraints on her sexuality than her non-disabled peers. Her family members tell her that no one will want to marry her, and her friends make a point of not talking about sex when she is around. On one occasion, Panzarino is not allowed to go out for pizza with a fourteen-year-old boy who is also disabled: "somehow, because we were disabled, there were different rules" (86).

Lacan's theorization of the mirror stage can help us understand why the dominant culture desexualizes disabled people. Lacan argues that although subjects aspire to embody the ideal-I, we nonetheless continually return to our state as bodies in pieces. In "Aggressiveness in Psychoanalysis," an earlier essay that also theorizes the mirror stage, Lacan finds evidence for a compulsion to embody the *corps morcelé* in patients' frequent dreams of "dismemberment, dislocation, evisceration, devouring, and bursting open of the body."[10] Such dreams evoke Freud's discussion of nightmares suffered by survivors of war or railway disasters. Because these nightmares phantasmatically return patients to scenes of pain and danger, Freud cites them as examples of a "compulsion to repeat," a concept that he links to his theory of the "death drive."[11] Elsewhere, I have argued that the force Freud calls the death drive would more accurately be termed "the disability drive."[12] After all, dreams of reliving trauma, or of repetitively reverting to the body in pieces, are fantasies less of biological death than of physical and mental disability.

The disability drive exerts a compulsion that is inseparable from sexuality.[13] Psychoanalytic theory demonstrates that sex is disabling: it induces losses of mental mastery and bodily control, causes subjects to feel helpless and dependent, and occasions influxes of overwhelming sensory stimuli, which make the body and mind suffer. Thus, the sexual drive is also a drive toward disability. Additional links between sex and disability come to light in Freud's account of the emergence of childhood sexuality: the child's "inadequate stage of development" prevents it from realizing its sexual fantasies, thus producing "painful feelings" of "loss and failure"; loss, failure, and insufficient development are all common tropes for disability.[14] Similarly, Lacan connects humans' "prematurity of birth" to a "body in pieces," which haunts our libidinal relations. This frustrating sense of incapacity is never overcome; people are always impelled, in excess of our egos' demands for control and self-sufficiency, to reenact this constitutive merging of sex and disability.

This may be one reason that disabled people – and disabled people's sexuality – incite such hostility. Because disability reminds us of the ways in which sexuality disables all subjects, images of disability may have an unrecognized erotic appeal; yet this sexual pull is felt as intolerable by the rigidly armored ego, which desperately wants to preserve its fantasy of totality. Subjects therefore deny their determination by the disability drive, rejecting disabled people as undesirable and figuring disabled sexuality as unthinkable. Alternatively, disabled people are often fetishized or portrayed as hypersexual; these reactions also arise from repression of the disability drive, as they depict disabled people as irremediably "other" and install what Alison Kafer calls a "desire/disgust" binary, in which disability is seen as desirable to fetishists but disgusting to everyone else.[15] Repression of the disability drive results in aggressiveness toward disabled people, which, as Panzarino shows, is enacted as medical abuse, parental rage, and state-sponsored genocide.

The Me in the Mirror thwarts the culture's repression of the disability drive by subverting the myth that disabled people do not experience or elicit sexual desire. Boldly foregrounding her sexuality, Panzarino recounts a lengthy succession of crushes, sexual relationships, and love affairs, from the boy in high school who lay pressed up against her in bed (but said that no one would marry her because of her disability) to the female teachers she fantasized about, her long-term relationship with Ron Kovic (author of *Born on the Fourth of July*), her coming out as a lesbian, and decades of emotional and sexual relationships with women (one of which began with sex in the back of her van at the Michigan Women's Music Festival with a woman who had chased after her, shouting, "I'm in love with you! I've read all about you and saw your picture in [a] book") (222).

"Hysteria" and Undocumented Disability: A Panzarinian Reading of Lacan

The Me in the Mirror opens with an anecdote that occurred when Panzarino was in a Master's program training to be an art therapist. Panzarino is working with Eddie, a five-year-old boy with cerebral palsy who has been making the same artwork week after week: a clay pie, which he cuts in half, saying, "I don't want this part, that's the yucky part" (3). Panzarino interprets the boy's behavior as symbolic of a wish to eliminate his paralyzed left arm. She talks to the boy about her own paralyzed hand, noting, "I like the way it looks and the way it feels" (3).

Soon after, Eddie stops removing "yucky" parts from his artwork (3). If one were to analyze this scene through the lens of Lacanian theory, one might read Eddie's excision of undesired portions of his artwork as an attempt to fortify the ideal-I by rejecting the disabled body, or the body in pieces. A Lacanian analysis of this scene might also point to the futility of Eddie's actions: rather than producing the totality that he seems to seek, cutting off the "yucky" portions of the clay pies generates what Lacan might call an "imago of the fragmented body," that is, an object that is broken into pieces (85).

Yet Panzarino and Lacan have different assumptions about the purpose of therapy. While Panzarino helps her clients produce artwork that mirrors an internal sense of wholeness, one can imagine Lacan dismissing this approach as "American ego psychology." Rather than helping patients solidify a sense of themselves as coherent subjects, Lacan instead presses them to "untie" or "sever" their attachments to stable identities (80). But it would be an oversimplification to claim that "The Mirror Stage" destabilizes egos and *The Me in the Mirror* shores them up. As we shall see, Panzarino's memoir undermines the stable – or able – ego in ways that Lacan's essay defends against: while Panzarino emphasizes bodies' vulnerability and stresses the limits of psychic control over corporeality, Lacan at times represses these aspects of embodied experience. This contrast will become evident in my discussion of the two writers' divergent accounts of what I call "undocumented disabilities," that is, impairments for which contemporary medical technology cannot identify definitive biological causes.[16] While Lacan attributes such impairments to "hysteria," Panzarino challenges medical professionals' tendency to assume that unexplained physical symptoms must have psychological origins. Extending Panzarino's critique, I argue below that Lacan's use of the concept of hysteria functions in ways that directly contradict his stated aims: although the concept of hysteria may seem to undermine the fiction of the ego's supremacy, the disease category in fact has the effect of upholding this fiction.

A central insight of "The Mirror Stage" is that the ego, or ideal-I, is a fantasy. Rather than proposing a linear progression in which the *corps morcelé* gives way to an integrated self as the infant matures, Lacan suggests that the body in pieces paradoxically comes *after* the ideal-I. Only from the vantage point of a subject that imagines itself as an integrated, totalized ego can a contrasting representation of an (ostensibly transcended) fragmented body can be constructed.[17] But even though Lacan's theory of the mirror stage undermines the fiction of the ego as a self-sufficient totality, his construction of "hysteria" has the opposite effect: it upholds fantasies of autonomous selfhood. To show how this happens, let me begin by sketching out the grounding assumptions of Lacan's construction of hysteria. According to Lacan, hysteria is one possible manifestation of a subject's attraction to images of the *corps morcelé*: the imago of the fragmented body, he claims, finds expression in "the hysteric's fantasmatic anatomy" (78). This assertion resonates with Freud's theory of hysteria; according to Freud, unexplained bodily symptoms result from "conversion" of repressed psychic material into physical symptoms. Much as Freud contends that one of his patients experiences chronic pain in her legs as a way of expressing a sense of figuratively "having no support",[18] Lacan claims to have cured a supposedly hysterical girl of astasia-abasia (an inability to stand without assistance, and a lack of motor coordination in walking) simply by remarking that she had not had her father's "support."[19] Panzarino's disability strongly resembles that of Lacan's patient; Panzarino is unable to walk, cannot stand without assistance, and has great difficulty balancing, even when seated. Once, when her father places her on the toilet and walks away too quickly, Panzarino falls on her head (22). Panzarino's narrative and Lacan's anecdote about his patient are so similar – each involving mobility disability, balance impairment, and literal and figurative lack of paternal support – that one can imagine that, had Panzarino consulted with a Lacanian psychoanalyst, she might have been told that the source of her disability was "hysteria."

Panzarino does not recount having been diagnosed with hysteria, but for the first several years of her life her doctors cannot identify a biological cause for her condition, and they imply that her disability is psychogenic. The suspicion that Panzarino's impairment lacked an organic cause was often conveyed in moralistic terms: "When I couldn't do the exercises, my father said I was lazy and my mother lost patience and hit me" (46). In some ways, Panzarino's parents' understanding of her disability diverges from Lacan's construction of hysteria: rather than supposing that she was deliberately choosing not to walk, a Lacanian account of Panzarino's disability might posit that she was *unconsciously* converting psychic wishes into physical symptoms. But although the claim that hysteria arises from unconscious motives might seem to make the diagnostic label less stigmatizing, this formulation actually compounds the social oppression of people with undocumented disabilities, as it depicts us as "epistemologically disabled," that is, as lacking a self-awareness that people without undocumented disabilities are presumed to possess.[20] This dynamic plays out repeatedly in psychoanalytic theory – as when Lacan claims to have cured his patient of astasia-abasia without "her having understood anything" (88).

Psychoanalysis postulates that hysteria has multiple, sometimes apparently contradictory, causes. In addition to those that I have just discussed, another etiological contributor to hysteria, psychoanalytic theory claims, is an excessively defensive ego. This complex causal model is encapsulated in Freud's famous remark that "hysteria is the negative of the perversions."[21] By this, he does not mean that hysteria and perversion are opposites of each other; rather, he contends that so-called hysterics have strong urges toward sexual "perversion" *and* that they are particularly inclined to repress such urges. If one were to recast Freud's aphorism in Lacanian terms, the claim might be that hysterics are libidinally compelled to manifest the body in pieces *and* that they are at the same time deeply invested in fortifying the ideal-I as a defense against this compulsion. The notion that undocumented disabilities result from a too-strenuous defense of one's ego or bodily integrity informs social and medical reactions to Panzarino's disability. For instance, one doctor questions her parents, "Do you allow your daughter to get exercise? I mean, little children need to run around, play" (16). Similarly, when Panzarino's mother holds her on her lap at a social gathering, one of the guests asks, "Why don't you put her down and let her run around? Don't be so overprotective" (29). In these stereotypical representations of people with undocumented disabilities, "hysteria" emerges as a sign for an excessively defensive ego, a self unwilling to risk its own shattering.

But perhaps it is not people with undocumented disabilities, but instead the diagnostic category of hysteria, that phantasmatically stabilizes the fiction of a self-sufficient ego. The ego, Lacan suggests, is the part of our selves that puts its faith in the value of *cogito*. This Cartesian construct asserts a supremacy of mind over matter, imagining that what one *thinks* is coextensive with what one *is*. Psychoanalysis, Lacan emphasizes in the first paragraph of "The Mirror Stage," is fundamentally "at odds with any philosophy stemming directly from the *cogito*" (75). Yet this Cartesian value seems to be inadvertently reified in Lacan's construction of "hysteria." The notion that so-called hysterical symptoms result from a "conversion" of the mental into the physical images a triumphing of mind over matter; the theory of hysteria discounts the importance of the body as a locus that exceeds the imagined totality of the ideal-I. Although Lacan seeks to undermine belief in the primacy of the ego, in his construction of "hysteria" he apparently overlooks something important: to attribute undocumented disabilities to "hysteria" is to envision the ego, that component of our selves which is capable of language, meaning-making, and metaphoric formulations, as possessing a power so total that it can govern even the remote reaches of the body – hence, Lacan's patient's supposed use of a mobility impairment as a trope for a lack of emotional support. But is the ego really this far-reaching entity? Certainly, one must allow that bodies suffer illness, pain, and incapacity for all sorts of reasons that have nothing to do with one's fantasies or desires, conscious or unconscious – and surely, one must acknowledge that this happens regardless of whether current medical technology can document an impairment's etiology. Also, how likely does it really seem that our psyches can direct our bodies in the way that Freud and Lacan imagine – that one's mind, wishing to communicate distress about, say, a parent's failure to provide emotional support, can instruct the body to metaphorize this distress by paralyzing its legs? Our bodies' radical vulnerability, and the frustrating limits of our egos' ability to control whether (and in what manner) we become ill or disabled, are occluded in Lacan's construction of hysteria but underscored in Panzarino's memoir. As we have seen, Panzarino's disability, which her doctors initially described as psychogenic, resulted not from repressed psychic fantasies but instead from a genetic disorder that impaired the function of her spinal nerves. Disregarding the possibility that undocumented disabilities may have as-yet-unrecognized biological causes, the theory of hysteria forgets – or, more precisely, represses – the ways in which all subjects are at risk of falling, without their consent or desire, into the state of a body in pieces.

In critiquing the construction of "hysteria" in psychoanalysis, I am going further than critics who claim that the ego cannot overrule "the language of symptoms." Instead, I am challenging the assumption that undocumented physical symptoms necessarily have psychological meanings in the first place. The oft-heard psychoanalytic claim that, as Jane Gallop puts it, bodily symptoms "are ways of speaking" – that is, of expressing latent psychic wishes – blocks recognition of the *corps morcelé* by eliding the existence of the body as a realm that is inaccessible, and indeed alien, to meaning-construction, or to "ways of speaking."[22] In this way, the theory of hysteria upholds the fantasy of ego totality that Lacan's formulation of the mirror stage seeks to undo. In contrast to Panzarino's account of undocumented disability, which emphasizes the aleatory aspects of embodiment (for no particular "reason," she was born with a genetically produced impairment), the theory of hysteria hews to a rationalistic, Cartesian model of causality, in which physical symptoms that cannot easily be explained by medical tests are assumed to have psychological meanings.[23] While for non-disabled people, this may be a comforting way of envisioning disability (as it exempts one from confronting the possibility that one might oneself, for no psychologically meaningful reason, become disabled or ill), the theory of hysteria compounds the oppression of people with undocumented disabilities – for example, it licenses Panzarino's parents and healthcare providers to claim that her symptoms were her own fault.

The notion of hysteria buttresses the fantasy of an intact ego in another way, too: the diagnostic category enables psychoanalysts to fortify their own egos at the expense of people with undocumented disabilities. To make a diagnosis of "hysteria" is to imagine a sharp contrast between a patient who, in Lacan's words, has not "understood anything" and a doctor who appears to possess superior knowledge. By reifying this unequal distribution of epistemological privilege, Lacan exempts himself from the important argument with which he concludes his essay: "aggressiveness ... underlies the activities of the philanthropist, the idealist, the pedagogue, and even the reformer" (81). If one applies a Panzarinian critique of ableism to Lacan's observation, it becomes clear that "the doctor" and "the psychoanalyst" also belong on Lacan's list of cultural authorities whose activities, despite their apparent good-Samaritan intentions, are propelled in part by aggression toward those whom they claim to help.

Yet Lacan's and Panzarino's radically different representations of undocumented disability should not be taken as reasons for psychoanalytic theory and disability studies to maintain a distance from one another. On the contrary, I have undertaken a comparative study of "The Mirror Stage" and *The Me in the Mirror* to press these disciplines into closer contact. As we have seen, each of these fields has generated insights that the other needs: disability studies' analyses of the social structures that oppress disabled people, and psychoanalytic theory's expositions of the psychic dynamics that shape the construction of selves, can illuminate each other in important ways. Perhaps the dialogue between Jacques Lacan and Connie Panzarino that I have staged in this chapter could be a starting point for future conversations between psychoanalytic theory and disability studies.

Notes

1 Unless otherwise noted, all in-text citations of Lacan refer to Jacques Lacan, "The Mirror Stage as Formative of the *I* Function as Revealed in Psychoanalytic Experience," in *Écrits*, tr. Bruce Fink (New York: W. W. Norton, 2006), 75–81 and all in-text citations of Panzarino refer to Connie Panzarino, *The Me in the Mirror* (Seattle: Seal, 1994).

2 For exceptions, see Brian Watermeyer, *Towards a Contextual Psychology of Disablism* (London: Routledge, 2013); Margrit Shildrick, *Dangerous Discourses of Disability, Subjectivity, and Sexuality* (New York: Palgrave Macmillan, 2009); Dan Goodley, "Social Psychoanalytic Disability Studies," *Disability and Society* 26, 6 (2011), 715–728, available at www.tandfonline .com/doi/abs/10.1080/09687599.2011.602863.

3 See Sigmund Freud, "On Narcissism: An Introduction," in *The Standard Edition of the Psychological Works of Sigmund Freud, volume XIV*, tr. and ed. James Strachey et al. (London: Hogarth, 1914), 79–104; Freud, "Some Character Types Met with in Psycho-Analytic Work," in *The Freud Reader*, ed. Peter Gay (New York: W. W. Norton, 1989), 589–593. For critiques of psychoanalytic theorists' pathologization of disabled people, see Tobin Siebers, "Tender Organs, Narcissism, and Identity Politics," in *Disability Studies: Enabling the Humanities*, ed. Sharon L. Snyder, Brenda Jo Brueggemann, and Rosemarie Garland-Thomson (New York: MLA, 2002), 40–55, 45; Adrienne Harris and Dana Wideman, "The Construction of Gender and Disability in Early Attachment," in *Women with Disabilities: Essays in Psychology, Culture, and Politics*, ed. Michelle Fine and Adrienne Asch (Philadelphia: Temple University Press, 1988), 115–138, 117.

4 UPIAS, *Fundamental Principles of Disability*. London: Union of Physically Impaired against Segregation, 1976, available at http://disability-studies .leeds.ac.uk/files/library/UPIAS-fundamental-principles.pdf.

5 See Liz Crow, "Including All of Our Lives: Renewing the Social Model of Disability," in *Exploring the Divide: Illness and Disability*, ed. Colin Barnes and Geof Mercer (Leeds: Disability, 1996), 55–73; Susan Wendell, *The Rejected Body: Feminist Philosophical Reflections on Disability* (New York: Routledge, 1996); Anna Mollow, "'When *Black* Women Start Going on Prozac': Race, Gender, and Mental Illness in Meri Nana-Ama Danquah's *Willow Weep for Me." MELUS* 31.3 (2006): 67–99, available at https:// www.jstor.org/stable/30029652; Margaret Price, "The Bodymind Problem and the Possibilities of Pain," *Hypatia* 30, 1 (Winter 2015), 268–284, available at http://onlinelibrary.wiley.com/doi/10.1111/hypa.12127/full; Alyson Patsavas, "Recovering a Cripistemology of Pain: Leaky Bodies, Connective Tissue, and Feeling Discourse," *Journal of Literary and Cultural Disability Studies* 8, 2 (Summer 2014), 203–218.

6 See David T. Mitchell and Sharon L. Snyder, "Introduction: Disability Studies and the Double Bind of Representation," in *The Body and Physical Difference*, ed. David T. Mitchell and Sharon L. Snyder (Ann Arbor: University of Michigan Press, 1997), 1–31, 11; Lennard Davis, *Enforcing Normalcy: Disability, Deafness, and the Body* (New York: Verso, 1995), 4.

7 See Anne Finger, *Elegy for a Disease: A Personal and Cultural History of Polio* (New York: St. Martin's Press, 2006); Jim Ferris, *The Hospital Poems* (Charlotte: Main Street Rag Publishing Company, 2004).

8 Lucy S. Dawidowicz, *The War against the Jews, 1933–1945* (New York: Bantam, 1975), 131–134; Hugh Gregory Gallagher, *By Trust Betrayed: Patients, Physicians, and the License to Kill in the Third Reich* (St. Petersburg: Vandamere, 1995), xiv–xv.

9 On disability, race, and selective abortion, see Alison Kafer, *Feminist, Queer, Crip* (Bloomington and Indianapolis: Indiana University Press, 2013), 161–168).

10 Jacques Lacan, "Aggressiveness in Psychoanalysis," in *Écrits*, tr. Bruce Fink (New York: W. W. Norton, 2006), 82–101, 85.

11 Sigmund Freud, *Beyond the Pleasure Principle*, tr. and ed. James Strachey (New York: W. W. Norton, 1961), 12.

12 Anna Mollow, "Is Sex Disability? Queer Theory and the Disability Drive," in *Sex and Disability*, ed. Robert McRuer and Anna Mollow (Durham, NC: Duke University Press, 2012), 285–312.

13 Ibid.

14 Freud, "Beyond the Pleasure Principle," 22.

15 Alison Kafer, "Desire and Disgust: My Ambivalent Adventures in Devoteeism," in *Sex and Disability*, ed. Robert McRuer and Anna Mollow (Durham, NC: Duke University Press, 2012), 331–354.

16 Anna Mollow, "Criphystemologies: What Disability Theory Needs to Know about Hysteria," *Journal of Literary and Cultural Disability Studies* 8, 2 (Summer 2014), 185–201.

17 See Jane Gallop, *Reading Lacan* (Ithaca: Cornell University Press, 1985), 78–84.

18 Sigmund Freud and Joseph Breuer, *Studies in Hysteria*, tr. James Strachey (New York: Basic Books, 2000), 178.

19 Lacan, "Aggressiveness in Psychoanalysis," 88.

20 Mollow, "Criphystemologies," 191.

21 See Sigmund Freud, *Dora: An Analysis of a Case of Hysteria*, ed. Philip Rieff (New York: Simon and Schuster, 1963), 43; Sigmund Freud, *Three Essays on the Theory of Sexuality*, tr. James Strachey (New York: Basic Books, 2002), 31.

22 Jane Gallop, "Keys to Dora," in *Dora's Case: Freud – Hysteria – Feminism*, ed. Charles Bernheimer and Claire Kahane, 2nd edn (New York: Columbia University Press, 1990), 200–220, 208.

23 See Freud, *Dora*, 34.

CHAPTER 10

Lacan and New Media

Clint Burnham

What can new media tell us about Lacan and how, in turn, can Lacan help us to think about new media? In this chapter I seek to understand how such instances of new media art as the selfie and digital simulations – but also digital or internet culture more broadly conceived – bring new, and what I will argue are *dialectical*, understandings to such mainstays of Lacanian theory as the mirror stage and the big Other. I begin, then, by considering how the selfie as practice brings to a critical function the Lacanian mirror stage: now understood vis-à-vis the painted self-portrait as well as celebrity and art photography. Narcissus is not a self-idolater, but a hacker. But that selfie, or the hacker, requires a network, and the network resides in the Cloud, and so now we have a digital collectivity, especially when the selfie and the Cloud are conceived of as antinomies. These digital relations, then, allow us to better understand the logical formalism of late Lacan, where lack means not only that there is no big Other but also that there is a virtual big Other.

The Selfie and the Mirror Stage

The selfie – a photographic self-portrait, often made with a smartphone, that is then posted to social media. If we can trace a history of self-portraits in traditional painting (Parmigianino's is only the most famous, but there's also Rembrandt), and then in photography (many of which are also examples of "mirror selfies"), this latest aesthetic form is marked by (is an event because of) being networked (shared), shot with a digital device ("handheld," which then means touched), and made by the subject viewing their own image as part of making the image. In these details of its making, but also its distribution and consumption, the selfie offers new ways of thinking about Lacan's mirror stage. The selfie is made with a digital device: that is, the phone is a mirror. This is both a specific function or practice (or "app" – let us say app is the new practice, and

185

therefore ideology) – you can get a make-up mirror on your phone. But you can also now realize that the device – the technology qua object – is entirely a mirror. From the narcissism of social media to its proliferation of visual media, the smartphone is the thing/frame through which we gain access to the digital imaginary. What the selfie does, I argue, is to make apparent that imaginary hegemony of the digital.[1]

The device, however, is also, like money or our underwear, insistently carnal (or at least *flesh* in Eric Santner's sense, a supplemental or ghostly extra layer to our own bodies), nestled as it is in our purses or pockets, next to our genitals or wallets.[2] It is like the mirror on which one snorts cocaine or touches up one's eye shadow, and then reinserts into one's purse. With the selfie, the imaginary acquires agency: the mirror here *does something*, it makes the picture happen. The mirror as agent means that when you look at the picture of yourself before you take the picture (I do not take photographs, I make photographs – so declares the Chilean artist Alfredo Jaar), you are "composing" the picture, your face, what is in the background, your expression. Your eye is working in the way of the modernist photographer – Hannah Hoch or Walker Evans. If Hoch made collage in her images of urbanity, Evans *found* it, found that collage in the street, the sharecropper's shack. That is, what one does when taking a photograph has a relationship to an important historical question in photography. This has to do with the relation between the photographer and the subject in terms of awareness, looking (the gaze), and the three-way triangulation between the subject, the photographer, and the lens. When we confront the rectangle of our phones, and then try to look not at our own image but at the lens in the corner or the top center, this considered practice means we are still dealing with scopic regimes of art photography. We revisit, that is, questions of how Evans worked under the hooded 8x10 camera (a camera that to this day takes a photograph with ten times the data storage of any digital image), or Thomas Struth, when he takes family photographs, stands next to the camera, so his subjects look at the lens "without" the illusion that they are looking at the photographer. With the selfie, we are both photographer and subject, and like Struth's subjects, we look not at ourselves, as alluring as that is, and instead at that lens. The photographed subject looks at the artist's eye via the lens.

Then the finger moves – it swipes or pushes or clicks (a movement makes a sound *and* a picture) and the photograph is taken – the selfie exists, a performance, an event, a document that is now in the digital archive.[3] Now you look at the photograph, engage in pragmatic aesthetics of keep it or trash it, though this temporal scheme has been changed by

Snapchat. Then, what happens to the file, the object, the photograph, the selfie? Maybe: no one sees it again (which is the case for many?). Some: are sent around, posted, seen by hundreds or thousands (most of whom are seeing many images every day). A few go viral. They are shared, commented upon, sometimes other visual responses. It goes beyond "liking" or the haters – the two extremes of online commentary – it participates in that online culture. (But they are also touched again). They are touched, and the touching, that neurotic flicking that is akin to scratching a dog or a horse behind the ears. The smartphone, one could say, is a nipple or a breast: it is in the imaginary, it *nourishes* us, as we turn to our Facebook or Instagram feed. That online culture, appropriately enough, is extremely caught in a narcissistic imaginary – sometimes because its members are quite young, but one encouraged by the apparent democracy of online commentary practices (as though everyone can talk to/listen to everyone).[4]

The selfie, then, can be thought of as a genre or practice that actually diagnoses or analyzes (it is an analytical discourse) the constitutive narcissism, the imaginary, of social media, of the digital. Within this paradigm, the media celebrity Kim Kardashian West is exemplary: her project of the selfie, as practice, as book, as ongoing digital meme, bears the brunt of that analysis (is an analysis of its own practice even as it carries out a critique of the larger digital event), and bears it, it should be said, on its own body, on her (and her posse's, her child's, her husband Kanye's) body as that imaginary "sack of organs," a body or face that transforms into a "duck face."[5]

But if the critical event of the selfie is that realization or coming-into-critique of the digital imaginary, there is also a utopian event of the selfie: and here we can turn to John Ashbery's poem on Paramagianino's painting, "Self-portrait in a Convex Mirror" (Ashbery's poem bears the same title as the painting: rendering the title into a master-signifier, a retroactive, that is, baptism of the phrase).[6] In its description of the painting and its import for thinking about the self-portrait qua discourse of subjectivity, Ashbery's poem is also a discourse *about* the discourse of writing about art (Ashbery worked as a critic for *Art News*). The poem performs what David Herd calls its "essayistic thrust," "making scholarly references (it quotes Vasari and Freedberg); offering etymological digressions (the word 'speculation', we are advised, derives from 'the Latin *speculum,* mirror'); and unpacking allusions that ordinarily readers might be expected to get for themselves ('As Berg said of a phrase in Mahler's Ninth;/Or, to quote Imogen in *Cymbeline*')."[7] But Ashbery's poem is not merely a tissue of academic citations, a poetic version of Lacan's university

discourse: rather, it is a poem that derives its form from the reflexivity of
Parmagianino's mirror. His "barber's mirror," for it will be remembered
that the artist had a mirror made on a "ball of wood" to help him paint
his distorted image. The shift from the mirror stage (the poem is "an
elegy for the mirror stage," as Jody Norton puts it) to reflexivity allows us
to think of the selfie not merely as a narcissistic meme but also as a form
of dialectics.[8] By this I mean that just as Parmagianino's painting is a bra-
vura display of foreshortened perspective, rendering the classical project
a moot one, so too Ashbery's poem's reflexivity (its self-consciousness)
reflects upon its own writing.

To better work out this reflexive, dialectical, aspect of my argument I
want to turn from Kardashian's selfies to the Canadian artist Tim Lee's
work. Note how these two cultural examples are dialectically related (but
also immanently). In the first example, Kardashian's practice, the mirror is doubled. All too often, that is, in a reflexive gesture, Kardashian
takes a selfie in the mirror: it is a mirror of a mirror. Kim Kardashian is
not, as is often claimed, the Andy Warhol of the selfie; rather, she is the
Dan Graham of social media, bringing out its reflective surfaces as an
auto-critique. Or perhaps it is an Orson Welles affectation: an allusion
to *The Lady from Shanghai*. In Tim Lee's work, by contrast, we have mirrors taken away (instead of, as in Kardashian, their doubling or figuration). What seems to be a mirror turns out to be a photograph (in a kind
of reverse-engineering of the selfie as always-already a photograph, an
image: see Figure 10.1).

The mirror is itself an image, Lee's picture tells us, offering a remake of
a scene from the Marx Brothers' film *Duck Soup*. According to an online
source, the plot of the film at this point is the following. A villain

> sends Chicolini [Chico Marx] and Pinkie [Harpo Marx] to the house to
> steal the war plans. Chicolini locks Firefly [Groucho Marx] in his bath-
> room and dresses up like him with eyeglasses and a fake thick greasepaint
> mustache and eyebrows. Pinkie also dresses up as Firefly as well. Both
> Chicolini and Pinkie try to fool Mrs. Teasdale into giving them the war
> plans. But Firefly breaks out of his bathroom and attempts to find the
> men impersonating him. In a famous sequence, Pinkie breaks a large mir-
> ror and mimic's Firefly's movements.[9]

And so, Groucho Marx thinks he sees himself in a mirror, which is actually a doorway (framing the large mirror that Pinkie has broken]. In that
doorway is Pinkie/Harpo, dressed like Groucho in a night shirt and cap,
with greasepaint eyebrows and moustache. Harpo doesn't want Groucho
to realize it is him, he wants to fool him, and so he copies Groucho's

Figure 10.1   Tim Lee, "*Duck Soup*, The Marx Brothers, 1933," 2002

every move. Much hilarity ensues. But Lee's goal is different: he wants to momentarily fool the viewer, so that we have the *pleasure* of having been fooled. Lee wants to play a trick on *us* just as the mirror image played a trick on Groucho Marx. By comparing the two scenes, we can learn much about the logic of the mirror and the image, the double and the reflection or the representation.

What is similar and what is different about the two representations – the Marx Brothers' film and Lee's artwork? In neither case do we actually have a mirror, but in both instances the mirror is simulated – they are trying to fool Groucho or the viewer into thinking we see a mirror. Groucho by seeing himself copied, the viewer by thinking we see Lee's reflection. Then, Groucho has to look extra lively at the guy who is copying him, while Lee does not have to look at all; first he looked quizzical, but then he is not looking, merely facing, as a picture is taken – actually – behind his back. Lee is presumed to be looking, but is not.

With the Marx Brothers example, we look at someone trying to fool someone else – and then at the one being fooled – our point of view, our sympathy or identification, shifts. With Lee, we look at the one being fooled, or are fooled into thinking we see someone fooled, as we ourselves are fooled by the photograph, which we think is a mirror, within a photograph. If we identify with the one looking into a mirror, then we ourselves are part of a larger representation – that queasy feeling of being looked at. Lee's photograph makes us aware we are being looked at when we take a selfie – but not looked at by ourselves, rather by the big Other.

How does Lee's trick work? By our thinking we see him looking into the mirror (he is looking at a photograph of himself), by our being fooled into thinking he is narcissistic – *but really he is dialectical, reflexive*. Dialectics in two senses: looking at Lee's work, we have to both see and not see the image as mirror/photograph; and Lee's work with/without Groucho Marx's. Accomplished via the technology of photography, of its print as a large format (like Jeff Wall, Lee is based in Vancouver), of his own unremarkable (Asianized) body in "normcore" garb, and all of that, that trickery, itself a form of a "remake" of a Hollywood comedy. And thus it engages in a temporality both internal and external: the latter in the sense of reaching back to an earlier artwork (just as Ashbery's poem did), the former in terms of Lee's picture's making. In the first photograph, which we initially "think" is a mirror, Lee looks quizzical, puzzled – he is getting ready to be surprised.

What the selfie allows, then, is a way to rescue Lacan's mirror stage from the moralism of the narcissistic charge. Jodi Dean makes a similar argument, blogging that by taking pictures of ourselves, and then uploading them, we are participating in a collective project. The point, for Dean, is that the selfie is *not* individualistic:

> Multiple images of the same form, the selfie form, stream across our screens, like the people we might pass walking along a sidewalk or in a mall. When we upload selfies, we are always vaguely aware that someone, when it is least opportune, may take an image out of its context and use it to our disadvantage. But we make them anyway as part of a larger social practice that says a selfie isn't really of me; it's not about me as the subject of a photograph. It's my imitation of others and our imitation of each other.[10]

Geoffrey Batchen anticipated Dean's analysis statement when he remarked in 2010 that the selfie "represents the shift of the photograph serving as a memorial function to a communication device."[11] These three positions must in turn be unpacked (or selfied): the selfie as symptom of the narcissism of (social) media, the celebration of the selfie, and the selfie as indication of the dialectical reflexivity of media. The selfie is a form of speculation: aesthetic-intellectual, but also financial.

One can, and should, however, bring an aesthetic approach to the selfie, and think about such common features of the genre as foreshortening from the classic selfie to the possibilities via the selfie stick, to the creepy eye effects.[12] But of course the problem immediately is that we regress to an ahistorical formalism, for we find the same characteristics in Parmigianino, as John Ashbery reminds us: "the right hand / Bigger than the head," and "There is no way / To build it flat like a Section of wall." These are all visual tropes, are all then trapped in the classic mode of Lacan's imaginary (my through line here is that the selfie helps us to understand that Freud's narcissism, and Lacan's imaginary, are not only visual, but also have to do with the body, with touching).

I propose, then, to reread Freud's essay "On Narcissism" in a post-selfie context.[13] Here we can see how he introduces the haptic swerve or swipe that is key to the selfie practice: "who looks at it, that is to say, strokes it and fondles it" (73) but perhaps never obtaining complete satisfaction (unless via the "fragile absolute" that is the smashed iPhone).[14] Freud connects this narcissism to a perversion that we must read in a strict Lacanian fashion, as the pervert who knows the Other's desire, who enacts or is that desire (the big Other that is the internet's desire).[15] But Freud also, finally, lays out a strict economy of narcissism that can, I hope, shift that term (narcissistic) from the moralizing with which it is often applied to contemporary social media and the selfie.

We can see how this works when Freud distinguishes between two kinds of object choices, the anaclitic or attachment type, and the narcissistic type. (The first might turn out to be the digital device, then, along with such aspects of that device as its wifi signal). He then admits that since we all begin with two sexual objects, ourselves and our caregiver, we all possess a primary narcissism (87–88). Also, Freud's discussion of the narcissistic type *par excellence*, the narcissistic woman, soon becomes a description of why we love the narcissistic child or other types: their charm lies in their narcissism, in their self-containment, in which, in a curious proto-LOLcats way, he includes "the charm of certain animals which seem not to concern themselves with us, such as cats" (89). It's as if Freud were anticipating the early twenty-first century with its fascination with pictures of cats, and the subcultural vernaculars of "LOL." And so it is that here Freud is almost providing us with an early example of the "listicle" so predominant in social and online media today, when he switches from good German to a list of whom "A person may love":

1   According to the narcissistic type:
   a   what he himself is (i.e. himself)
   b   what he himself was,
   c   what he himself would like to be. (90)

In form and content, then, this is very much a newsfeed or Facebook update (or Snapchat list). Such lists perform a series of related ideas or observations, like the bullet-point list we fall into when taking notes or writing. What is narcissistic about the list, how does such a form, be it online (the listicle article) or in Freud's writings (the bullet-point list), function in the imaginary? Of course this works in part because it is an image of text, or the text as image. Therefore the text shifts from being read to being looked at (or also to being looked at). And the very form of the list, its serial nature, renders it susceptible to the narcissism of small differences. And this is then made meta or reflexive, for of course in our list it is a narcissism, in the sense that it lists whom the narcissist wants to love, and it is all variations of himself. *Freud's list for the narcissistic type, I argue, is the prototype for every listicle ever:* what one was in the past (one's failures), what one is now (hysterical), what the future is (dread or triumph: that non-relation). Like the selfie, the listicle is an online narcissism *par excellence.*

When we turn, finally, to Lacan's talk on the mirror stage, we do find a curious repetition of Freud's haptic swerve in Lacan's argument that the "eventually acquired control over the uselessness of the image, immediately gives rise in a child to a series of gestures in which" the child "adopt[s] a slightly leaning-forward position," a "libidinal dynamism" where "the contour of his stature that freezes it and in a symmetry that reverses it" results in "the spatial capture manifested by the mirror stage."[16] The spatial capture of the mirror stage is akin to the selfie in its haptic desire (here I think of the recent ad for Crave TV, a streaming service, in which the hands of the viewers reach toward screens: *the screen is no longer watched, it is touched*). We are captured by the screen, our hands are tied – but if we touch instead of watching, is our gaze now haptic? Now can we add, to the tripartite selfie theory (narcissism, commodification, and reflexivity), the touchiness of the selfie, the touchscreen that is also, perhaps, paranoid, a little touchy?

The Cloud and the Big Other

Can there be said to exist a digital big Other? Can we think about Lacan's theory of the symbolic register, aka the big Other (*le grand Autre*), in a digital framework? In order to understand Lacan's theory of the big Other, it is perhaps useful to trace how this figure emerges in his 1950s and 1960s texts, as a structural form of the father or master (but also, perhaps, the "paternal function," the paternal signifier).[17] Unlike the small other (our friend, neighbor, colleague), the big Other is invested with authority, be it formal or informal, written or unspoken. That is, the big Other stands in for the law. We can understand this better, perhaps, if we think about the psychotic reaction to the big Other (the psychotic's "foreclosure" or violent expulsion of the big Other from their world) and about what that foreclosure tells us about the virtual or fragile nature of the big Other, which has in turn to do with its etiology. Lacan is clear: "the essential point ... is that the delusion began the moment the initiative came from the Other, with a capital O."[18] The symbolic prop of the big Other is what is denied by the psychotic, because for the psychotic, the primal scene is all too present, that scene where the big Other intrudes into the imaginary dyad of infant and caregiver. This intrusion may be due to the demands of work – civilization, Freud would say, capitalism, we may say now. Or even through one's own desires: the multifarious question of the desire of the other. The content does not matter – indeed, the very arbitrariness of the big Other at this stage ensures that the big Other will in the end be a structural proposition or function, but also points to its weakness, its fragility or virtuality.

That is, consider how the psychotic forecloses the big Other, refusing the necessity for an external authority, whilst remaining fascinated with that big Other, when the foreclosed returns as the voices that speak to one. Such a condition of foreclosure persists, from the *Ur*-psychotic, Daniel Paul Schreber, to wireless technology. Think of a common occurrence in modern life: we come across a person talking in an animated fashion, perhaps waving his arms, but no one else is around. Here the "stupid first impression" is that someone is talking to himself, is walking around gesticulating like a madman. But we correct that impression when we realize that, no, he is on his phone, he has that triangular thing hanging off his ear. He is using Bluetooth technology. And then that second impression itself is corrected, and we go back to the first representation, which now includes wireless technology in the larger picture of daily life as madness. For in their foreclosure of the big Other, the psychotics were ahead of the curve: post-1960s, we have witnessed the decline of the big Other in the sense of these notions of symbolic arbitration – and the concomitant rise of the demand to enjoy. Like the Bluetooth user, we want to be connected all the time, interpellated by the digital, endlessly downloading, uploading, checking on our friends or family through social media.

So, "there is no big Other," or the theory of the virtuality of the big Other, holds, via the interpassive logic of *le sujet supposé* (the subject supposed to know, to believe, to enjoy, to desire), that the power of the big Other lies precisely in its supposition by others, by our believing that there is someone in charge.[19] But this notion of the "virtual" big Other suggests two further problems. Firstly, there could be a big Other of the digital world (an order, a system). Secondly, the virtuality of the big Other means we have to entertain the paradoxical possibility that while there is no big Other, there is a non-big Other, or a big Other that does not exist, and that big Other which does not exist is virtual.[20]

To summarize, then: (1) Is there a big Other of the digital world? (2) Is the big Other virtual or digital? In terms of this first question, we should answer in the affirmative – because everywhere we go, in digital life, we are subject to big laws and small ones – "netiquette," as they used to call it, is an example of the latter. If we answer "yes," then we are in the realm of a pluralism, a "multiculturalism" of the digital, as attested to by Virginia Heffernan's recent thesis of the democratic Web and the privatized smartphone.[21] But the relativist big Other means more than the unobjectionable argument that diasporic, migrant, or ethnic communities will have their own systems of law and laws, and more, too, than simply extending this finding to class, gender, and other taste- and subcultures. That is, the plurality of big Others should not blind us to the "fact" that there is really only one big Other (and he doesn't exist): the big Other is structural, and thus relatively agnostic when it comes to content.

Let us turn then to our second proposition: the theory that the big Other is virtual. What does this mean? If there is no big Other, or there is a non-big Other, a virtual big Other, does this mean that in our post-austerity present, of ever-accelerating download speeds, storage capacity, such a technological feature of the digital age constitutes a formal "limit of no limits," or what in Lacanese is called the "demand to enjoy"? For our desire on our part to upload ever more photographs, to send more texts, to add more comments is precisely what is called-into-being by the digital panopticon, a crowd-sourced NSA, and perhaps the most concrete example of such digital abstraction is the Cloud. By this I mean, of course, today's "Cloud computing," in which digital storage and program software are not part of one's own computer or digital device, but are instead somewhere else, "in the Cloud," as the vernacular has it. So one's Facebook photographs (and status updates), but also programs with which to organize projects (from the smallest, personal, efforts to large corporate accounting and HR programs) are, again, somewhere else (so a matter of space and location). In the Cloud, but what or where is the Cloud, and why is this gaseous metaphor used to describe – what? The actual servers on which such data and programs are stored? The ideology of placelessness, of speed, mobility, and ethereal access (from anywhere to anywhere)? Is the Cloud the big Other?

In his book *Tubes: A Journey to the Center of the Internet*, architecture critic Andrew Blum investigates the thing-ness of the internet, from cables crossing oceans to data exchanges; toward the end of his book he looks at "where your data sleeps," or the big data centers operated by Microsoft, Google, and the like. In Blum's usage, "the Cloud" refers to the network of data centers (and he takes us to one, in The Dalles, Oregon). But the Cloud is also an obfuscation: "web-based companies in particular seem to enjoy hiding within 'the cloud' ... generally speaking, the cloud asks us to believe that our data is an abstraction, not a physical reality."[22] Further, he argues, such "feigned obscurity becomes a malignant advantage of the cloud, a condescending purr of 'we'll take care of that for you' that in its plea for our ignorance reminds me of the slaughterhouse."[23] Blum's suspicions are borne out by his farcical tour of the Google server farm in The Dalles, where he essentially gets to walk around the parking lots, is not told the purpose of any buildings, and ends up having lunch with a group of non-communicative employees. "Google's first rule of data center PR was: don't go in the data center."[24] If the Cloud is the internet's big Other, then it does not exist, not in the sense that since Google does not want us to see the insides of their servers it therefore does not exist, but because the Cloud is an antinomy, both the servers *and* their denial.

Benjamin Bratton explores this conundrum further in *The Stack: On Software and Sovereignty*, where, drawing on Carl Schmitt, he argues that a post-Westphalian system of governance, or *nomos*, characterizes the Cloud. And bringing together Blum's terms, Bratton argues that "it is the physicality of abstraction that is at the center of things," and, further, that there is a violent settler colonialism at the heart or origin of the very forces of abstraction that make possible the contemporary world of planetary computerization.[25] While Bratton is making gargantuan leaps here, moving from the ancient historical moments foundational for Heidegger, Derrida, and Schmitt to presentday computer networks, his switching back and forth between the abstract and the material is worth our attention:

> It should be said that for Schmitt, if not for Heidegger, it is the physical taking and defence of land that matters most, not the transgenerational claims of autochthonous bloodlines that may have lost out against new forces. These political conundrums are still on our plates, and the

ecological absolutes staring back at us are based not in the simple honor
of defending homelands, but in *the physicalization of abstraction and the
abstraction of physicalization.* The Cloud is not virtual; it is physical even if
it is not always "on the ground," even when it is deep underground. There
is nothing immaterial about massless information that demands such
energy from the Earth.[26]

The *nomos* of the Cloud then is its weight – like Santner's theory of the
flesh, the Cloud has weight. For Bratton, such qualities of the Cloud fore-
close any kind of irredentism, or the desire for a return to (or of) some
pre-lapsarian authenticity. Herein lies the conundrum: we actually want
the Cloud to be simply virtual, not only because such emptiness allows
us to maintain the fiction of "there's no big Other" (there are no rules,
let's have fun), but also because it is a way to avoid thinking about the
"massless information that demands such energy from the Earth." *But the
opposite is also true.* It's odd, is it not, how the most knotted logic of post-
Lacanian thinking gets close to negative dialectics? For if we think of, or
dwell on, or fetishize, that very "weight" of massless information, its car-
bon footprint if you will (guilt trips about e-waste and the like), then we
are not so much thinking dialectically of the non-big Other, but rather we
are stuck on, simply, the big Other. Otherwise we risk short-circuiting the
path from "there is no big Other" to "there is a non-big Other."

The weight of the Cloud, which is also its materiality, then is what I
propose we can think about thanks to John Gerrard's important work
Farm (Pryor Creek, Oklahoma) 2015 (Figure 10.2).

In this digital simulation, Gerrard depicts a Google server farm, com-
bining 2,500 photographs taken from a helicopter. Gerrard was in a
helicopter because the Google corporation, which has as its mission "to
organize the world's information and make it universally accessible and
useful," would not grant him permission to photograph the building's
exterior (more recently, images of a server building's interior, all glitter-
ing and hi-tech, have become widely available including through a 360°
view). In a way, Gerrard's work tests the thesis that there is no big Other/
the big Other is virtual. If we start with the proposition of the Cloud as
a bit of digital jargon/marketing hype that denotes distributed computing and remote data centers, its very nomenclature reminds us that our
data or programs are weightless or virtual (even while this global industry
is now big enough to consume more energy than the airlines).[27] Indeed,
the originator of the term, computer scientist David Gelernter, originally
meant it as a figure of a Cloud's shadow over a tile surface.[28]

Figure 10.2   John Gerrard, *Farm (Pryor Creek, Oklahoma)*, at
Thomas Dane Gallery, 2014

Therefore, if we start with the thesis that the Cloud does not exist (is virtual, etc.), we have the counterevidence of Gerrard's art, which makes the proposition that it does in fact exist (also Blum's and Bratton's thesis) – for here we have but one of the thousands of server complexes around the world. Gerrard's artwork then makes the argument that this very materiality, or thing-ness, of the server is its undoing – because the very way in which the "simulation" is made obviates either realism, or photography (or it adds another layer/stack to those aesthetics or that medium). Gerrard puts it this way: "the internet doesn't *not* exist. It's physical," and then, tellingly, "I became interested in what the internet looks like." And so he resists Kubrick-like dolly shots down cool curves of blinking machines, and films the buildings' exteriors. But Gerrard's syntax is important: saying "the internet doesn't *not* exist" is different from saying "the internet exists." By going through the idea that the internet does not exist before arriving at its negation, Gerrard avoids the same short-circuit identified above, in the path from "there is no big Other" to "there is a non-big Other." Without considering that the internet could *not* exist, our thinking would short-circuit, would avoid the hard work

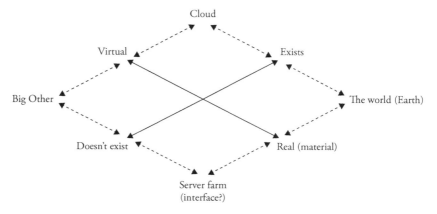

Figure 10.3   Semiotic rectangle (the Cloud and the big Other)

of switching from an argument to its opposite and back again. And yet, how do you take a picture of something, the internet, which doesn't *not* exist? How do you represent the dialectics of the non-big Other?

And so what do Gerrard's images show us, what do they tell us? Nothing. As our point of view slowly moves around the building, we see pipes, edges, the blue prairie sky. Grass, low-slung buildings, lights. Nothing memorable or extraordinary – and that is the point. The nothing that we see, the nothing that is the server farm as well as its simulation (which is the medium in which Gerrard labels his work), we can think about in the following way, best illustrated by the semiotic rectangle in Figure 10.3).[29]

I am calling on Gerrard's art to do a lot of work here, evidently: to make an argument about the status of the big Other, about the digital infrastructure, and about the relationship between art, the digital, and Lacanian theory. First of all, *Farm (Pryor Creek, Oklahoma) 2015* posits an antinomy between what is virtual and what exists. Virtual reality, or the simulation, or even virtual in the vernacular sense of "almost" – all of these concepts are brought to mind by this artwork. Presumably, what is virtual both does and does not exist – a VR landscape or figure does not exist in the way that an actual landscape or person does, and yet of course it does exist as code; it also exists in a way similar to how other representations exist. Further, existing in the Cloud, it is part of the infrastructure of our obscene demands for instant connectivity. These terms thus generate their own negations or oppositions: what is real or material, on the one hand, and what does not exist, on the other. Each antinomy, then paired, is illustrated by what Gerrard's artwork makes it possible to conceptualize. The Cloud, then, is both virtual (data stored on the Cloud may not be weightless, but it certainly takes up much less space then conventional books, archives, and the like) and yet also exists (the Cloud is there, we can find it, look at it, perhaps even touch it). What exists, and is also real, or material, is the world, by which we mean not the Heideggerian world (or Worlding) but the Earth, the planet. Gerrard's artwork is part of the *Grow Finish Unit* series, which focuses on "architecturally similar, computer-controlled pork production units in the Midwestern USA."[30] The server farm is what is both real and yet does not exist. Why is this so? Lacan's theory helps us to think in such structuralist and yet also Hegelian modalities of negation, paradox, and contradiction. The server farm does not exist in the sense that, with Gerrard's work, we do not – cannot – see the farm, but instead its simulation.[31] We can only see the simulation for legal reasons (Google forbids photography) that are also ethical or political: the server farms, like pork production or slaughterhouses, are spaces we wish not to look into too closely, we do not want to think about them, we disavow them. And yet, of course, the server farm is real, or material: it is made up of building materials, and, as Bratton reminds us, the Cloud is nothing if not "massless information that demands such energy from the Earth."[32] The server farm is in a way an interface between the Cloud and the Earth. We complete our turn around the semiotic rectangle with a return to Lacan, to the big Other, which is both virtual and does not exist. So now we have a tautology or redundancy, but one that we are ready for. The big Other is virtual in the sense that it is digital, or cybernetic; and it does not exist in the sense that there is no rational order dictated by it, no right way of doing things.

The Selfie and the Cloud: Antinomy, Dialectics, Lack

Can we speak of a dialectic of the lack? Or, to reverse the question, of a lacking dialectic? In some ways, the selfie and the Cloud (which map in a Hegelian way on to the subject and *Geist*) relate to each other as a dialectic, first because they are fundamentally abstractions. And the Cloud is also a meta-abstraction, an abstraction – an *idea* – of the abstraction that is data. This is to bring out or stress the Hegelian side of Lacan's thought, which, via articulations by Rebecca Comay and Fredric Jameson, has been in turn related to Adorno and the (negative) dialectic.[33] To say that there is a dialectic of the lack is different from saying that there is a lacking dialectic. The first denotes how the terms or concepts – the selfie and the Cloud – are related to each other: in a relation of antagonism, causality, connection, and disconnection (or the positive *and* the negative, which would be more of a Hegelian dialectic rather than an Adornian one). They are related to each other in terms of lack, a mutually constitutive (or immanent) lack. The Cloud needs its selfie, its subject. What is the Cloud without the selfie, without data? An empty server, an empty set? No, the Cloud (the king with two bodies – the internet has two bodies) lacks the selfie qua content.[34] But the selfie also needs the Cloud – to connect – and for the social. Selfies lack the Cloud in the sense that a selfie without the Cloud is merely old tech, a photograph, an image (not a networked image): not just analogue, but un-networked.

But what if the dialectic itself lacks, if the mechanism or technique or methodology here – the dialectic qua connectivity that also disconnects – itself lacks? Is this then a lack of lack, along the same lines of a negation of negation? (Lacanian theory forbids such doubling: there is no metalanguage, there is no other of the big Other.) Is the lack in the dialectic – to return to digital examples – those instances where we get no signal, no bars of wifi, airplane mode? Or is lack *of* connectivity different from the constitutive or immanent lack of the dialectic? (For we only need "airplane mode" when we ourselves are connecting, are making airline connections, are moving our bodies.)

I am discussing the selfie and the Cloud at fairly developed levels of abstraction here: the selfie as subject but also referring metonymically to any kind of content for online or networked communication, such as emails, tweets, status updates, or self-portraits. Moreover, the Cloud is not simply the servers, that network, the computers, but also, perhaps, thinking itself, solipsistic thinking conceived of as social in some ways (the "hive mind" may capture this paradox). But the lack that is immanent to the Cloud or the selfie is not only mutually implicated – each abstraction or concept also lacks constitutively. The Cloud, for instance, can be divided between its storage capacity – what is called, both in psychoanalysis and in cybernetics, "memory" – and its processing facility – which may be what in theory or in philosophy is called "thinking." But memory also has speed. So, the one is size, the other speed, which are neoliberal metrics for a different kind of capacity, a capacity which must be "built" but also "sustainable." (Which also leads us to ask not, *à la* Heidegger, "what is called thinking?," but "what is the energy used for thinking?") The dialectic of the Cloud, this non-identity with itself, along with other immanent contradictions such as between its material basis and its ideal content, then is matched by the dialectic of the selfie, which is signaled perhaps by the nomenclature, by the "ie" at the end of the "self." Like other suffixes of contemporary demotic – the "ie" in "bestie" (for best friend), the –ish of *blackish*, or the "y" added to many words – the "ie" here in selfie is about connotation or the spread of meaning. It is also a quiddity: the selfie is both the networked self-portrait *and* the lack of the other. Here a common, everyday critique of the selfie – that the picture's distorted foreshortening or "selfie arm" denotes the subject's pathetic solitude – contains a grain of truth. The lack, that is, of another person to take the selfie: the selfie denotes a lack of the social (which then is remedied with the Cloud). The Cloud and the selfie lack each other and, in turn, lack themselves. The selfie cannot be a selfie without the Cloud, just by itself, and the Cloud, of course, is the constitutive antagonism or lack of the selfie. The selfie is social (or, as Jodi Dean calls it, communistic).

This, then, is by way of a conclusion, to bring the selfie and the Cloud into a dialectics of lack. The selfie, caught up in the mirror of dualisms, of self and other, then encounters a third term: the Cloud. But how do we describe this? As an antagonism, a synthesis, a positive dialectic or a negative one (the former Hegelian, the latter Adornian or Žižekian)? What, first of all, would be a Cloud of the selfie, what is the Cloud of Kim Kardashian, of Tim Lee, of Parmagianino or Ashbery? The question contains its own answer: the plethora of examples and discourses (from social media celebrity to contemporary art, from Old Masters to American poetry) are themselves a Cloud, a word cloud, a collective of hashtags. This is not to homogenize their differences: as Jameson remarks with respect to Lacan and the dialectic, what is genuinely radical about Lacan's body of work is how it allows what is incommensurable to lie as it is, without forcing it into a similarity that cannot but help to leave a remainder. Thus, to use one of Jameson's examples, the role of Marx and Freud in Lacan's theory is never ironed out or made symmetrical, and indeed the shifting valences of the big Other, too, which becomes, at different times, he argues, "both language and society, both the Symbolic and the social."[35]

Does Gerrard's project propose a selfie of the Cloud – the helicopter-derived photography as a virtual (that word again!) selfie stick? Does that project signal a return, under the guise of a video game-worked collection of images qua simulation, the totality, the One, indeed the Cloud as Master (or big Other)? Instead of data sets (or even data), we have the datum. One bit of knowledge, which stands in for or replaces all the others. The unconscious as data set, or the other way around.

Notes

1 Of course the classic SLR camera also used a mirror as part of its apparatus. The work of the mirror should also be considered in line with the role of inversion in optics, from the *camera obscura* to the photography of Rodney Graham. Negar Mottahedeh has stressed the politics of that networked practice. See "The Political Consciousness of the Selfie," at http://stanford press.typepad.com/blog/2015/07/the-political-consciousness-of-the-selfie .html, accessed April 25, 2017.

2 Here I am thinking of Eric L. Santner's *The Royal Remains: The People's Two Bodies and the Endgames of Sovereignty* (University of Chicago Press, 2011), where he traces the path from royal to popular sovereignty via sublime fleshiness.

3 Walter Benjamin anticipates this swiping in his comments on the telephone and the camera in the essay "On Some Motifs in Baudelaire": "In the mid-nineteenth century, the invention of the match brought forth a number of innovations which have one thing in common: a single abrupt movement of the hand triggers a process of many steps. This development is taking place in many areas. A case in point is the telephone, where the lifting of the receiver has taken the place of the steady movement that used to be required to crank the older models. With regard to countless movements of switching, inserting, pressing, and the like, the 'snapping' by the photographer has had the greatest consequences. Henceforth a touch of the finger sufficed to fix an event for an unlimited period of time." Walter Benjamin, *Selected Writings, vol. IV: 1936–1940* (Cambridge, MA: Harvard University Press, 2003), 328.

4 In Kristin Dombek's *The Selfishness of Others: An Essay on the Fear of Narcissism* (New York: FSG, 2016) she argues that narcissism as a cultural diagnosis has metastasized in the past decade, with a little help from Big Data, generational fallacies, and online self-help culture.

5 Lacan: "Even the body the way we feel it is like skin, retaining in its sack a pile of organs." *Seminar XXIII*, seminar of November 18, 1975, tr. Cormac Gallagher, www.lacaninireland.com.

6 John Ashbery, *Self-Portrait in a Convex Mirror* (New York: Penguin, 1972), 68–83.

7 David Herd, *John Ashbery and American Poetry* (New York: Palgrave, 2000), 163.

8 Jody Norton, *Narcissus Sous Rature: Male Subjectivity in Contemporary American Poetry* (Lewisburg: Bucknell University Press, 2000), 202. More recently, Christopher Nealon has argued that the poem, when read via the political specificity of 1970s New York, counterposes a dialectic of fluidity and spectacle, the former historical, the latter imprisoning. Christopher Nealon, *The Matter of Capital: Poetry and Crisis in the American Century* (Cambridge, MA: Harvard University Press, 2011), 73–106.

9 http://www.imdb.com/title/tt0023969/synopsis

10 See Jodi Dean's 2016 blogging on the selfie at http://blog.fotomuseum .ch/2016/02/iii-images-without-viewers-selfie-communism/. See also my response, "The Narcissistic Selfie," http://capturephotofest.com/the-narcis-sistic-selfie/. Both accessed April 25, 2017.

11 Geoffrey Batchen, quoted in "Me, myself and iPhone", David Colman, *The New York Times*, June 30, 2010.

12 See Adam Kostko, *Creepiness* (London: Zero, 2015), where he draws also on Santner.

13 Sigmund Freud, "On Narcissism: An Introduction," in *The Standard Edition of the Psychological Works of Sigmund Freud, volume XIV*, tr. and ed. James Strachey et al. (London: Hogarth, 1957), 79–104, cited by page numbers in the text.

14 This "sexuality of the swipe" or its libidinization helps us to understand the generational divide that is digital (is the gap): that divide has as much to do with a sexual youth (and asexual elders) as it does with competence. The swipe is the finger, the *digit*-al practice, the haptic that is also phallic.

15 Note that Freud almost immediately adds that narcissism, at least in the case of neurotics, is not a perversion, "but the libidinal complement to the egoism of the instinct of self-preservation" (Freud, "On Narcissism," 73–74).

16 Jacques Lacan, "The Mirror Stage as Formative of the I Function as Revealed in Psychoanalytic Experience," in *Écrits*, tr. Bruce Fink (New York: W. W. Norton, 2006), 75–81, 75–76.

17 See *The Seminar of Jacques Lacan, Book II: The Ego in Freud's Theory and in the Technique of Psychoanalysis, 1954–55*, tr. Sylvana Tomaselli (New York: W. W. Norton, 1991) , where Lacan first formulates the Other (or *Autre*), also known at this stage as the "absolute" or "true" or "*véritable*" Other (235–247). The following year, in Jacques Lacan, *The Seminar of Jacques Lacan, Book III: The Psychoses, 1955–56*, ed. Jacques-Alain Miller, tr. Russell Grigg (New York: W. W. Norton, 1993), Lacan began using the appellation the "big Other" (74).

18 Lacan, *The Psychoses*, 193.

19 This logic of the "demise of symbolic efficiency" is worked out in Slavoj Žižek, *The Ticklish Subject: The Absent Center of Political Ontology* (London: Verso, 2000), chapter 6, "Whither Oedipus?"; Žižek's matrix of the different "subjects supposed to ..." is to be found in Žižek, *The Sublime Object of Ideology* (London: Verso, 1989), chapter 5, "Which Subject of the Real?"

20 It is important to keep in mind that Žižek was already describing the decline of symbolic efficiency in terms of digitization (*The Ticklish Subject*, 324–325) and, further, that Lacan's conception of the symbolic was also in dialogue, in the 1950s, with cybernetic theory (see Lydia Liu, *The Freudian Robot: Digital Media and the Future of the Unconscious* (University of Chicago Press, 2010), chapter 5, "The Cybernetic Unconscious").

21 This concept, along with "digital natives" and Virginia Heffernan's thesis of "white flight" from the Web (*qua* ad-strewn ghetto, but also the commons)

to apps (*qua* gated community, the privatized smartphone), constitutes a national-cloud aspect of the digital (to join its carceral and laborist tendencies). See Virginia Heffernan, *Magic and Loss: The Internet as Art* (New York: Simon and Schuster, 2016). These concepts of digitality and sovereignty are also at work in Benjamin Bratton's work, discussed below.

22 Andrew Blum, *Tubes: A Journey to the Center of the Internet* (New York: HarperCollins, 2012), ebook, Kindle loc. 3001.

23 Ibid., Kindle loc. 2995.

24 Ibid., Kindle loc. 3044.

25 Benjamin Bratton, *The Stack: On Sovereignty and Software* (Cambridge, MA: MIT Press, 2015), 64.

26 Ibid., 73.

27 For more on the energy consumption of the computing industry, see Greenpeace's 2012 report *How Clean is Your Cloud?*, available from greenpeace.org. There they note, for instance, that "[t]here have been increasing attempts by some companies to portray the cloud as inherently 'green,' despite a continued lack of transparency and very poor metrics for measuring performance or actual environmental impact" (6).

28 See the discussion between Dave Gelernter, John Markoff, and Clay Shirky, at www.edge.org/conversation/david_gelernter-john_markoff-clay_shirky-lord-of-the-cloud. Tung-Hui Hu offers a series of origins in *A Prehistory of the Cloud*, including "a 1922 designed for predicting weather using a grid of 'computers'" (in the sense of human mathematicians), an AT&T series of microwave relay stations in 1951, and the symbol of a cloud, used by engineers to represent "any unspecifiable or unpredictable network." Please see Tung-Hui Hu, *A Prehistory of the Cloud* (Cambridge, MA: MIT Press, 2015), Introduction.

29 Such terms as "simulation" or simulacrum, as well as the "virtual", suggest as well Deleuze and his pairs of the virtual and the actual. See Gilles Deleuze, *Bergsonism*, tr. Hugh Tomlinson and Barbara Habberjam (New York: Zone Books, 1988), especially chapter 3, "Memory as Virtual Coexistence," and the extensive secondary literature.

30 See "resources" at johngerrard.net.

31 As a simulated (moving) image of digital infrastructure, Gerrard's work seems to be similar to recent photography of demolished Kodak factories or vacant photo studios by Robert Burley or Scott McFarland. The difference lies in the melancholy that pervades those latter images – a nostalgia for a vanished form of image production that Gerrard's work resolutely avoids.

32 Bratton, *The Stack*, 122.

33 See Rebecca Comay, "Adorno avec Sade..." *differences: A Journal of Feminist Cultural Studies* 17, 1 (2006), 6–19; Fredric Jameson, "Lacan and the Dialectic," in *Lacan: The Silent Partners*, ed. Slavoj Žižek (London: Verso, 2006), 365–396.

34 Is the relation of the Cloud to the selfie one of a mirror – to continue a theme from the first part of this chapter? Could this be a way of bringing "Marx's mirror stage" – the "Peter and Paul" footnote in *Capital* – into discussions of "mirror sites" as a metaphor for back-ups and duplication online and in the Cloud? See Karl Marx, *Capital, vol. I*, tr. Ben Brewster (London: Penguin, 1990), 144, and, for a Lacanian commentary on same, Žižek, *The Sublime Object of Ideology*, 24.

35 Jameson, "Lacan and the Dialectic," 386.

Islam after Lacan

Nouri Gana

Psychoanalysis has almost always entertained a contentious relationship with religion, especially since Freud, the founder of the so-called god-less science, was not only openly atheist but also unabashedly critical of religion. But while Freud and his followers studied the topic of religion and religious ritual in the West, they have hardly stepped outside the anthropological and intellectual boundaries of Europe (Erich Fromm is a case in point).[1] For decades, Freud's quasi-dismissal of Islam in *Moses and Monotheism* acted as an enduring license for later European practitioners of psychoanalysis to thrust Islam into complete oblivion. After propounding that Islam is an "abbreviated repetition" of Judaism, which achieved over a short period of time "great worldly successes," Freud famously surmised that "the internal development of the new religion soon came to a stop, perhaps because it lacked the depth which had been caused in the Jewish case by the murder of the founder of their religion."[2]

Regardless of whether Freud was right or wrong about Islam, it was not his view of it as a religion that lacks the foundational crime of Oedipal parricide that traveled to the Muslim world but his early theories of the unconscious and dream interpretation. Given the Judeo-Christian and Western points of reference of such theories as the Oedipus complex, they did not resonate well with Muslim sensibilities, and only further affirmed the reigning interwar assumption that psychoanalysis is an exotic science, at loggerheads with the Islamic worldview in which Allah exerts immense tutelary power on the everyday lives of Muslims. This view did not change much until the late 1970s, even while it was somewhat debated and steered into more reconciliatory and desirable directions by Malik Badri in his book *Dilemma of Muslim Psychologists*.[3] Apart from intermittent fascination, Freud's work on the interpretation of dreams, on the role of the unconscious in everyday life, and on theories of subjectivity writ large proved less contentious, even productive, particularly in avant-gardist circles such as the Egyptian school of psychoanalysis.[4]

Freud's tentative view of Islam had never really been taken seriously in the Muslim world until the outbreak of the Iranian revolution (1979) and the emergence of the phenomenon of political Islam or what is also referred to as Islamism at times and Salafism at others. The Rushdie affair (1989) – which started with angry protests against Indian-born British author Salman Rushdie's provocative 1988 novel, *The Satanic Verses*, and reached its apotheosis with his condemnation to death by a Khomeyni-issued *fatwa*, or religious decree – fueled the desire to lay down Islam on the analytic couch. It was somewhere between these two events that Fethi Benslama started his project of "psychoanalyzing Islam," thereby following in the footsteps of Freud who most infamously psychoanalyzed Judaism. But while Benslama's model may be Freudian, his methodology is largely Lacanian. Indeed, Benslama mobilizes such Lacanian concepts as desire, lack, and especially (feminine/Other) jouissance in order to deconstruct and reconstruct the question of origins in Islam (partly because of the centrality of such a question to various Islamist movements and partly because it was the topic of Rushdie's 1988 controversial novel, *The Satanic Verses*, as well as the topic of Benslama's own 1988 seminal book, *La nuit brisée/The Shattered Night*). Benslama's challenge is not so much to read Freud in the wake of Lacan (after all, it may be impossible to do otherwise) as to read Lacan in the wake of Islam and vice versa.

Benslama's 2002 book, *La psychanalyse à l'épreuve de l'Islam* (later translated into English and published in 2009 as *Psychoanalysis and the Challenge of Islam*), dramatizes both the challenges and insights of translating Islam into Freudian and especially Lacanian psychoanalysis. Along the way, Benslama confesses that the Rushdie affair was somewhat a "rude awakening ... particularly with regard to the commitment of an intellectual project that led to an investigation of the question of origins of Islam, where psychoanalysis was challenged, both clinically and theoretically, when it found itself transported to a cultural context different from the one in which it had taken shape."[5] Benslama is not unaware of the challenges of applying psychoanalytic theory to Islam, since Islam was not, beyond Freud's passing remarks in *Moses and Monotheism*, a topic of psychoanalysis. In a sense, psychoanalysis is partly "culpable" for the presentday "resistance to the intelligibility of Islam" precisely because psychoanalysis did not accord attention to Islam as a topic of analysis, which would have promoted, for better or worse, its intelligibility, and even eventual mainstreaming (6). Because of this allegedly missed encounter between psychoanalysis and Islam, Benslama's method therefore is not applicative but translational, attempting, as it does, to read Islam and psychoanalysis in tandem.

This chapter seeks to shed some light on Benslama's deployment of Lacanian psychoanalysis to examine the notion of origins in Islam, given that this notion exerts enormous gravitational pull on so many Islamist movements. The insightful ways in which Lacan's concepts of the real, desire, and lack are brought to bear on the construction of origins in Islam and more so on the repression of female/Other jouissance, so central to Benslama's revisionary project of Islam, are admirable feats, generative of cross-cultural critical inquiry and dialogue. In this sense Benslama's book testifies not only to the productive possibility of studying Islam through a psychoanalytic lens but also to the ways in which Lacanian psychoanalysis holds open the promise of worlding psychoanalytic inquiry, reorienting it to the non-Western world at a time when psychoanalysis is agonizing in Euro-America. Yet in as much as there are benefits in compelling Lacan (after Lacan) to travel into uncharted territories, there are also risks and pitfalls, and these may have to do, as it will become clear in due course, as much with Lacan's brand of psychoanalysis as with Benslama's own deployment of it, especially in light of his avowedly secular ideological leanings. The main methodological flaw of Benslama's psychoanalytic engagement with Islam is the tendency to conflate Islamism as a singular-plural political movement, emerging out of specific historical circumstances, with Islam as a religion that has a more or less finite core system or structure of belief and ritual despite the numerous internal divergences and different schools of interpretation. It may not be Benslama's explicit authorial intention, but the constant movements throughout *Psychoanalysis and the Challenge of Islam* from an analysis of Islamism to an analysis of Islam tacitly imply that for Benslama Islamism is (a symptom of) Islam. Obviously, Islamists themselves wouldn't agree more with such a conclusion. The enormity of such a risk, though, makes driving a wedge between the two topics – Islam and Islamism – not only urgent but crucial to any project of psychoanalyzing Islam (or, alternatively, Islamism). The attempt to trace Islamism back to Islam without proper and consistent circumstantial differentiations may only further blur the dividing lines between the two, or, worse still, displace and disperse Islamism into Islam. Bearing these concerns in mind, I shall examine how Benslama makes use of Lacanian vocabulary in order, firstly, to deconstruct the myth of origins in Islam and, secondly, to reinstate the overlooked role of the female Other, not to mention the enigma of female jouissance, in mediating the access to origin in Islam. Women, according to Benslama, are the unacknowledged – if not repressed – midwives of monotheistic and Islamic origin par excellence.

Undoing Origin

> The return to origin should be understood not as a movement of the present toward the past nor as a past that must be made present, but as the return of a past from before the beginning, an anachronic and anarchic antecedence toward the matrical ark of the law. It is a question of being born again into origin from a preorigin. To paraphrase Hamlet, Islam is out of joint. (50)

Inspired by Freud's seminal inquiry into the foundational origins of Judaism in *Moses and Monotheism*, and equipped with a Lacanian poststructuralist method of analysis, Benslama sets himself the task of deconstructing what he calls the "primal fictions of Islam [*fictions originaires de l'Islam*] and the workings of its symbolic system" (vii) in order to discern "the kernel of the impossible around which language forms an imaginary shell, a projection of the psyche toward the external world" (ix). Such a task entails a hermeneutic shift from "metaphysics into metapsychology" (vii), or from "the psyche of god to that of the unconscious" (viii). The rise of Islamism (aka Salafism) as a regressive political movement that purports to return to the pure origins of Islam – and to the first Muslim community as an exemplary model on which to refashion the present – provides the circumstantial alibi for Benslama to engage with the onto-theological origins of Islam as the last monotheistic religion whose founder claimed patrilineal descent from Ishmael and Abraham, the founding father of monotheism. "As soon as I began to pay attention to the language of Islamist speech, I realized," Benslama points out, "it was haunted by the question of origins" (10). Islamists conjured up the glorious Muslim past and mobilized the masses around

> the promise of a return to the golden age of the founding of Islam, when the beginning and the commandment were united in a single principle in the hands of, first, the Prophet-founder-legislator, then his four successors. This period was assumed to have been one of ideal justice on Earth, before the fall into the division and internal sedition (*fitna*) that the community would later experience. (4)

Benslama's ultimate goal is quite simply to show to the Islamists that there is no single origin to return to – really, that origin is structured by a void, a constitutive lack that can neither be accounted for nor recreated. Yet, while Benslama achieves a brilliant deconstruction of the myth of origins in Islam, as I will show shortly, he does not inquire much about the historical origins that inform the formation of this fantasy of origins in Islamism itself. Not that Benslama is unaware of the traumatic colonial encounter between the Muslim world and Christian Europe, but he takes it as a "form of intellectual imposture" to attribute the causes of Arab Muslim humiliation solely to the West or to the United States: "Victimization by outside forces alone can only deflect attention from internal causes and perpetuate the passivity that characterizes the posture of humility, to the extent that it remains fully wedded to its own desperate collapse" (64). Surely, reducing everything to imperialism is counterproductive, but the inverse gesture (i.e. reducing everything to internal or intrinsic causes, as is the case with Benslama) is no less counterproductive. Clearly, Benslama is just not that interested in the concrete historical grievances of Arabs and Muslims, even while he is profoundly aware of the subjective devastation, identificatory crisis, and despair of the masses at the World War I loss of the Islamic caliphate, which used to anchor, despite its exponential decline, a conscious or unconscious sense of individual and collective belonging to a community of believers with a past, a present, and a possible future.

I would argue that it was imperialism, and not Islamism, that has blown Muslim time out of joint. Yet, Benslama only focuses on the anachronistic gesture of return to origins that characterizes the Islamist project even while he is, it bears repeating, aware that it is a reactionary gesture, a symptom of Euro-American imperialism par excellence. While treating colonial modernity as more of a foregone conclusion rather than as a cause of the emergence of regressive fundamentalist movements, Benslama concedes that the encroachment of modernity into the Arab Muslim world gave rise to at least two incommensurable desires: there is, on the one hand, the "desire to be an other," which he qualifies as the "most powerful desire that modernity has managed to create" (2), and there is, on the other hand, the "despair of willing to be oneself [*le désespoir où l'on veut être soi*]" (5, translation modified). The "desire to be an other" to which Benslama refers has nothing to do with the deconstructive ethical experience of radical alterity, but, rather, with what Badiou calls "*le désir d'Occident*" – i.e. the desire to be as Occidental as the Occidentals, which is, after all, what Benslama admires in the beginning of his book about Habib Bourguiba's project of mimetic modernity in postcolonial Tunisia, a project that was indeed structured by "a desire for the West."[6] The "desire to be an other" is then nothing less than the coercive incitement to conformity exerted by colonial modernity.[7] It is puzzling here to note how in the name of secularity – or of what he calls the "absolute impiety" of Bourguiba (2), who incited Tunisians not to fast during Ramadan – Benslama sanctions the repression of "sacred temporality" (2) and decries the "constitutive repressions" ("*refoulement constitutifs*") of religious institutions (vii). In other words, while Benslama seems to license the repression of Islam by Bourguiba, he tends to systematically pathologize the reverse repression of modernity by the Islamists.

It is as if the "desire to be an other" is exempt from the despair (of belatedness and exile from the present) that Benslama reserves for the Islamists (or traditionalists writ large) in their attempt to recover who they were in the precolonial period. Yet, both the "desire to be an other" (which is also marked by the "*despair* of willing to be an other") and the "despair of willing to be oneself" (which is also marked by the "*desire* to be oneself*") are byproducts of colonial modernity and both can be, if excessive, pathological and counterproductive to the same extent. Notwithstanding Benslama's tacit secular liberal leanings,[8] he is quite right about his treatment of the "despair of willing to be oneself" as a symptom of exile from the present, in which the immutable temporality of the sacred has come to be violently overshadowed by the encroaching temporality of the secular colonial. The violence and electrifying speed with which modernity entered the Arab Islamic world resulted in a "subjective devastation. The negation of the psychic is a dependent exponential variable of those devastations that are manifested in individual and collective psychoses, in massacre and genocide" (54). What muddies the waters still is that the entrance of Arabs and Muslims into the modern world was not mediated by a process of individual and collective mourning, nor were there any cultural reparative works that would have made such a necessary psychoaffective process possible in the first place. Benslama speaks of a "modern caesura of identification" (54) with the world of sacred temporality that occurred suddenly and without the necessary and corresponding cultural work (*Kulturarbeit*). In other words, not only have Arabs and Muslims failed to resist the swift transformations of their world brought about from the outside by colonial modernity, but they have also failed to transform themselves from the inside in light of those coercive transformations dictated and implemented from the outside.

This double failure has thrown the doors wide open for the Islamists' "cry of revolt" and "mass protest" (52) at the loss of a world which used to anchor, consciously or unconsciously, their individual-collective

identity (and entire economy of jouissance), and made possible the eventual Islamist recourse to "archaic configurations" (55) as forms of both
authentic identification and melancholy resistance to imperial modernity.
Islamist despair, Benslama argues, "has been able to produce itself only
from an unsustainable exposure to the void of the caesura, to the mass
subjective revocation it has brought about, becoming, in response, a
headlong quest for truths that restore subjectivity, including the return
to the paradise of origin" (59). Yet, as will become clear, the Islamists
avoided the void brought about by colonial modernity only to fall prey to
the void of origins brought about by the Quranic revelation. The return
to pure origins in Islam is the site of the impossible par excellence, even
though it feeds on the fantasy of recapturing lost or stolen jouissance.
As Bruce Fink reminds us, there is something idealistic about jouissance
beyond the paltry phallic function:

> we think that there must be something better, we say that there must
> be something better, we *believe* that there must be something better. By
> saying it over and over, whether to ourselves, to our friends, or to our
> analysts, we give a certain consistency to this other satisfaction, this Other
> jouissance. In the end, we wind up giving it so much consistency that the
> jouissance we do in fact obtain seems all the more inadequate. The little
> we had diminishes further still. It pales in comparison with the ideal we
> hold up for ourselves of a jouissance that we could really count on, that
> would never let us down.[9]

The return to origins is driven by and toward a jouissance that never
fails, an infallible and unfailing jouissance. The assumption that the
colonial Other withholds or blocks the path toward recapturing lost
jouissance and plenitude further foments the fantasy to take stock of it,
except that this fantasy keeps stumbling against the intractability of the
real. Hence the object of jouissance, because irreducible and unyielding,
is eventually displaced by the very ideology – here, Islamism – that purports to recover it. Yet, the access to the object of jouissance in Islamism
is impossible for another reason. Apart from the fact that any such return
to origins would not be possible without the mediation of language, the
story of origins in Islam is itself marked by the literal intrusion of language. Firstly, Benslama reminds of the Prophet's terrifying childhood
vision of an open chest, from which dark flesh was removed and space
was cleared for the letter (*al-ḥarf*) of the Quran to be placed. Secondly,
the Quran itself is nothing but a revelation of the hyperoriginary book
that had already been written and preserved in a "guarded tablet" (13).
In addition to the Prophet's exposure, withdrawal, and agony, the story

of origins in Islam invokes accordingly an openness to foreignness and a process of linguistic mediation that goes from grafting to deciphering the letter (*al-ḥarf*) of the Quran. In other words, the story of origins in Islam is the site of piecemeal and processual grafting rather than wholesale gratification: it is marked by that originary hospitality to the stranger (in this case, language) – it is never about an intact purity or "originary plenitude" (12).

The search for authenticity and purity associated with the return to origins is therefore futile, according to Benslama, because of the literal intrusion of language. "The intruder in the heart of man is language," and "whatever assumed the status of 'Islam' acquired its essentiality only from its provenance in the 'Foreign,' which had lodged in this recess of infantile narcissism" (13). The purity of origins has therefore to be measured against the possible impurity of the medium through which origin was mediated in the first place. Moreover, the site of origin in Islam is split between the moment of infantile vision in which the Prophet's chest was opened for the placement of the letter (*al-ḥarf*), and the later moment of reception and reading – indeed, "Read," Gabriel's injunction to the Prophet, constitutes the inaugural gesture of Quranic revelation and the actual beginning of the Muhammadan message. Benslama is right in suggesting here that "the concept of origin in Islam was split between a cut (*entame*) and a beginning (*commencement*)" (14). Yet, this split that distances origin from itself is preceded by an even deeper split or time-lag between the moment of foundation of Islam and its anterior announcement as "a biblical promise" (14). Being the last monotheistic religion, Islam had already been anticipated by the Torah. It is the materialization of God's promise to Hagar after she was driven away with her son, Ishmael, into the desert. The Prophet foregrounded the biblical connection between Abraham and Ishmael as the source of "a primary monotheistic filiation through the older son, which was prefigured in the scrolls of the Father (*ṣuḥuf 'ibrāhīm*)" (14). What would the return to the origins of Islam mean if Islam itself was nothing more than a return to origins (i.e., a return to the originary religion of Abraham)?

Islam's positioning as the last monotheistic religion and simultaneously as the originary religion of Abraham opens up the question of singularity of origin to the multiplicity of beginnings. Origin is far from being a self-evident and transparent event in which truth, being, and the absolute collide. Rather, Benslama concludes, "the truth of an event is always compromised by the necessary transition of that event to a text, a work of writing and authorship, and that even if the event is true, its exposition in language pulls it into the realm of fiction" (15). There is a considerable time-lag between Islam as a biblical promise and the actual beginning of Islam as the last monotheistic religion, not to mention the time-lag between the infantile vision of the Prophet and the actual Quranic revelation. These variable time-lags make the notion of origin in Islam hardly identical with any clear point of origin. It is rather dispersed and incomplete. At the origin of Islam, then, Benslama concludes in Lacanian fashion, there is a lack of origin.

Notwithstanding his insightful deconstruction of the notion of origin in Islam, Benslama makes it sound as if the lack of origin is indeed what fuels the desire of Islamists to return to origins. While this may be true from a structural Lacanian perspective, in which the fantasy of origin may be seen to mediate an economy of jouissance toward which and by which the Islamist project is driven, it is simply not the case from a historical perspective. It is not the lack of origins in itself that caused the desire to return to origins to arise, but rather the historical encounter with colonialism and the subsequent collapse of the Ottoman caliphate in 1924. Such a historical fact would not be in contradistinction with the Lacanian-inflected insight that the desire to return to origins works from within an economy of jouissance, in which the fantasy of an eventual return offers a form of (traumatic) enjoyment, but it cannot be reduced to it in the way Benslama tends to frame the Islamist torment of origin. Benslama makes a structural argument there where a historical argument would have been more pertinent, at least as the historical backdrop against which particular social movements and collective psychic (or psychopathological) formations may emerge. There is a tendency in Benslama to reduce what is historical to what is structural or endemic to Muslim societies; the effect is at times more demystifying than illuminating. While this may have in the end to do with Benslama's dependency on Lacanian vocabulary, it does not have to be so if more historical nuancing were to be made.

Gendering Origin

It is insofar as her jouissance is radically Other that woman has more of a relationship to God than anything that could have been said in speculation in antiquity following the pathway of that which is manifestly articulated only as the good of man.[10]

Hagar is the origin that has been repudiated in order to preserve filiation in accordance with the imaginarized impossible. The imaginarized impossible is the foundation of the origin in metaphysics. The concept of the father in originary monotheism entails the repudiation of the foreigner and the phallic choice of the proper. (96)

Monotheism could have possibly done without Hagar and started with Sarah tout court. In Benslama's words, "it would have been possible for the absolute god of monotheism to offer the gift of a single origin, within a united family" (80). Yet, God did not. The gift of origin was initially withheld from Sarah and granted to Hagar who gave birth to Ishmael and established the biological paternity of Abraham. This purely human patrilineal modality of descent, which would later establish Islam as the only truly Abrahamic monotheistic religion, proved to be, according to Benslama, only "a bastard beginning" (88). Therefore, it isn't until the last moment, Benslama observes, "that a purer, nobler, more spiritual beginning is produced, one satisfied with being not merely the gift of a child but the gift as the impossible. Sarah's conception is that of the miracle of the dead body that suddenly comes to life, contradicting the laws of human procreation" (88). The birth of Isaac renders Abraham a "father by proxy," just like Joseph in relation to Jesus (86).

What complicates the notion of origin in Islam is the fact that the origin of monotheism itself is marked by the lack of a single origin. Instead, there are two divergent principles of origin, each quite distant from the other, one paternal, the other divine – "One, originating in Hagar, is the principle of the flesh, or the gift of the possible; the other, coming through Sarah, is that of the spirit or the gift of the impossible" (89). As the above epigraph indicates, it is origin through the sexual insemination of Hagar by Abraham that has been repudiated in favor of origin through Sarah, in which Abraham serves as "a father by proxy," a mere "representation of the real father" (86). It is as if beginning through Abraham–Hagar–Ishmael proved too mundane and not worthy of monotheistic origins as such; it was more of an impasse of beginning rather than a proper beginning, especially given that Hagar was a bondwoman, a slave gifted to Sarah by Pharaoh (indeed, Hagar was a counter-gift to Sarah who was Abraham's initial gift to Pharaoh). But while Hagar was pushed aside in the story of monotheistic origin, she remains not only "the disturber of originary paternity and its triumvirate conception," but also the locus of Other jouissance – the recipient of God's covenant following their mystical encounter in the desert (78).

Hagar was initially brought up as some sort of a solution to Sarah's infertility; once Sarah realized that the God of Genesis had denied her the gift of origin, she offered her slave Hagar to Abraham as a surrogate womb to offer him the gift of a son and the gift of origin at one and the same time. At stake in the arrival of the son is the very arrival of the father; without the son, Abraham cannot become father, much less the father of monotheism. Needless to say, withholding the son in Genesis is tantamount to holding both the father and monotheistic origin in suspense: "In the beginning is 'that which withholds.' In other words, there is that there-is-not [*Il y a qu'il n'y a pas*]. We cannot push origin further back than this" (92). "Monotheism," Benslama rightly concludes, "is initially presented as faith in this impossible that is the lack of the father in the world, or the imaginary lack of origin" (92). Both father and son are lacking yet forthcoming. From this clearly Lacanian perspective, origin is structured by lack or, as Benslama has it, by the "void of interval" between *entame*/cut and *commencement*/beginning (123). This lack may have preceded the arrival of Sarah and Hagar, but comes to structure their relationship and later rivalry, and fuel the desire of each one of them to overcome it.

Understandably, all Sarah wanted was to "overcome the lack of god in herself" by way of Hagar; yet through her act, Benslama observes, "Genesis makes the transition from the initial lack of origin to the question of female *jouissance* in its relation to the establishment of the father" (80). In other words, "the woman who commands [Sarah] does not begin, leaving the primacy of the gift of the father to the woman who engenders through the flesh [Hagar]" (95). Sarah sought to overcome the lack of origin in her by the proxy womb of Hagar. The transfer of the gift of origin from Sarah to Hagar entails therefore the tacit endowment of Hagar with female jouissance (and with Other jouissance following the mystical encounter with God). At the origin, there is therefore female (and not solely phallic) jouissance – there is, in other words, Hagar overcoming the lack of origin in Sarah and establishing Abraham as father. As Lacan's epigraph above intimates, female jouissance involves a relationship to God that is neither phallic nor knowable outside of experience. For Benslama, Hagar's encounter with the God of Genesis gives her access to this excess jouissance or radically Other jouissance.

The overarching goal of Benslama's *Psychoanalysis and the Challenge of Islam* is to "formulate a structural function of the feminine at the moment of origin, which conditions the genealogical establishment of the father" (97). All the more so given that "Hagar's story is one of repudiation at monotheism's origin, which became disavowal when Islam began" (110). For instance, Benslama underlines the following fact about Hagar's elision from the Quran: "Although Ishmael is cited a dozen times in the Koran, and Abraham seventy-eight, Hagar is nowhere to be found" (120). Similarly, the Quran refers to Isaac's birth and blesses Sarah as "the wife of Abraham," but refers to Hagar only indirectly when relating the episode about her exile with her son Ishmael, her distress and frantic search for water in the desert (102–104). Interestingly enough, it is during this episode, when Hagar and Ishmael were abandoned in the desert, that the God of Genesis hears her suffering, and promises to make her "the origin of descendants beyond number" (81). With the founding of Islam, this promise to Hagar was somewhat fulfilled, except that Islam staked a genealogical claim to Abraham and Ishmael to the detriment of Hagar: "The return to Abraham was the key element in the Muhammedan refounding, a return that saw itself as the culmination of monotheism, binding its origin to its end" (69). While deconstructing the notion of origin, Benslama does not do away altogether with the gesture of return and offers instead a corrective to the established patriarchal and phallic theological narrative of origins in Islam.

The *recovery from* the myth of a pure Islamic (or monotheistic, for that matter) origin is as important as the *recovery of* how origin was en*gendered* in the first place. In this sense, the eradication of Hagar from the story of monotheistic-Islamic origins is symptomatic of a more structural gesture that sought to gender origin at the outset by excluding or eliding the role of the feminine and the excessive jouissance that comes with it. The need to recover and reinscribe the role of the female and foreign Other in the story of origin is therefore a salutary melancholic endeavor; all the more so if, as Benslama claims, "Islam had recourse to a stream of proscriptions to reduce, dismantle, then deny that Other *jouissance*, so as to gradually establish the sovereignty of a phallic, juridical, and ethical order congruent with the formation of the state" (149). It is quite misleading, however, to seek to establish, as Benslama propounds, an allegorical correspondence between the marginalization of the female Other in the monotheistic-Islamic story of origins and the contemporary "condition of women in Islamic societies" (109). Such a gesture not only exempts the other monotheistic religions from this same problem, but also excludes the circumstantial dynamics of history and geopolitics which continue to produce and reproduce the so-called contemporary condition of women in Islamic societies. Finally, it replicates – really, ratifies – the anachronistic Islamist gesture, which wants to refashion the present in the image of the past (in which case Benslama's suggestion – that the current condition of women in Islamic societies corresponds to the exclusion of the feminine in the story of monotheistic-Islamic origins – sanctions the same anachronism it seeks to deconstruct in relation to Islamist puritanical rhetoric).

It is incumbent therefore to reclaim and reinscribe the particular roles played by a number of illustrious women in the story of

monotheistic-Islamic origins and, simultaneously, to resist the temptation to recast the systemic repression of the female Other in that story as
a timeless framework for the analysis of the contemporary condition of
women in Muslim societies. Bearing this in mind, I will now conclude
by highlighting the important role that two other women (in addition
to Hagar) played in Islam's story of origin. The aim here is to further
explore (and not to entirely map) the elements of what would constitute an alternative female spiritual path to the phallocentric story of
foundation in Islam. Little wonder that this alternative spiritual path is
anchored in feminine/Other jouissance. It is as if the gendering of origin
in Benslama must pass through the gendering of jouissance in Lacan:
"There is a jouissance that is hers about which she herself perhaps knows
nothing if not that she experiences it – that much she knows. She knows
it, of course, when it comes (*arrive*). It doesn't happen (*arrive*) to all of
them."[11] Like Lacan and his followers, including Bruce Fink, Benslama
does not explain why this unspeakable jouissance should be structured
along gender lines, especially that much of Benslama's analytical innovations hinge on the hermeneutical insights of Ibn Arabi, whose work
interweaves neatly philosophy, theology, and Sufism. Paul Verhaeghe
may be right to observe that the "post–Lacanian hype about 'feminine
jouissance' is nothing more than a hysterical attempt to recuperate something that cannot be recuperated, owing to its very nature."[12] Surely,
there may be an inverse essentialism at work in the notion of feminine
jouissance, whose feminist strategic politics are beyond the focus of my
argument here. Suffice it to say that the essentializing gesture of feminine jouissance in Benslama (more so than in Lacan) serves a reparative
purpose. Indeed, what sets Benslama's recuperative historiography apart
from other Lacanian critics is that it expands Lacan's repertoire of female
examples beyond Hadewijch of Antwerp and Saint Teresa, and maps a
stellar assemblage of diverse female figures whose supplementary experiences of Other jouissance has been elided in the monotheistic-Islamic
story of origins. Benslama contends that "Islam, ever since the originary
repudiation, has been haunted by the other woman, who has threatened
to capture the son, making him an illegitimate bastard" (116). Benslama
has in mind here not only Ishmael in relation to Hagar, but also, as
will become clear, Ruqayya in relation to Prophet Muhammad; it was
Ruqayya who wanted to entice Abdallah (who would become the father
of Prophet Muhammad) to have sex with her and give her access to the
phallic jouissance that would enable her to capture the founding son, and
reach the status of woman of the Other.

The role of the other woman in the story of monotheistic-Islamic origins cannot be overstressed. Hagar was not only the recipient of God's promise but also the only woman in biblical narrative to have seen God without dying (123). Insofar as Islam is a biblical promise, the promise was made to Hagar and not to Abraham. Without the coming of Prophet Muhammad, however, Islam would have remained a biblical promise in search of a founding son. The story of the procreation of Prophet Muhammad is therefore central to the foundation of Islam; all the more so since it involved yet another tale of female rivalry, not unlike the rivalry between Hagar and Sarah, which denied monotheism the benefit of a single origin. While Amina was the actual mother of Prophet Muhammad, Ruqayya is the name of the other woman who saw the sign of the forthcoming son (the glow between the eyes of Abdallah, the father of the Prophet), and who wanted to capture the seed of origin from Abdallah (ironically, Abdallah was somewhat the oblivious bearer of the seed of the son and as such the bearer of the object of Ruqayya's desire but not the object of that desire per se). Ruqayya, according to Benslama, "enjoys a knowledge about light and the body, about the body of light of infantile origin, that is invisible to the father who carries it" (115). Like Hagar before her, Ruqayya emerges as the other woman who threatens to capture the son from the rightful mother, Amina. In short, "both Hagar and Ruqayya possess an arrogant power of clairvoyance that enables one of them to see god without dying and name him with the name of that vision, and the other to perceive the glow of sanctity and want to capture it" (131).

The clairvoyant power of the other woman, which haunts the fiction of monotheistic-Islamic origins, cannot be understood from within the prisms of phallic jouissance alone. The other woman's access to the phallic absolute supplements and surpasses the procreative realm of phallic jouissance and overflows into the mystical realm of absolute alterity and of Other jouissance. For, as Lacan surmises, "it is in the opaque place of jouissance of the Other, of this Other insofar as woman, if she existed, could be it, that the Supreme Being is situated."[13] The rivalry between Ruqayya and Amina revolves "not so much around the man as sexual object as around access to the status of woman of the Other and to the phallic *jouissance* that access confers, that is, the supreme power of engendering the son who will become the founding father" (115). Other jouissance is a central asset that endows women with the capacity to recognize the foundation of truth in Islam. No wonder, then, it had taken one woman to recognize and try to capture the seed of the founding son of

Islam (Ruqayya) and yet another (Khadija) to discern and establish the truth of Quranic revelation. Indeed, it was Khadija who was able to reassure Prophet Muhammad that the larger-than-life being that appeared to him every now and then was not a demon but an angel. Benslama relates the compelling story of the encounter between the Prophet, archangel Gabriel and Khadija, and how the archangel disappeared as soon as Khadija unveiled herself. While unable to see the angel herself, Khadija concluded thenceforth that, had it been a demon, it would have possibly not been unsettled by female immodesty, and withdrawn itself immediately from the scene and the sight of the Prophet. Benslama does not make light of this story, a primal scene of sorts, regardless of its historical veracity; on the contrary, he accords it a great deal of analytical and critical attention, and teases out a number of conclusions that underline the central importance of female clairvoyance to the story of foundation in Islam. Henceforth, Other jouissance for Benslama becomes the locus of the Tiresias-like clairvoyance of Khadija.

Benslama pays particular attention to the contradictions of this scene and to the paradoxes of the moment of foundation in general. For one thing, Khadija's unveiling reveals and simultaneously conceals the truth, given that the angel disappears at the sight of Khadija's hair; yet, "the concealment of truth is the verification of truth" (134). For another, the founder of truth does not recognize the revelation of the truth, which "inevitably leads toward the conclusion that man, if he is to believe in god, must rely upon belief in a woman, one who has access to a knowledge of truth that precedes and exceeds the knowledge of the founder himself. She verifies the founder's truth" (134). She has access to the truth of the Other precisely because of her position as eternal Other. Benslama translates Lacan here in more concrete terms: "The Other is not simply the locus in which truth stammers. It deserves to represent that to which woman is fundamentally related ... Being the Other, in the most radical sense, in the sexual relationship, in relation to what can be said of the unconscious, woman is that which has a relationship to that Other."[14] Far from being a disadvantage, Otherness here becomes something "extra (*en plus*)."[15] Otherness gives access to the experience of Other jouissance, the experience of this quasi-prophetic insight that Khadija becomes privy to but is incapable of giving an account of it. Perhaps, as Fink claims following Lacan, "the idea here seems to be that one can experience this Other jouissance, though one cannot say anything about it because it is ineffable; just because it does not exist does not mean one cannot experience it: one's experience of it simply ex-sists."[16]

Given that Khadija was the first person to believe in the Prophet, she became the first Muslim. Arguably, without her mediation, the Prophet would not have himself believed in God's messenger (archangel Gabriel) as well as in himself as messenger of God. Benslama is right here in perceiving Khadija as "the intermediary between intermediaries."[17] Undoubtedly, her role cannot be overestimated. However, Benslama claims that she became "the antiorigin upon which the initial faith in origin resided" (135). He goes on to suggest that woman went through "three stages in the female operation of theology: initially veiled, unveiled to demonstrate originary truth, then reveiled by order of the belief in that truth of origin. For, once established, truth aspires to conceal the nothingness through which it has passed" (135). While the act of veiling plays an important role in the revelation of the truth here, Benslama chooses to privilege unveiling and to look unfavorably at veiling even though Khadija was veiled before the revelation of truth. In addition, what I find of particular interest here is that Khadija wore the veil in the privacy of her home; had she not been wearing the veil in the privacy of her home, though, the archangel might not have been revealed to the Prophet. Khadija's modesty must have had no bounds already, and before Islam. Not surprisingly, Benslama Islamizes veiling there where he should have historicized it.

The scene of origins is the scene of contradictions and contingencies par excellence. Khadija "founds the truth of the founder,"[18] even while she has no direct access to that truth herself and even though her act of unveiling amounted to nothing less than an assault on the modesty of God's messenger. In other words, the one who can identify the truth of revelation (Khadija) does not see it and the one who can see it (Prophet Muhammad) cannot identify it. The story of origin is decentered. The paternal and maternal play equal roles in its dispersed formation. The fact that it has been gendered in monotheistic history is not enough alibi to re-gender it here, and reproduce the inverse yet same essentialist gesture. That said, I find myself in agreement, however, with Benslama in his reproach of European psychoanalysts "who overlooked the existence of a feminine spiritual path that the original monotheism glimpses but rejects."[19] His psychoanalytic project entails a *melancholic return* and rescue of this feminine spiritual path while that of the Islamists is more of a *melancholite return*: a reactionary attempt that aims in the end to resurrect and perpetuate the phallocentric fictions or established theological order of origin.

While Islamists embark on a theo-pathological return to origins, staking melancholite claims to an otherwise non-existent originary purity, Benslama actuates a revisionary return to origins, reclaiming the repressed figure of the feminine as key to a non-patriarchal and non-patrilineal understanding of origins. For Benslama, Islam lacks a finite point of reference identical with origin. While it may seem that Benslama reproduces as he reverses the gender biases at the origin of monotheistic and Islamic history, it is understandable that his melancholic gesture is more recuperative than essentialist. After all, the foundation of the last monotheistic religion came about through many different installments over time, ranging from the biblical promise to Hagar by the God of Genesis to the revelation of the Quran to the Prophet Muhammad by the archangel Gabriel. The challenge is to steer clear of the phallocentric story of Islamic origin and to unveil in the process the feminine spir-itual itinerary which it has left out of the account. This is perhaps in the end the challenge in the title of Benslama's book, *Psychoanalysis and the Challenge of Islam*. It is a Lacanian account of that overlooked and at times repressed feminine spiritual itinerary so instrumental to the story of monotheistic and Islamic origins.

Notes

1 See, for instance, Erich Fromm, *Psychoanalysis and Religion* (New Haven: Yale University Press, 1978).
2 Cited in Fethi Benslama, *Psychoanalysis and the Challenge of Islam*, tr. Robert Bononno (Minneapolis: University of Minnesota Press, 2009), 68.
3 Malik Badri, *Dilemma of Muslim Psychologists* (London: NWH London Publishers, 1979).
4 Omnia El Shakry, "The Arabic Freud: The Unconscious and the Modern Subject," *Modern Intellectual History* 11, 1 (2014), 89–118.
5 Benslama, *Psychoanalysis and the Challenge of Islam*, 9. All further page refer-ences to this book will appear in the body of the text between parentheses.
6 The notion of "*le désir d'Occident*" or "desire for the West" is scattered through several of Badiou's books and talks; for a more recent example, see Alain Badiou, *The Rebirth of History: Times of Riots and Uprisings*, tr. Gregory Elliott (New York: Verso, 2012), 50.
7 See Talal Asad, "Conscripts of Western Civilization," in Christine Gailey, ed., *Dialectical Anthropology: Essays in Honor of Stanley Diamond, volume I: Civilization in Crisis* (Gainesville: University Press of Florida, 1992), 333–351.
8 For more on this, see Joseph A. Massad, *Islam in Liberalism* (The University of Chicago Press, 2015). See especially chapter 4 titled "Psychoanalysis, 'Islam,' and the Other of Liberalism."
9 Bruce Fink, "Knowledge and Jouissance," in Suzanne Bernard and Bruce Fink, eds., *Reading Seminar XX: Lacan's Major Work on Love, Knowledge, and Feminine Sexuality* (Albany: SUNY Press, 2002), 35.

10 See Jacques Lacan, *The Seminar of Jacques Lacan, Book XX: Encore: On Feminine Sexuality, the Limits of Love and Knowledge, 1972–1973*, ed. Jacques-Alain Miller, tr. Bruce Fink (New York: W. W. Norton, 1988), 83.

11 See Lacan, *Seminar XX: Encore*, 74.

12 Paul Verhaeghe, "Lacan's Answer to the Classical Mind/Body Deadlock: Retracing Freud's *Beyond*," in Suzanne Bernard and Bruce Fink, eds., *Reading Seminar XX: Lacan's Major Work on Love, Knowledge, and Feminine Sexuality* (Albany: SUNY Press, 2002), 113.

13 Lacan, *Seminar XX: Encore*, 82.

14 Ibid., 81.

15 Ibid., 77.

16 Fink, "Knowledge and Jouissance," 40.

17 Fethi Benslama, "The Veil of Islam," *S: Journal of the Circle for Lacanian Ideology Critique* 2 (2009), 19.

18 Ibid., 18.

19 Fethi Benslama, "Islam in Light of Psychoanalysis," in *Psychoanalysis, Monotheism and Morality: Symposia of the Sigmund Freud Museum, 2009–2011*, ed. Wolfgang Müller-Funk, Ingrid Scholz-Strasser, and Herman Westerink (Leuven University Press, 2013), 16.

Index

For EU product safety concerns, contact us at Calle de José Abascal, 56–1°,
28003 Madrid, Spain or eugpsr@cambridge.org.

www.ingramcontent.com/pod-product-compliance
Ingram Content Group UK Ltd.
Pitfield, Milton Keynes, MK11 3LW, UK
UKHW010042140625
459647UK00012BA/1549